Napping in Delilah's Lap

The Pandemic of Pornography
in the Pew & the Pulpit

HANNAH THUKU KOLEHMAINEN, PHD.

ISBN 978-1-0980-7249-0 (paperback)
ISBN 978-1-0980-7250-6 (digital)

Christian Faith Publishing, Inc.
832 Park Avenue
Meadville, PA 16335
www.christianfaithpublishing.com

Printed in the United States of America

For Jesus,
The primary reason I am;
And for Justin, Paul, and James,
My secondary reason for being.

Reviews

A timely work on a problem too tender to touch, for too many, for too long. Kolehmainen's thoughtful, compassionate words reach the reader and help the taboo become a topic for all to discuss. A must-read for leadership and for each believer who wants more of the Life of Christ within.

Cathy Goekler, author, "Rev Your Wife's Engine"

Poignant, relevant, important, urgent!

Doctoral Thesis Committee, Newburgh Theological Seminary

Dr. Kolehmainen tackles issues that few wish to acknowledge, let alone investigate. The manner in which she explores the scourge of pornography and addiction in our culture is unique and thorough. I believe that this book will be a game-changer for many struggling to find true intimacy with God.

Douglas Timmons, Lead Pastor, Crossroads Church
and local Celebrate Recovery Overseer

Napping in Delilah's Lap uncovers the heart's complexities with wisdom, courage, generosity, and personal dignity. Page after page responds to the deepest questions with biblical data, personal anecdotes, and current research. It tracks the movement of God's grace throughout and provides a paradigm-shifting approach to understanding and finding full recovery. Without a judgmental tone, Hannah writes as a fellow pilgrim eager to lead us out of the mess we find ourselves in. Warm, personal, and practical—expect to be encouraged!

Rene Chanco, Faculty, Pastoral Studies Dept.
Asian Theological Seminary, Philippines

Kolehmainen moves the conversation to center stage of what it means to make Jesus Lord of our passions, desires, affections, and sexuality. Her vulnerable storytelling and gentle "bristle alerts" move us to identify and expose where our true affections lie, and call us forward to repentance and powerful restoration.

Titus & Stephanie Folden
Ministry to Children and Families at Risk, World Venture, Spain

In this thought-provoking and challenging book, Hannah exposes the pervasive and destructive nature of pornography in the lives of believers and non-believers alike. She provides biblical strategies that will help the Body of Christ win the battle against sexual immorality. Highly recommended!

Rudy Tinocco
Lead Pastor, Old Town Church

Contents

Acknowledgements

A world of thanks to my family of origin which made me what I am today. My memories are rich beyond measure. I thank God for every single one of you. I praise him for Mum, Mick, and Irene who are now whole and perfect in the very presence of our Jesus. Your departure left holes in our hearts and heaven is more dear to us now that you are there. I can't wait to see you again. Dad, DJ, Faith, Megs, Joy, Mary, Wambui, and my precious nephews and nieces are unseen wells of sustenance for my soul.

C.E.B., your faithfulness in sharing your heart with me started all this. You are a gem of a sister to me and I thank God for your vulnerability.

Heartfelt thanks to Bill and Marsha Sweitzer. You painstakingly pored over details and corrected content. Your sweet and gentle spirits delight my soul. Mike and Shari Totman, you are remarkable role models in my life. Your generosity and love are unrivaled. With astounding faith in relinquishing their child to a foreign land when I left home decades ago, my parents blessed me and said, "Find God's people." My God heard their prayer and landed me in your hands. I am forever grateful. You've taught me authentic Christian living and how to laugh at myself. As though that wasn't enough, from its inception you conscientiously read and reread my work. You provided encouragement and brilliant feedback on the content and helped me flush out my thinking. Thank you!

Cathy Goekler was the midwife who looked at my baby with fresh eyes just before its birth to ensure all systems were go. I cherish you. Your wisdom is molding my life.

Thank you to my numerous dear brothers and sisters who read, prayed, encouraged and/or challenged me through this arduous journey, especially Joy, Faith, and Amanda. You are priceless to me! Pastor Rudy, thank you for throwing your life into shepherding me with gentleness and vulnerability. I have loved watching the Lord expand your territory over the years and I'm deeply blessed to be a part of it.

"The law of the Lord is perfect, refreshing the soul.
The statutes of the Lord are trustworthy,
making wise the simple.
The precepts of the Lord are right,
giving joy to the heart.
The commands of the Lord are radiant,
giving light to the eyes.
The fear of the Lord is pure, enduring forever.
The decrees of the Lord are firm,
and all of them are righteous.

They are more precious than gold,
than much pure gold;
they are sweeter than honey, than
honey from the honeycomb.
By them your servant is warned;
in keeping them there is great reward.
But who can discern their own errors?
Forgive my hidden faults.
Keep your servant also from willful
sins; may they not rule over me.
Then I will be blameless, innocent
of great transgression.

May these words of my mouth and
this meditation of my heart
be pleasing in your sight,
Lord, my Rock and my Redeemer"
(Psalm 19:7-14).

Chapter 1

Saints on the Road to the Grave

Dramatically called, gifted, and appointed for work prepared in advance by the Master of the universe—so was Samson, so is the Church today. Napping in Delilah's lap, clueless about the impending tragedy—so was Samson, so are many in the Church today. In fact, that was the story of my life.

Samson was an Old Testament judge. His story is told in the book of Judges, chapters 13 to16. He was a miracle child, born to a barren Mrs. Manoah. His conception was foretold by an angel who visited her during a time when the Israelites were in political distress. Their country was being run by their old enemies, the Philistines. The Angel of the Lord visited her in the field one day.

That evening, sitting on a rock outside their house and enjoying an evening breeze at sunset, a very distracted Mrs. Manoah blurted to her husband, "Manny, an *ish* (man) visited me today." Her mind had been swirling since the stranger left earlier that day.

"Oh?" queried Manoah absently, as he looked through a pile of wood.

"He looked just like a *Malach HaElohim* (an angel)—very awesome," she continued dreamily.

"Oh?" said Manoah, fiddling with some smooth pieces of wood. He looked at her. "Where was he from?"

"Well," she pondered, "you know, I didn't ask."

"Hmm." He nodded his balding head quizzically. "What was his name?"

She wrung her hands on her skirts and turned to him, really seeing him for the first time since he got home. "It did not occur to me to ask that either."

Manoah looked up at her and cocked his head. "What did he want?"

"Manny." She turned her body to him with urgency. She was trying not to be hysterical. "He said I was going to be pregnant."

He didn't hear the thud as the piece of wood he was holding hit the ground. He choked on his own spit. She had his full attention. She was barely sitting now, leaning in so close to him, eyes wide, wild.

"He said we will have a son."

"I don't understand, *Ishah*!" He threw his hands out, bewildered. She backed off, almost scared. "What are you talking about?"

"If he wasn't so real, I would have thought I'd lost my mind, Manoah," she said louder than she intended. She breathed deeply and turned away. After a long silence, staring into the sinking sun, she barely whispered, "He said we are to name him Shimshon."

Manoah stared at her and leaned his head in slowly. He shook his head, incredulous. When she wouldn't look at him, he turned to the magnificent sunset that was glimmering in the distance. Its rays sparked something in his heart. "A son… Shimshon," he murmured. His heart was on fire now, like the angel fire dancing wildly on the horizon.

———————————

Later, in the deep of night, the whole world slept. It had been a long day, but Manoah hadn't slept a wink. An old owl hooted in her hunting escapade. What had become of his wife? This wasn't like her. Why would she think such things? Surely she'd misheard the man. Who was he anyway? This was madness. He sat up and stared at her, barely making her face out in the silvery glow of the half-moon's light.

She hadn't slept a wink either. Her body felt and echoed his every restless move as he wrestled. She felt him staring at her, mumbling. With her eyes closed, she said, "He said he will take the lead in delivering Israel from the hands of the Philistines."

He almost jumped out of his skin. He didn't know she was awake. And now, more madness! "Who? The man?"

"No," she said calmly, her eyes still closed. "Shimshon."

Hours later, he was still tossing and turning. This had to stop. It was almost sunrise. "Elohim," he finally entreated his God. "What is this? Who was this man?" A sudden sob escaped his lips before he could stop himself, and a stray tear dribbled down his temple and into his ear. This matter had tapped into a deep pain in his heart—an ache for a son. Had the grief of a barren womb finally gotten to his wife's mind, the way an infection in a tooth can cause the heart to stop? "Does he mock us, this man? Is this you? Do I dare hope for *ben* (a son)? Oh, Adonai, if this had anything to do with you, please let the *Ish HaElohim* come again." And his tear-smudged head finally drifted off to sleep.

───────────────

She sat on the ground in the field. She would need to turn in soon, but she lingered a while, enjoying the peace. She sighed, took a deep breath, and closed her eyes, enjoying the sun in her face. In the background, the chattering of birds flitting about around a pile of grain answered the distant chitchat of a group of women. She heard Mara telling a tall tale and laughing her great belly laugh. The ladies around her were responding in kind.

The sun, at once, got brighter and threatened to burn her closed eyes. She opened them, shocked at the sensation, and started to stand with her hand held out in front of her, shielding her eyes from the sudden glare. She put out her left hand to steady herself as she rose. Suddenly, she retracted it and gasped as though a viper had lunged at her. On the dusty ground, right where she was going to place her hand, planted like an erratic rock was a man's massive foot. She stared at it, her heart pounding in her ears. She swept her glance slowly and beheld the other foot. She followed the huge feet up. It took an eternity. By the time she got to his huge hands, she knew who it was, and her wild heartbeat doubled its cadence.

She scrambled to her feet and locked eyes with him.

"Shalom!" they both greeted at the same time, almost awkwardly. He reached out a hand to steady her. She was reeling. His warm smile calmed her somewhat.

―――――――――

Manoah had just snorted himself awake when she came barreling through the door. "He's here, he's here!"

"Who? Where?" he mumbled, sitting up, patting his head then the pillow.

"The *ish* that came to me the other day," she said over her shoulder. He turned to face the door, and was met by a blur of hair and skirts and words. She'd turned on her heels and bolted.

His feet barely touched the floor and he was at the door in no time. "Wait," he called out after her. She didn't. He couldn't keep up with her as she ran into the field. She'd scooped up her skirts and was flying faster than he thought her capable of. Slowing down as she approached the man, she danced in place, still holding her skirts. She felt delirious and barely contained herself. Her face was beaming a brilliant smile of incredulity as she looked anxiously from the man to her fast approaching husband, then back to the man, as though to say, "I told you!" She hadn't seen Manoah move this fast since they played Chase as children. It was almost comical.

Manoah finally got there, huffing. His hand went to his heart, as though to hold it in place. There stood a rather grand man, and he was taken aback. All his questions suddenly disappeared. "Are you the man who talked to my wife?" he asked, feeling suddenly unintelligent.

She nodded vehemently and was so giddy she almost squealed. Again she contained herself.

Manoah was at a loss for words. He finally blurted out, "A son?"

The man smiled his huge smile, and nodded, his eyes warm with fiery delight. "Shimshon."

"Shimshon!" Manoah grabbed his wife who had finally erupted in half-giggles half-sobs. He swept her off her feet and twirled her till he was dizzy. The man steadied them before they landed in a pile on the ground. Then he sat down, still laughing.

"Shimshon," She laughed.

"Shimshon," the man confirmed. Peals of fresh laughter engulfed the couple. The man laughed a happy, thunderous laugh out loud, and Manoah threw his hat on the ground.

"What should we do? What will he be?" Manoah was in the man's face now, his words tripping out of his mouth.

"Your wife must do all that I've told her. She must not eat anything that comes from the grapevine nor drink any wine," he started.

"No grapevine, no wine…" He looked at his wife and nodded earnestly at her to make sure she was getting all this.

"No drinking any fermented drink nor eating anything unclean. Of all the things I said to her, let her be *shomer* (on guard)."

"Absolutely," said Manoah in complete agreement. He looked at his wife seriously. "Be *shomer*."

Presently, the man stood and looked into the distance, his work here obviously done. "*Shalo*—" he started to say, ready to depart.

"No, wait." Manoah, who was far from done, panicked. "We would like you to stay until we prepare a young goat for you."

"Even though you detain me, I will not eat any of your food. But if you prepare a burnt offering, offer it to the Lord," replied the man.

"*Mi shmehchah* (What is your name) that we may honor you when your word comes true?" Manoah inquired.

"Why do you ask my name? It is *feli* (wonderfully incomprehensible)."

Manoah and his wife glanced at each other, brows furrowed.

> *Manoah took a young goat, together with a grain offering and sacrificed on a rock to the Lord. And the Lord did an amazing thing while Manoah and his wife watched: As the flame blazed up from the altar toward heaven, The Angel of the Lord ascended in the flame. Seeing this, Manoah and his wife instantly fell with their faces to the ground. When he did not show himself again to them, Manoah realized that it was The Angel of the Lord.*
>
> *"We are doomed to die!" he said to his wife. "We have seen God!"*
>
> *But his wife answered, "If the Lord had meant to kill us, he would not have accepted a burnt offering and grain offering from our hands, nor shown us all these things or now told us this."*
>
> *The woman gave birth to a boy and named him Samson. He grew and the Lord blessed him, and the Spirit of the Lord began to stir him while he was in Mahaneh Dan, between Zorah and Eshtaol* (Judges 13:19–25).

Samson was called, set apart, and greatly gifted. He had a holy calling upon his life even before he was conceived. Unfortunately, like many in the church today, he was a spiritedly stubborn sort who pursued his own desires and strove to satiate his bottomless fleshly cravings. He was doggedly single-minded in his pursuit of whatever it was that his heart burned for at any given moment. He swiftly brushed off any words of caution spoken by those in his life who dared to express concern over his conduct. He had an appetite for foreign women—particularly Philistine women, which is disturbing because:

- God commanded the Israelites to marry God-fearing spouses. He forbade marrying foreign women because,

  > *They will turn your sons away from*
  > *following Me, to serve other gods;*
  > *so the anger of the Lord will be aroused*
  > *against you and destroy you suddenly*
  > (Deuteronomy 7:4).

- Philistines were the very enemies who were oppressing the Israelites. In carousing with these women, Samson was literally sleeping with the enemy.
- As a leader, Samson should have been a role model to his followers.

Toward the end of his life, Samson met Delilah and fell madly in love with her. Delilah had plans for him, but they were not for his good. Like the enemy of our souls, she had no qualms about killing, stealing from, or destroying him. From her hands, he drank from the rivers of sexual pleasures. In her hands, he lost his strength, his sight, his freedom, his calling, and, ultimately, his life.

> *She [The Temptress] has been the ruin of many;*
> *many men have been her victims.*
> *Her house is the road to the grave.*
> *Her bedroom is the den of death*
> (Proverbs 7:26-27, NLT).

Chapter 2

In The Temptress's Arms

The book of Proverbs spends chapters 5 through 7 warning the reader about *The Temptress*. Her sensual seductions drip with sensuous delights. Below is a great summary of a day in her life. Heeding these timeless words would have served Samson well.:

With persuasive words she led him astray;
she seduced him with her smooth talk.
All at once he followed her like an
ox going to the slaughter,
like a deer stepping into a noose till
an arrow pierces his liver,
like a bird darting into a snare, little
knowing it will cost him his life.
Now then, my sons, listen to me;
pay attention to what I say.
Do not let your heart turn to her
ways or stray into her paths.
Many are the victims she has brought
down; her slain are a mighty throng.
Her house is a highway to the grave,
leading down to the chambers of death
(Proverbs 7:21-27).

Table i. below shows some similarities between Samson and the church today. Unfortunately, modern-day Delilah has caught the eye of many Christians. We have accepted her invitation and are comfortably at home in her love shack. Clandestine trysts with her through various compulsions are as wanton in the church today as they were in Samson's heart and life, and have effectively swiveled the heart of many away from God. We have not been *shomer.* May the words of Proverbs, above, serve as a warning to the body of Christ.

Table i. Similarities between Samson and Christians

Trait	Samson	Christians
Promised	*The angel of the Lord appeared to her [Samson's mother] and said, "You are barren and childless, but you are going to become pregnant and give birth to a son* (Judges 13:3).	*Now you, brothers and sisters, like Isaac, are children of promise* (Galatians 4:28).
Set apart	*Now see to it that you drink no wine or other fermented drink and that you do not eat anything unclean. You will become pregnant and have a son whose head is never to be touched by a razor because the boy is to be a Nazirite* (Judges 13:4, 5a).	*Before I formed you in the womb I knew you, before you were born I set you apart* (Jeremiah 1:5a). *Separate yourselves from them, says the LORD. Don't touch their filthy things, and I will welcome you* (2 Corinthians 2:17).

Called and anointed for service to God	*You will become pregnant and have a son whose head is never to be touched by a razor because the boy is to be a Nazirite, dedicated to God from the womb. He will take the lead in delivering Israel from the hands of the Philistines* (Judges 13:5).	*And we know that in all things God works for the good of those who love him, who have been called according to his purpose.* (Romans 8:28). *For we are God's handiwork, created in Christ Jesus to do good works, which God prepared in advance for us to do* (Ephesians 2:10).
Spirit-filled	(in the Old Testament, the Holy Spirit came and went from individuals) *The Spirit of the Lord came powerfully upon him* (Judges 14:6a). *Then the Spirit of the Lord came powerfully upon him* (Judges 14:19a).	(Since Jesus's ascension, the Holy Spirit dwells in believers) *You will receive power when the Holy Spirit comes on you* (Acts 1:8a). *Don't you realize that all of you together are the temple of God and that the Spirit of God lives in you?* (1 Corinthians 3:16).

This book is geared towards people who claim to be Christians. Being a Christian means God becomes the Lover of your Soul and you become his bride. Here's a bristle alert: much like we would do with a physical spouse, we need to love God the way *he* wants to be loved—not the way we think he needs to be loved, or only the way we want to love him. In the Bible he goes to much effort to describe how much he loves us but also how he wants to be loved. Our utmost efforts to love someone our own way are ineffective if that's not what they want or need. We need to speak their love language.

Once you become a Christian, you join the family of God. As leader, he holds you to different family rules; to exacting standards regarding your behavior, sex and idolatry. You now belong to a new tribe and it has a different language and culture. Upon coming to faith in him, he expects our sexual conduct and lives to be very different than that of non-believers. Non-Christians can have an idolatrous and sexual free-for-all, as their personal morals and convictions permit. But like Samson, Christians are to be *shomer*, on guard. This book unmasks common thinking of many believers and disrobes an evil undercurrent of self-worship through indulging in attitudes and behaviors that God expressly forbids. Jesus taught,

> *Anyone who loves me will obey my teaching.*
> *My Father will love them, and we will come*
> *to them and make our home with them.*
> *Anyone who does not love me will not obey*
> *my teaching. These words you hear are not my*
> *own; they belong to the Father who sent me*
> (John 14:23-24).

The fact that you are holding this book is not a coincidence. The Holy Spirit is wooing you into deeper intimacy with God. You have been prayed for. I have prayed in the words of Lysa Terkeurst, that God would unsettle you. You doing what you are doing this second is your heart responding to Holy Spirit's wooing. Allow yourself to free fall into the arms of the Lover of your Soul. You will never be the same.

Unsettle me.

These are the two words rattling about in my brain today. I almost wish it was a more glamorous prayer...

The funny thing is I've spent my whole existence trying to find a place to settle down. People to settle down with. And a spirit about me worthy of all this settled down-ness.

All of this is good. A contented heart, thankful for its blessings is a good way to settle.

But there are areas of my life that have also set-tled that mock my desires to be a godly woman. Compromises if you will.

Attitudes that I've wrapped in the lie, "Well, that's just how I am. And if that's all the bad that's in me, I'm doing pretty good."

I dare you, dear soul of mine, to notice the stark evidence of a spirit that is tainted and a heart that must be placed under the microscope of God's word. Yes, indeed, unsettle me Lord.

Unearth that remnant of unforgiveness.

Shake loose that justification for compromise.

Reveal that broken shard of pride.

Expose that tendency to distrust.

Unsettle me in the best kind of way. For when I allow your touch to reach the deepest parts of me—dark and dingy and hidden away too long—suddenly, a fresh wind of life twists and twirls and dances through my soul.

I can delight in forgiveness and love more deeply.

I can discover my gentle responses and find softer ways for my words to land.

I can recognize the beauty of humility and crave the intimacy with God it unleashes.

I can rest assured though harsh winds blow, I will be held.

Goodbye to my remnants, my justification, shards, and tendencies. This is not who I am— nor who I was created to be.

Goodbye to shallow love, sharp words, self-focus, and suspicious fears. I am an unsettled woman who no longer wishes to take part in your distractions or distructions (sic).
Welcome deeper love, softer words, unleashed intimacy, and the certainty I am held.[1]

Clandestine trysts with The Temptress
through various compulsions are as wanton
in the church today as they were in Samson's
heart and life, and have effectively swiveled
the heart of many away from God.

Chapter 3

Of Pornography and Idolatry

Commonly, the church, like the culture uses the term *pornography* to mean "erotica." This is a woefully inadequate definition. "Porneía" and "pórnos" are the root of the English term *pornography*. They are "derived from "pernaō", meaning "to sell off," denoting a selling off or surrendering of sexual purity; promiscuity of *any (every)* type."[1]

Several Hebrew and Greek words are used in the Bible to refer to sexual sin, including *naaph, zanah, taznuth, and moicheuo*. All these words carry an idiomatic double-meaning! They also refer to idolatry—holding anything or any person in higher esteem than God, and prostrating ourselves to it. Thayer's Definition of Bible Words adds that *porneia* is "metaphorically the worship of idols."[2] In this book, I will use the terms "pornography" and "idolatry" interchangeably. Hosea 4:7b teaches,

> *They exchanged their Glory [i.e.*
> *God] for something disgraceful.*

To help you visualize this mechanism, imagine habitual engagement in erotica as one spoke on a wheel of a motorcycle. Now zoom out and notice the other spokes. They represent the various other forms of sexual immorality: wrongful fantasizing, emotional affairs, masturbation, fornication, adultery, homosexual activity (not to be confused with the temptation of same sex attraction), incest, bestiality, etc. All this sexual activity is pornography. I would add depriving your spouse sexually to this list. The hub of this wheel is *self-gratification*.

Zoom out some more and notice the other wheel. Its spokes are various other compulsions (See chapter titled *The Physiology of Addiction—Part 2* for the technical definitions, characteristics, and updates regarding addictions): electronics, shopping, over-eating, workaholism, excessive thrill-seeking, over-exercising, alcohol and drugs, etc. The hub of this wheel is *sensual indulgence*.

Pornography. Idolatry.

Take another step back. The engine of this motorcycle is *self-worship*. Its nuts, bolts, and parts are various other sins—perfectionism, lying, gossip, worry and anxiety, boasting, stealing, busyness, trusting in your wealth, over-eating, excessive competitiveness, manipulation, rebelliousness to authority, excessive attention to image, desiring control, having a sharp tongue, pessimism, laziness, entitlement, undermining others, self-loathing, jealousy and envy, worldliness, vengefulness, seeking conflict and being quarrelsome. There are too many to list but we will point out several throughout the book.

Writer Dr. Neil Anderson claims, "The entire world is still choosing to eat from the tree of the knowledge of good and evil without the tree of life. The result is intellectual arrogance, pride, self-sufficiency, self-adulation, self-centeredness, self-gratification…self, self, and more self. Self-sufficiency is the greatest enemy to our sufficiency in Christ."[3]

The make and model of this motorcycle is "*Porneia—MeMobile*." It remains a classic. Notice the shiny chrome. It's a head-turner. Can you hear it rev? Do you see it pop a wheelie? It's a pretty slick ride, but DON'T GET ON IT! It's the sweet express to Delilah's house. Delilah's plan for you is exactly what it was for Samson—to steal, kill, and destroy.

> *Her house is the road to the grave.*
> *Her bedroom is the den of death*
> (Proverbs 7:27).

God created us. He purchased and saved us with the blood of His Son. He owns us and is sovereign over us. When you become a Christian, this is the relationship you are entering into, as we shall see in the chapter titled *The Anatomy of Salvation*. As such, he gets to call the shots in your life and determines what is acceptable and what isn't. As the Lover of our Souls, he tells us how to love him.

His mandate for sexual purity is marriage between one man and one woman for life. There are biblical and cultural stipulations that the man and woman should not be immediate relatives. The man and woman gift the other with their body in sexual union. For each of them, the goal of every sexual encounter is to wholeheartedly please and fulfill the partner. Any mental or physical sexual act outside of this scope is a selling off or surrendering of God's standard. I repeat: Any mental or physical sexual act outside of this scope is a selling off or surrendering of God's standard. He will not tolerate it. He has rigged or engineered the system so that it only works out his way. Every single attempt to circumvent him and his ways is futile and ends in pain, as we shall see throughout this book.

> *A man who strays from the path of understanding*
> *comes to rest in the company of the dead.*
> *There is no wisdom, no insight, no plan*
> *that can succeed against the LORD*
> (Proverbs 21:16, 30).

The prophet Hosea states,

> *A spirit of prostitution*
> *[zanah—Hebrew word for fornication;*
> *figuratively—idolatry]*
> *is in their heart*
> (Hosea 5:4b).

One definition of "spirit" is "an unaccountable or uncontrollable impulse."[4] God paints a picture for the visual learners among us,

Behind your doors and your doorposts, you
have put your pagan symbols. Forsaking
me, you uncovered your bed, you climbed
into it and opened it wide; you made a
pact with those whose beds you love,
and you looked with lust on their naked bodies
(Isaiah 57:8).

Clearly, pornography and idolatry are two sides of the same coin, two wings on the same bird. Their ultimate goal is to turn hearts away from God.

How does a Christian become a pornographer/idolater? How do they stay addicted? The same way as anyone else. Remember the wonder of the first time you watched a video of a sperm swimming to and then fertilizing an egg? Writer Fred Rochester captures the moment of conception of the dreadful, life-dominating sin of pornography. Though he uses the term to refer to erotica, I believe that the principle he describes is accurate for all forms of pornography. He claims that it doesn't matter if you have only one exposure *or* several, but when you *consent* to participating, a seed of addiction is deposited in you as an initial seed.[5]

This seed is also sown when one is exposed to various forms of pornography against their will, but it takes consent for it to germinate. If a helpless victim is repeatedly exposed to porn, for example children in the sex trade, their hearts become fertile ground for pornography to thrive, despite their lack of consent and even them hating what is done to them. The goal of pornography is self-gratification. Obviously most of these victims get no gratification from it, though some may choose to be gratified by it as a coping mechanism.

The Spirit of Samson

We learned that one definition of "spirit" is an unaccountable or uncontrollable impulse. Many of us struggle with what I call a spirit of Samson. It affects men and women alike. I will use the pronouns *he/him/his* for simplicity. The spirit of Samson leaves observers either scratching or shaking their heads. What does it look like in real life?

1. He is called to be set apart to God. Has a divine directive or calling from God. This is likely marked by clear, very unusual spiritual circumstances surrounding certain aspects of his life. This calling is evident to and affects significant others around him. He is remarkably gifted in specific areas.

2. He tends to be immature, impatient, undisciplined, and persistent. He throws adult tantrums. He wants what he wants, when he wants it, and how he wants it, even if it is unreasonable or it means disobedience to God's clear instruction. He believes he is the center of the universe and is oblivious how his actions affect other people.

3. He disregards the expressed counsel of those around him. He is certain he is right and rarely, if ever, wrong. He may frequently believe that others are mistaken or uninformed and that he has the corner on the truth.

4. He is spiritually blind. He doesn't see or acknowledge the blessings around him. Because he is doggedly focused on the pursuit of his physical desires, he despises good things that are available to him. He lays his pearls before swine, blind to what is of value and who can be trusted.

5. He is a sensual and very passionate person. He feels and experiences things very strongly, yet he has poor insight. He is driven by what he sees, hears, feels and desires. He is undisciplined and lives very much in the moment. This leads to poor judgement due to lack of foresight. He loves a good time and may be the life of the party. He may exhibit extreme mood swings. When things are great, they're

phenomenal. When they're not so great, life is tragic. He quickly forgets lessons learned in the past and therefore has little hindsight. He is vengeful and may have episodes of explosive rage and do damage to others, including their reputation or property.

6. He is a strong, powerful, influential personality, sometimes larger than life. He cares little what others think of him. Though surrounded by many people, he may not have close friends and may hold others at bay emotionally. He is charming and fun to be around. The party starts when he gets there.

7. He weaves a consistent thread of deceit into his life and can be conniving. He may not hear, understand, or remember what doesn't suit him.

8. He gets away with things that most people don't get away with. God protects him in mind-boggling ways and he survives situations that most others wouldn't. He is resilient and bounces back from adversity in remarkable ways. He is a man of prayer but his prayers are shallow, self-centered, and mainly when he is in trouble.

9. He is drawn to/attracts histrionic personalities into his inner circle, allows them to stay there, and gives in to their pressures. Sometimes he is uncannily aware that he is in danger but globally he is simpleminded and even foolishly blind when others seek to do him harm. He ignores obvious signs of danger, positioning himself in the cross-hairs of the enemy. He is misused by others for their pleasure.

10. He underperforms for his capacity. He does not live out his true identity. He does not do what he is supposed to be doing.

As you read this, someone immediately comes to mind for you! You readily said, "Yup! Yup! Yup!" as you went down the list. You have shaken and scratched your head repeatedly regarding this person. We are surrounded by Samsons. I have painted the spirit of

Samson in absolutes. The people you know may not have all these traits or the traits may not be dominant.

Now allow me to press in and risk stepping on your toes with a bristle alert. *We are all Samson.* We hate to admit it but there are traits on this list that hit awfully close to home. It amazes me how easy it is to see a mote or speck in a brother's eye while we are bonking them with the beam or plank jutting out of our own eye. As we go through this book, I pray that we will invite the Holy Spirit to admonish us. That means to shine a light on some dark places.

Search me, O God, and know my heart;
try me, and know my thoughts: And
see if there be any wicked way in me,
and lead me in the way everlasting
(Psalm 139:23-24).

Chapter 4

The State of the Heart—
Sensitive or Sensual?

So I tell you this, and insist on it in the Lord,
that you must no longer live as the Gentiles
do, in the futility of their thinking. They are
darkened in their understanding and separated
from the life of God because of the ignorance
that is in them due to the hardening of their
hearts. Having lost all sensitivity, they have given
themselves over to sensuality so as to indulge in
every kind of impurity, and they are full of greed
(Ephesians 4:17–19).

A few years ago, my father was diagnosed with pericarditis, a cardiac disease of slow onset whereby the pericardium, the thin membrane that surrounds the heart, slowly and irreversibly hardens. It seriously restricts the pumping of that powerful, life-giving muscle, effectively stultifying the sufferer. Since it was stifling all other bodily processes, Dad had to have that stiff membrane removed in a major surgery before it killed him. His surgeon, Dr. Njuguna, had so saw that chest open, essentially peel the heart, and sew him back together.

The idolater may be involved in "Christian activity" like church attendance while simultaneously indulging in pornography in its various forms. Author Steve Gallagher states that this saint is shrouded in hypocrisy, saying, many in his life "consider him to be morally

33

upright and would never guess what he does when no one is looking." He has perfected the stained-glass-masquerade. This double life leads to spiritual pericarditis, a hardening of his heart, "blinding him to his true spiritual condition. Because he spends time in God's presence and meetings, it is easy for him to imagine that he truly is walking closely with the Lord. This is compounded by the spiritual reality that the Lord is not quick to judge sin."[1]

Because of the stiff spiritual pericardium, an addicted Christian is no longer sensitive to God or His ways. His conscience is no longer clear but is weakened and marred. He has become hardened or desensitized to things of God. Despite eating and breathing, nutrients and air cannot effectively get to the rest of the body nor can waste be cleaned out. Gallagher describes this phenomenon,

> The more a person gives himself over to the power of sin, the harder he grows towards God. He may still attend church, sing all of the songs of worship, and even enjoy good preaching, but there is a thick callus around his heart that keeps him from feeling the Holy Spirit nudge him towards repentance. The more a person sins, the thicker that callous grows. Eventually he will find himself so hard that he can no longer discern truth for himself.[2]

Paul warned us about pleasure and its relationship with Christian maturity;

> *But mark this: There will be terrible times in the last days. People will be lovers of themselves, lovers of money, boastful, proud, abusive, disobedient to their parents, ungrateful, unholy, without love, unforgiving, slanderous, without self-control, brutal, not lovers of the good, treacherous, rash, conceited, lovers of pleasure rather than lovers of*

God—having a form of godliness but denying
its power. Have nothing to do with such people
(2 Timothy 3:4–5).

Jesus claimed:

The seed that fell among thorns stands for
those who hear, but as they go on their
way they are choked by life's worries, riches
and pleasures, and they do not mature
(Luke 8:14).

James also admonishes about the interplay of pleasure and prayer.

What causes fights and quarrels among you? Don't
they come from your desires that battle within
you? You desire but do not have, so you kill.
You covet but you cannot get what you want, so
you quarrel and fight. You do not have because
you do not ask God. When you ask, you do not
receive, because you ask with wrong motives, that
you may spend what you get on your pleasures
(James 4:1–3).

A. W. Tozer said,

[H]uman nature is in a formative state
and…is being changed into the image of the
thing it loves. Men and women are being molded
by their affinities, shaped by their affections and
powerfully transformed by the artistry of their
loves. In the unregenerate world of Adam this
produces day-by-day tragedies of cosmic propor-
tions.[3]

We will review these in the chapter titled *13 Problems with Porn*.

The heart of the problem, friends, is the heart. The heart is "the center of your character, who you really are. Where you believe and exercise faith. Center and seat of physical and spiritual life, thoughts, passions, desires, purposes, intelligence, will, character, emotions."[4] As a memory technic, think of yourself as a gynecologist and the heart comes in on its PAPDATE. You need to get a smear so you can assess purposes, affections, passions, drive, appetites, thoughts, and endeavors. The heart is the maestro of the orchestra of our lives!

> *As water reflects the face,*
> *so one's life reflects the heart*
> (Proverbs 27:19).

Our current worldview sees the heart as good and even encourages us to follow its leadings. God sees the unredeemed heart very differently. He just doesn't peel the old layer off the heart. He takes the whole gizmo and replaces it with a brand spanking new one! Unregenerate, we are spiritual prostitutes like the prophet Hosea's wife Gomer. Here's what God has to say about it.

> *The heart is deceitful above all things, and*
> *desperately wicked, who can know it?*
> (Jeremiah 17:9).

> *Out of the heart proceed all evil*
> *thoughts, murders, adultery, fornication,*
> *theft, false witness, blasphemies*
> (Matthew 15:19-24).

The miracle at Calvary is that these sick, hard hearts are removed and we are given new hearts. God is the Great Physician who specializes in heart transplants. He implores the Israelites to forsake the idolatry they are steeped in and so avert its horrible consequences.

*Rid yourselves of all the offenses you have
committed, and get a new heart and a new
spirit. Why will you die, people of Israel?*
(Ezekiel 18:31).

God promises restoration:

*I will give them an undivided heart and put a
new spirit in them; I will remove from them their
heart of stone and give them a heart of flesh*
(Ezekiel 11:19).

*I will give you a new heart and put a new
spirit in you; I will remove from you your
heart of stone and give you a heart of flesh*
(Ezekiel 36:26).

What a great exchange! Paul continues in this vein and declares
hope:

*God's love has been poured out into our hearts
through the Holy Spirit, who has been given to us*
(Romans 5:5b).

*Command certain people not to teach false
doctrines any longer or to devote themselves to
myths and endless genealogies... The goal of
this command is love, which comes from a pure
heart and a good conscience and a sincere faith*
(1 Timothy 1:5).

The heart works in concert with the conscience. The job of the
conscience is to sense and sound the alarm when we are in violation
of God's expectations. Paul warns in 1 Timothy 4:1-2 that the conscience (our built-in conviction-meter) can be seared as with a hot
iron. The seared nerve endings or sensors of a too-oft ignored con-

science are destroyed and therefore insensitive to God. As a result, we downplay the gravity of sin, the utter sinfulness that the most "innocent" person is capable of, and the direness of sins' consequences.

Bristle alert! Many Christians are not convinced that they are capable of untold wickedness in thought and deed. We are insulted by that thought. To make matters worse, we are in a twisted culture that describes sin as good and good as evil. Most of us believe we are pretty good people and live as though God is blessed to have us. We certainly work overtime to project to others the image that we are spot-on, or better than most. We spend a lot of time on façade management, carefully sitting on the holes in our carpet. We appear as "good" church attenders, but people would be shocked to know our private conduct. You would do well to grasp that under the right temperature and pressure any human being is capable of all sins— and that includes you.

I am privileged to sit in one counseling session after another and I'm learning not to sputter and choke when people bare their hearts. I am also learning that I really shouldn't be surprised at our capacity for untold depravity, just as God isn't. The sooner we divest ourselves of this charade, the sooner we can get on the same reality as God regarding why he sent his Son. God, please forgive us this foundational sin of hypocrisy. Forgive us for behaving as though once we come to Jesus for salvation, we don't need you anymore.

Our natural hearts are sin-seeking devices. And we don't even have to sin physically. God says, "the imagination of the heart of man is given to evil continually."[5] To imagine something is to picture it in the mind. In ancient cultures, the heart is so closely intertwined with the mind that for the purposes of our discussion they are one. Lust in the mind/heart taints one's vision. As a plant on a windowsill reaches to the sun, hearts that are not constantly surrendered to God automatically incline to sin, no matter which way you turn them. The heart is fertile ground for sinful imaginations. Jesus says, "but I say to you that whoever *looks* at a woman to lust for her has already committed adultery with her in his heart."[6] yet the apostle Paul says that among us there must not even be a "*hint* of sexual immorality."

Pastor William Harrell makes an interesting observation in distinguishing a *wicked* heart from a *wretched* heart. Since the saint is regenerated (made new) how do these terms apply to him or her? What is the state of the Christian's heart?

Harrell claims that the wicked man is evil, desires evil, and is powerfully driven by evil. His state is despicable and God has pronounced him guilty. On the contrary, the righteous are declared "good, just, and submissive to God." Though the Christian may act wickedly, he is not wicked at heart. He is wretched. He or she hates evil and desires to do good, in keeping with God's command to be holy as he is holy. The wretched man or woman is, "distressed, weak, and miserable" about his propensity to sin. He or she offends as a result of the "weakness and imperfections" as sanctification does its work throughout the lifetime.[7]

Might this be what Paul was talking about when he powerfully concluded:

> *And I know that nothing good lives in me, that*
> *is, in my sinful nature. I want to do what is*
> *right, but I can't. I want to do what is good,*
> *but I don't. I don't want to do what is wrong,*
> *but I do it anyway. But if I do what I don't*
> *want to do, I am not really the one doing*
> *wrong; it is sin living in me that does it.*
> *I have discovered this principle of life—that when*
> *I want to do what is right, I inevitably do what*
> *is wrong. I love God's law with all my heart. But*
> *there is another power within me that is at war*
> *with my mind. This power makes me a slave to the*
> *sin that is still within me. Oh, what a miserable*
> *person I am! Who will free me from this life that*
> *is dominated by sin and death? Thank God! The*
> *answer is in Jesus Christ our Lord. So you see how*
> *it is: In my mind I really want to obey God's law,*
> *but because of my sinful nature, I am a slave to sin*
> (Romans 7:18-25 NLT).

What an elevated and freeing thought—any wrong we do, does not arise from a wicked heart (for all things have been made new) but from the flesh. Remember Harrell's words, "So long as we are in this life, we drag around with us the dead remains of what we once were apart from Christ." These remains vex and sadden the Christian and incline us to old ways of thinking, acting, and feeling. Only the Holy Spirit in you through the Word of God informs, inclines, convicts, and empowers us to live out God's ways. If some of that comes easily to you, thank him for it. For what is hard, lean into him harder. In that light, Harrell says,

> When we know ourselves to be *fundamentally righteous* and *incidentally wretched,* we cry to God for mercy and we find mercy abundantly supplied to us by God (Rom. 7:25). In that merciful provision we rejoice in the deepening realization that for us, there is now no condemnation from our God (Rom. 8:1). In turn, we who have tasted such divine mercy delight with patience and loving kindness to show mercy to our brethren who, like us, are distressed by frailties from which they desire liberation.[8]

The opposite of sensitivity is sensuality. We are either *sensitive* to the Lord and walking in obedience or hamstrung by fleshliness or *sensuality*—pleasing our flesh and its physical senses of touch, sight, taste, hearing, smell, and movement. Sensuality results in disobedience to God who calls and trains us to say "no" when our bodies want to say "yes."

> *Those controlled by the flesh do not*
> *please God, nor can they do so*
> (Romans 8:8).

> *[The grace of God] teaches us to say "No"*
> *to ungodliness and worldly passions,*

and to live self-controlled, upright and
godly lives in this present age,
(Titus 2:12).

Call your besetting sin(s) to mind. Now look at the continuum on Figure ii. below. As you walk around today, visualize it in the course of your day, choice by choice, action by action. Strain, with the help of the Spirit, to lean towards a heart of sensitivity.

Figure ii. Sensuality/Sensitivity Spectrum

Sensuality/Self-indulgence/   Sensitivity to God/Spiritual
Fleshliness

So I tell you this, and insist on it in the Lord,
that you must no longer live as the Gentiles
do, in the futility of their thinking. They are
darkened in their understanding and separated
from the life of God because of the ignorance
that is in them due to the hardening of their
hearts. Having lost all sensitivity, they have given
themselves over to sensuality so as to indulge in
every kind of impurity, and they are full of greed.
That, however, is not the way of life you learned
when you heard about Christ and were taught
in him in accordance with the truth that is
in Jesus. You were taught, with regard to your
former way of life, to put off your old self, which
is being corrupted by its deceitful desires; to be
made new in the attitude of your minds; and
to put on the new self, created to be like God
in true righteousness and holiness… And do

not grieve the Holy Spirit of God, with whom
you were sealed for the day of redemption
(Ephesians 4:17-24, 30).

Quite simply, physical addiction occurs
when you repeatedly satisfy a natural appetite
and desire with a temporary pleasure until
you become the servant of the temporary
object of pleasure rather than its master.[9]

Dr. Mark Shaw

So long as we are in this life, we drag
around with us the dead remains of what
we once were apart from Christ.

William Harrell

Chapter 5

The Pandemic of Pornography
in the Pew and the Pulpit

A spirit of prostitution
[zanah—Hebrew word for fornication;
figuratively—idolatry]
is in their heart
(Hosea 5:4b).

Members of the church today are virulently addicted to pornography, by the broader, more accurate definition we just established. It is a pandemic in the pew *and* in the pulpit. As I write this, the media is abuzz. The Me Too movement has grown exponentially as victims of sexual violence come out and take a stand against the atrocities done to them. They are telling stories of past abuse that they've been quiet about all along. Some of the abuse happened decades ago. Some of the abuse was perpetrated by high-ranking political figures or celebrities. Most was by regular men. The result is the same. Victims are devastated and they've had enough.

As a Christian, I wish I could say that this was happening "out there" in the world. Unfortunately, the story is *exactly* the same in the church. I support missionaries through Mercy Corps, an evangelical aid organization. I'm utterly heartbroken over investigative reports done by our local paper, *The Oregonian*, regarding claims that Mercy Corps co-founder, Ellsworth Culver, sexually abused his daughter, Tania Culver-Humphrey, for most of her childhood.

It only gets worse. In the 90's, while in college, Tania approached three Mercy Corps board members with these allegations. They conducted an internal investigation that lasted two years and included medical and mental health records, DHS reports, and hundreds of pages of her personal records including journal entries and personal interviews of Tania—detailing graphic scenarios of sexual activity her father Ellsworth forced her into.

According to an email her husband Christopher Humphrey wrote, an analyst that the organization used in the investigation concluded that Tania exhibited "most of the identified effects consistent with one traumatized at an early age by sex abuse." This analyst also expressed "significant concern" about how the investigation was affecting Tania.[1]

Mr. Culver denied the allegations. He resigned from his position as president, and was assigned the position of vice president, the public face of Mercy Corps world-wide. Alarmingly, the committee, which included a psychiatrist, did not report the allegations to the police or DHS. In a letter to Tania, Mercy Corps concluded that their investigation found that her account was "troubling but inadequate."

In 2018, twenty-five years after the initial report, a still traumatized Tania, along with her husband Christopher, contacted Mercy Corps again after reading about recent sexual allegations involving Mercy Corps' staff. Christopher said that since the organization was stepping up as a leader in "investigating current and past cases involving sexual misconduct," he and Tania wondered if Mercy Corps would review the investigation from the 90's to see if it met their current ethical standards. They also wanted to know what conclusions or follow-up actions the Mercy Corps board came to.

Mercy Corps' General Counsel emailed the couple, stating that, "Based on their review they concluded that there was insufficient evidence to require any further action by Mercy Corps." Moreover, Mercy Corps' Senior Legal Counsel informed the Humphreys in a letter that records of the two-year investigation were no longer in existence!

As a financial supporter of Mercy Corps, I received a letter from their chief development and marketing officer acknowledging that the organization failed Tania in the '90s and again in 2018 by not treating her with respect and by allowing her father to continue in the organization—in a very prominent role. They offered an apology and claimed they are committed to doing whatever it takes to rebuild the broken trust and to redress the harm caused.

I single out Mercy Corps because this story is epic, yet I strongly believe that such activity is not unique to Mercy Corps. This scenario is playing out in many other organizations, including local churches, and has been for a long time. More importantly, I know that this atrocity continues to be perpetrated in Christian homes across the street and around the world. The issues boil down to the pandemic of pornography in the pew and in the pulpit. Church, the Lord will not sit idly by.

In the past, God used the prophet Jeremiah to cry out against *porneia* not only among the people, but especially among the spiritual leaders. Its prevalence irked him greatly.

> *Both prophet and priest are godless;*
> *even in my temple I find their*
> *wickedness," declares the LORD...*
> *They commit adultery and live a lie.*
> *They strengthen the hands of the evildoers so that*
> *no one turns from his wickedness...*
>
> *But which of them has stood in*
> *the council of the LORD*
> *to see or to hear his word?*
> *Who has listened and heard his word?*
>
> *See, the storm of the Lord will burst out in wrath,*
> *a driving wind swirling down on*
> *the heads of the wicked.*
> *The fierce anger of the Lord will not turn back*
> *until he fully accomplishes the purposes of his heart.*
> *In days to come you will understand it clearly...*

But if they had stood in my council they
would have proclaimed my words
to my people and would have turned
them from their evil ways
and from their evil deeds.
"Am I only a God nearby," declares the
LORD "and not a God far away?
Can anyone hide in secret places so that I cannot
see him?" declares the LORD. "Do not I fill
heaven and earth?" declares the LORD…

But let the one who has my word speak it faithfully.
For what has straw to do with
grain?" declares the LORD.
"Is not my word like fire," declares the LORD,
"and like a hammer that breaks a rock in pieces?"
(Jeremiah 23:11, 14b, 18-20, 22-24, 28b-29).

This was a problem in the past and remains a problem today because most people do not want to hear that they need to forsake their cherished sins. Unfortunately, the call to single-minded devotion to God is met with eye-rolling. Preaching against sin and calling men and women to repent is met with outright disdain by carnal believers. They don't want to hear it. They want the blessings of God *and* to continue living as they please. Unfortunately, the backlash is so powerful that ministers steer clear of such topics. Some dare to dip their feet in the icy waters but draw them out quick at the numbing response they get. The prophet Jeremiah experienced this first hand. Fortunately, the message was uncontainable.

So the word of the LORD has brought
me insult and reproach all day long.
But if I say, "I will not mention him
or speak any more in his name,"
his word is in my heart like a fire,
a fire shut up in my bones.

I am weary of holding it in; indeed, I cannot."
But the LORD is with me like a mighty warrior
(Jeremiah 20:8b, 9, 11a).

I pray that every last one of us will passionately heed the words of the apostle Paul to Timothy,

In the presence of God and of Christ Jesus, who
will judge the living and the dead, and in view
of his appearing and his kingdom, I give you
this charge: Preach the word; be prepared in
season and out of season; correct, rebuke and
encourage—with great patience and careful
instruction. For the time will come when people
will not put up with sound doctrine. Instead, to
suit their own desires, they will gather around
them a great number of teachers to say what their
itching ears want to hear. They will turn their
ears away from the truth and turn aside to myths
(2 Timothy 4:1-4).

"My eyes are on all their ways; they
are not hidden from me,
nor is their sin concealed from my eyes"…
"I the LORD search the heart
and examine the mind,
to reward a man according to his conduct,
according to what his deeds deserve."
(Jeremiah 16:17, 17:10).

Chapter 6

My Besetting Sin

A wise man sits on the hole in his carpet.

I've loved that ancient Arabic proverb since I heard it as a teenager. This brilliant adage advises us to put our best foot forward. After all, the casual visitor doesn't need to know there is a hole in the carpet! At a deeper level, though, it describes what I call façade management—an attempt to engineer or finagle appearances so that we look as impressive as we possibly can. The issue is that *we all* have holes in the carpet of our lives. The problem with sitting on the hole is the disadvantageous reality that while the guest is present, the host is tethered to the hole, immured by their potential shame.

Everything within me cringes and recoils at the thought of writing this book. I cower, shudder, *and* wince as I embark on this work because it exposes a hole in my spiritual carpet that I've safeguarded for decades. Nevertheless, in an effort to live my life "before the Lord" as King David did[1], I write this work as a difficult step of faith showing my desire for God's approval rather than man's.

Therefore, since we are surrounded by such
a great cloud of witnesses, let us throw off

> *everything that hinders and **the sin that**
> **so easily entangles**. And let us run with*
> *perseverance the race marked out for us*
> (Hebrews 12:1, emphasis added).

The sin referred to here is one that *easily* ensnares or trips us up. It indicates that there is at least one specific sin in your life, probably multiple, that melts and soaks into you like butter on warm toast. The King James Version calls it a besetting sin. *Beset* is one of those great words that we don't use enough. It means to completely encircle; for example, "the ring was beset with diamonds." The word also has the ominous connotation of surrounding or hemming in with hostile intent, as a hunting party that attacks its prey from all sides.[2]

Writer Maeve Maddox says, "A besetting sin is one to which on account of our constitution, or circumstance or both, we are peculiarly exposed, and into which we most easily and most frequently fall."[3] There are many, many traps—besetting sins—Christians can fall prey to. Fits of rage, embezzlement, superiority, keeping score, gossip, people-pleasing, stealing, bending the truth, smearing people's reputation, sexual immorality, cheating, uncontrolled substance use, judgmentalism, hypocrisy, worry, harsh tongues, stirring up strife between people, throwing your weight around, picking fights, undue attention to body image, playing the victim, fear, perfection, lack of concern for the poor, widows, orphans, and the marginalized; laziness, bitterness and resentment, greed for money, haughtiness, overspending, control, and worry, to name a few.

More sinister traps that start off and look like good or normal things, that then become compulsive can also beset us—shopping, exercise and fitness, attention to appearance, eating, dieting, sports, recreation, pleasure, hobbies, entertainment, electronics, ministry, busyness, and financial security. These lists could go on and on. They are all forms of idolatry—ways in which Christians can turn their hearts away from acknowledging, worshipping, and trusting in the one true God.

Some of these issues are known as addictions in the current culture, as outlined in the chapter titled *The Physiology of Addiction—*

Part 2. I will now single out what we frequently think of as one of the worse ones to demonstrate this point. This illustration was the doorway to a dramatic life-change for me.

———————————————

On a mild February day in the Pacific Northwest, a dear older Jesus-sister and I took a walk at a nearby lake. It was wonderful to catch up with each other after many months. Partway through our walk, while mucking through a muddy trail, she double-jolted me. Almost out of the blue, she expressed that at various points in her life, she dealt with same-sex attraction. Moreover, she had never shared this with anyone!

My body turned to a solid mass of granite. My heart and mind raced so fast they blurred. I don't remember much about the rest of that visit. I was thoroughly befuddled. Her, of all people? She grew up in the church and was active in leadership. And why on earth had she confessed that to *me*? What was I supposed to do with *that* information?

I remained surprisingly composed the rest of our time together. Like Manoah and his wife, I didn't sleep a wink that night. Not that I was troubled, in fact, I was strangely calm throughout that wakeful night. By the next morning though, I knew exactly what I was to do with *that* information. Before I could even do my morning devotional, I prayed a brief prayer of trust that was answered by draconian conviction.

For some reason, after her confession, there was no turning back for me. There was no other option on the table. With a quiet mind and a pounding heart, I knew it was my turn to drop a bombshell. I took a deep breath, and for the last time, I looked around at a world that would never be the same again. I confessed to her that for years, at one point or another, I had indulged in sexual immorality.

That day would mark the beginning of a whole new life for me!

A besetting sin is one to which on account
of our constitution, or circumstance or both,
we are peculiarly exposed, and into which
we most easily and most frequently fall.
                                        Maeve Maddox

Chapter 7

Mine Was a Happy Childhood Until...

Yet you brought me out of the womb;
you made me trust in you, even
at my mother's breast.
From birth I was cast on you;
from my mother's womb you have been my God
(Psalm 22:9,10).

Put on your gum-boots and let's take a field trip to my homeland on the fertile slopes of majestic Mt. Kenya, with its signature red soil. It's God's mountain, fondly known to the locals as *Kirinyaga*. What a sublimely gorgeous part of the world! That stalwart mountain is a strong background to the graceful sway of elegant tribal women walking in single file with loads on their heads or backs, singing enchanting rhythms that make the heart dance; and where children play free all day. At least forty years ago they did. I was the sixth of seven children in a middle-class family and had a wonderful happy-go-lucky childhood. I grew up in communal living surrounded by siblings, relatives, friends, and others.

While mine was a relatively privileged upbringing, I was acutely in touch with deep suffering all around me, as only the third world can present. I went to church from the time I was a little girl. I accepted Christ at the age of fourteen, in high school, a legacy of my sister Faith, who coached me in the faith. Hers was and continues to be a vibrant adventure with Jesus. Though her life was hard, her walk was as spellbinding to behold as steadfast Mt. Kenya. I fell in love with her amazing, practical God.

I have a gripping Christian heritage. My maternal grandfather, Charles Kabiru, was a pioneer convert to Christianity. It amazes me to think of this remarkable Dorobo man who heard and responded to the voice of a Jew, Jesus Christ, of Nazareth as revealed to him by German missionaries in the early 1900s. It boggles and thrills my mind to think of the web of factors that interplayed to get this message to him. With joy and compulsion, he proceeded to pour his life into reaching the locals for Jesus. I am honored to be a part of his lineage. I imagine his prayers for his progeny, and delight to know that, decades later, I am an outflowing of that prayer, just as I am one of the stars that father Abraham beheld in the night sky, millennia ago, as he contemplated the promises of God.

That God chose me is as clear as it is astounding. I had and continue to have little to offer him, other than a surrendered life of intimacy. Anything I do have has come from him. Thankfully, the surrendered life of intimacy is all he asks for. Over the years, I have come to hold my faith legacy in very high esteem as one of the richest blessings of my life. My parents were regular church-goers. That's what people did on Sunday. Though they were wonderful parents, many aspects of their lives weren't surrendered to God.

As I said, mine was a happy childhood—up until about 4:00 p.m. It was about that time every day that Mum started to drink. By 7:00 p.m., my gentle, sweet mother turned into a monstrous lush. I could always tell when she was mad at Dad. At those times, she drank a little more than usual and, in her inebriated mumblings, disclosed exactly what she thought of him. At an early age, I learned to tell when it would be a long night. My heart pounded with dread, anticipating the harrowing interactions that would ensue when he got home. I am a testament to the astute conclusion that families living with a user is like living with a ticking time-bomb, or an approaching tornado "existing between the two extremes of crisis mobilization and hopeless despair."[1]

My dread always delivered. I was a child of the corner. I remember cowering in one corner or another, staring wide-eyed through pudgy, trembling fingers as they raged and affronted each other. Though Mum's verbal sawed-off shotgun was aimed at Dad, it blasted my little heart. His thirty-ought rebuttals tore it up from the opposite side. I don't know how I got caught in the cross-fire. In my little nighty, the small of my back pushed with all my little might into the corner against which I braced for recoil after recoil. I closed my eyes as tightly as I could, till they hurt. Covering my ears was pointless. I wished the cold, hard stone would suck me in and take me far, far away, or make me as hard as it was.

When she was three sheets to the wind, she didn't care. She actually goaded him. She got in his face and words flew like rapid fire. I remember stretching my neck, wide-eyed, from behind our brown velvet sofa, to see who this wild woman was that had broken into our house. He towered over her, but in those moments, she was like an enraged leopard and could have ripped him apart with her bare hands. When she couldn't think of any more words, she pounded his massive chest with her furious paws, claws protracted. It all stomped my bleeding heart underfoot.

I secretly despised her for years. She always called on me to pour her drink. I was a master at it. Culturally, children are always to do as they are told so I hid my contempt and poured it carefully, my lip curled up in disgust. I tilted the glass delicately, so it wouldn't foam up excessively. I can still hear the clink of the bottle against the glass. The yeasty smell of the frothy brew wafts afresh as I write this. She always asked how many more she had left. I dutifully informed her.

Physically my father was a giant. Socially, he was greatly revered in the community. I adored him. It wasn't until my teens that I accidently learned of his intrigues. My stumbling upon it was clearly of the Lord. The details were odious and the incidents innumerable. Mum always found out about them, though she didn't seek out such appalling information. They caused untold anguish. In one fell swoop, her behavior made complete sense in my young mind. My heart melted for her. I poured her drink with more respect and compassion, with less hardness and disdain. Surely, it was the least I could do to soothe her brokenness. A codependent was born.

It stunned me that it caused her so much pain. Even at my young age, I knew that "that's what men do." I heard and saw it all around me. At weddings, the bride was informed that she was never to question her new husband when he came home at 2:00 a.m. or didn't come home at all. "That's just what they do!" The woman's role is to do what her name implies. The Kikuyu word for woman is *mutumia*, meaning "she who is mum," no pun intended. This mum has nothing to do with motherhood. It has everything to do with looking the other way. Overlooking indiscretions. Not saying a word about them. A wise woman doesn't confront what she knows he is doing. *Mum* is the word. Codependence—the capacity to behave as though dysfunctional behavior is normal—was strongly reinforced in the culture.

So I learned to muffle my sobs, to contain my little heart which was heaving like an erupting volcano. After all it wasn't my pain, or my problem. It was theirs. I told myself that I was just a child and these were adult matters. I just needed to ignore them. I would beg God to make it all stop. It never did. Maybe if I was really good, this wouldn't happen. Maybe if I stayed out of the way. Maybe if I worked really hard and excelled in life…

Once I found some confusing information pertaining to dad and went to an older sister with it. In the middle of the next fight, with my back pressed into the corner, he looked at me and said, "You started this." Oh no! What had I done? I didn't even think he knew I was there. I died a thousand deaths. If I found stuff out I would never, ever share it again as it sparked such horror. I vowed I would never yell at anyone; I would never be angry. I wore masks to hide my shame and eventually lost my true face. The masks and personas I donned helped me avoid the pain of revisiting the trauma. Not that I needed to revisit it, heaven knows it visited unfailingly. It was a slippery slide to the land of people-pleasing. I mastered this in order to avoid conflict and begged for approval.

In the morning, I would awake to a magnificent orchestra, a cacophony of weaver birds outside. Inside the house, all would be sunny and back to normal too. It was magical. It was all smiles and business as usual. No talk of the night before. No revisiting of any unpleasantness. I learned that rough times are always followed by sweet times. These are swiftly followed by rough times again. I questioned my sanity but not for long. I chose to embrace my reality as I gleefully ran out to play with the neighborhood kids, grateful for simple pleasures. I was back to my happy childhood.

Until about 4:00 p.m…

In the course of time, I mastered avoidance and pretense. I mastered masquerades. I mastered dysfunction by withdrawing and nursing my wounds in the darkness of dissociation and denial. I knew that this picture played out in homes all around me. People knew it happened in ours. It was embarrassing to hear surrounding televisions, radios, or conversations hush as things escalated. No one talked about it, except in gossip.

When I was about ten years old, I was sent to a relative's house to retrieve something. I skipped along merrily and laughed as I scared off a brood of chickens pecking about. The little gremlin delighted in how they squawked and scampered, wild-eyed, and took wing. I was still chuckling as entered the house and recounted the instructions to get to the item. I jumped to reach above the armoire and made a blind sweep. Along with the item of interest, a book bonked me on the head and fell to the floor. I rubbed my annoyed head and leaned over to pick it up. My bent body froze in place mid-stride as I beheld its cover. All the blood drained from my head and my temples pounded like wild drums. Its images stunned me and I gasped. My young brain had never, *ever* seen or imagined what I saw. I was shocked and utterly repulsed—yet I couldn't look away. The room began to spin in slow motion. I turned the pages like a disgusted child poking a dead animal this way and that with a stick.

I walked in, a child. I stumbled out, dazed and trying to contain the neural blast that had just erupted. Unfortunately, I couldn't "unsee" the pictures. Have you ever accidently grabbed a slug or a snail? Hours after you flung it off you, you can still feel the plump, soft, slimy grossness in your hands. In the same sticky way, the images replayed in my mind for weeks, then months. I couldn't talk to anyone about it. No one in my life could possibly have any idea what it was.

I willed the images away. I prayed against them. Yet like a zombie, I found myself returning to them in practice or in my mind. Ironically, I learned that they became a predictable pleasure and comfort when things got unbearable at home. That too, I compartmentalized, of course. I had acquired yet another of many holes in my carpet! A couple years later, I got my official sex education—a whopping "Now, don't show boys your panties!" It was a dollar short and a day late by virtue of what I'd seen.

I learned to hide, suppress, and to numb my
pain. But this is what happens when pain
goes unvalidated (sic.) and unwitnessed: we
learn to internalize the false story that we
aren't worth the effort to be cared for.[2]

Aundi Kolber

Chapter 8

The Anatomy of Salvation

God desires an intimate relationship with human beings. That is a mystery in itself. Humans are born in a state of spiritual death and darkness due to Adam's sin. We are separated from and enemies of God. He loves us so much and is not willing that any human should remain in death but that everyone would come to repentance and live.[1] In His mercy and love, God did and continues to initiate reconciliation to mankind.

Sin demands death. His Son Jesus died a gruesome death and completely paid the penalty for our sin so we could be reconciled to God. He then came back to life, powerfully rescuing us from the kingdom of death and darkness which enslaved us, and delivered us to the kingdom of life and light. Humans, in believing that Jesus is the Messiah, the Son of God, receive life in his name.[2]

> *For this is how God loved the world: He gave*
> *his one and only Son, so that everyone who*
> *believes in him will not perish but have eternal*
> *life. God sent his Son into the world not to*
> *judge the world, but to save the world through*
> *him. There is no judgment against anyone*
> *who believes in him. But anyone who does*
> *not believe in him has already been judged*
> *for not believing in God's one and only Son*
> (John 3:16–18, NLT).

God then ups the ante. He woos individual hearts into a love relationship. God initiates this love affair by lighting a spark in our hearts that ignites at the fuel of the Holy Spirit. He sustains the relationship from beginning to end. He invites us to maintain it in faithfulness as we continually surrender to him. In and of ourselves, we are incapable of this. We need his help every step of the way.

> *Many a man claims to have unfailing love,*
> *But a faithful man who can find?*
> (Proverbs 20:6)

While we pour our entire selves into this relationship, we ultimately bring very little to it. We are beggars warmly invited to a sumptuous royal banquet by a loving king. Not a single one of us is invited because we deserve it. We are invited because he desires us. Read this slowly: We are invited because he desires us! We have no fitting attire for the soiree, so he dresses us. We have nothing worthy of bringing to the feast but all is lavishly provided. We just get to come and experience the time of our lives—here on earth and then into eternity. And all we have to do is believe this and accept the invitation. These lyrics from the hymn *Rock of Ages* phrase this beautifully:

> Not the labor of my hands
> Can fulfill Thy law's demands;
> Could my zeal no respite know,
> Could my tears forever flow,
> All for sin could not atone;
> Thou must save, and Thou alone.

> Nothing in my hand I bring,
> Simply to Thy cross I cling;
> Naked, come to Thee for dress;
> Helpless, look to Thee for grace;
> Foul, I to the fountain fly;
> Wash me, Savior, or I die.[3]

I cannot comprehend the fact that God chose me. I never will. But I will ever ponder it and leap for joy about it. Because he, so grand, stooped to choose me, so insignificant, I aspire to live my life ever before him. As we come to the banquet, something marvelous happens. We are transformed from the inside out as we will see in this book. As Spurgeon said, "in every case where a man is inwardly persuaded of the Holy Ghost that the Lord has chosen him out of the world, the sure and certain effect is that the Lord stands out to him in a clear light, and becomes to him the greatest force in his life, the chief motive power, the main thought of his mind."[4]

Alleluia!

I cannot comprehend the fact that God
chose me. I never will. But I will ever ponder
it and leap for joy about it. Because he, so
grand, stooped to choose me, so insignificant,
I aspire to live my life ever before him.

Chapter 9

Sin Leading to Death

For the wages of sin is death, but the gift of God
is eternal life in Christ Jesus our Lord
(Romans 6:23).

Sin leads to death. Period. We just saw that spiritual death is the state we are born in. It is characterized by broken fellowship and separation from God. This may span the gamut from mild disregard to hostile disdain for him, and always by disobedience (willful or otherwise) to him and his desires. The unbeliever is subject to both physical and spiritual death. Spiritually, when we come to Jesus, we pass from death to life as shown in the following pieces of Scripture:

*Very truly I tell you, **whoever** hears my*
word and believes him who sent me has
eternal life and will not be judged but
has crossed over from death to life
(John 5:24, emphasis mine).

As for you, you were dead in your transgressions
and sins, in which you used to live when you
followed the ways of this world and of the ruler
of the kingdom of the air, the spirit who is now
at work in those who are disobedient. All of us
also lived among them at one time, gratifying
the cravings of our flesh and following its desires

and thoughts. Like the rest, we were by nature deserving of wrath. But because of his great love for us, God, who is rich in mercy, made us alive with Christ even when we were dead in transgressions—it is by grace you have been saved. And God raised us up with Christ and seated us with him in the heavenly realms in Christ Jesus (Ephesians 2:1-6).

*Truly, truly, I tell you, he who believes has eternal life… This is the bread that comes down from heaven, so that **anyone** may eat of it and not die. I am the living bread that came down from heaven. If **anyone** eats of this bread, he will live forever. And this bread, which I will give for the life of the world, is My flesh* (John 6:47, 50-51, emphasis mine).

I have written these things to you who believe in the name of the Son of God, so that you may know that you have eternal life (1 John 5:13).

*For God so loved the world, that he gave his only begotten Son, that **whosoever** believeth in him should not perish, but have everlasting life* (John 3:16, emphasis mine).

*And this is the will of him that sent me, that **everyone** who sees the Son, and believes in him, may have everlasting life: and I will raise him up at the last day* (John 6:40,47, emphasis mine).

For I am convinced that neither death nor life, neither angels nor demons, neither the

> *present nor the future, nor any powers, neither*
> *height nor depth, nor anything else in all*
> *creation, will be able to separate us from the*
> *love of God that is in Christ Jesus our Lord*
> (Romans 8:38-39).

We see clearly that a Christian *cannot* be in a state of spiritual death. We are eternally and securely reconciled to Him and brought to everlasting life.

That said, though the believer has overcome death spiritually through Christ, he will experience the physical consequences of sin that he engages in, possibly even physical death. For example, consuming communion while habitually and willfully indulging in sin can result in physical "weakness, sickness, and death."[1] In certain cases, as in that of Ananias and Saphira in Acts chapter 5, a Christian can be called home as a result of his destructive fleshly behavior. These are physical consequences of the sin of pornography/idolatry.

Adam and Eve experienced this consequence. They incurred both spiritual and potential physical death in the garden as a result of sin; however, they were saved spiritually by the same faith that saves us. Fortunately, they believed God, evidenced by their obedience to the instruction of the blood sacrifice, which foretells the sacrifice of Christ. Another example is set by Cain. He evidenced his lack of saving faith, by his disobedience. Cain is the first recorded evidence of "works-based religion" in that he decided, as an act of his will, how he would approach the God of the universe. Through his good works, he wished to be saved. His works led to death.

> *What shall we say, then? Shall we go on sinning*
> *so that grace may increase? By no means! We are*
> *those who have died to sin; how can we live in it*
> *any longer? Or don't you know that all of us who*
> *were baptized into Christ Jesus were baptized*
> *into his death? We were therefore buried with him*
> *through baptism into death in order that, just*

as Christ was raised from the dead through the
glory of the Father, we too may live a new life
(Romans 6:1-4).

I'm not talking about the progressive sanctification of the maturing process, whereby God graciously shows us our sin more clearly as we mature. A new believer knows little of what behavior counts as sin and what doesn't. The more time we spend with Christ, the more our eyes are opened through Scripture, the Holy Spirit, and fellowship with other believers to what is sinful and what isn't. As we become aware of what displeases our Lord, let us be diligent to confess it and abandon it.

All Christians sin from time to time. We are to avoid a flippant attitude toward sin and strive to be reconciled to intimacy with God by swift confession. We are to repent whenever we become aware of sin in our lives, and have a rabid drive to make amends with everyone we have hurt. Willful disobedience is the believer giving himself over as a slave to sin. Since someone who claims to be a Christian has died to sin, a Christian who is *habitually* and *willfully* engaged in known sin falls in one of two camps:

1. He is fooling himself, and the truth (Christ) is not in him.

    If we claim to have fellowship [relationship,
    association, communion, intimacy, intercourse]
    with Him and yet walk in the darkness, we lie
    and do not live out the truth. But if we walk in
    the light, as he is in the light, we have fellowship
    with one another, and the blood of Jesus, his Son,
    purifies us from all sin
    (1 John 1:6, 7).

2. He is foolishly inviting strong discipline from his Father.

    [B]ecause the Lord disciplines the one he loves
    (Hebrews 12:5)

Chapter 10

The Anatomy of Porneia

As the Corona virus brings the world to its knees, this book explores equally virulent addictions and deep-rooted compulsions that are crippling the church of Jesus Christ. Members of the church are desperately addicted to pornography, by the more accurate definition we just learned. It is a pandemic in the pew *and* in the pulpit that makes Covid-19 look like child's play.

The Fowler's Snare & the Kerf

by Hannah Kolehmainen

"See, it doesn't hurt," hissed the voice, "if you just
sit very still."
And the firm grip around my ankle
Gets firmer.
Agonizingly firmer.
Now it hurts even when I am still.
The chain clangs mockingly
As the jagged mouth of the snare,
Its cold metal, uncaring, punctures the skin.
I gasp sharply.
It pauses momentarily,
Then
Slowly sinks its scabrous fangs.
And its venomous rust rips to my heart.

"There, there…, just sit very still," he shushes,
cackling impishly.
I sense the false relief of paralysis.

I learn to silence the whimper and go about my life
With terminal stoicism.
I dab at my gaping wound with filthy rags and
rewrap it with soiled ones.
Again and again.
I learn to sit very still
Not to walk too far
I learn sophisticated ways to dignify my limp
when I'm not lying low
I learn to appease the oppressive guard, Mr. Secrecy.

As gangrene gains ground
I forget what it was like to sing
I forget what it was like to flap my grand wings
I forget what it was like to take to the wind
"Shh…very still now," he sneers, snarling omi-
nously from time to time
And strokes me repulsively
Like a kidnapper attempting to kiss his victim.

Others around me are ensnared too,
But we don't linger at eye contact.
We smile politely,
And answer hurriedly,
"I'm doing great, thank you. How are you?"…

Historically, the church has considered pornography to be a
male problem among non-believers. The sad reality is that today,

women and children are equally ensnared. Those men, women, and children are in the church! The sooner we, the church, awake to this truth, the sooner we can tackle it head on.

Luke Gibbon's research, '15 Statistics About the Church and Pornography That Will Blow Your Mind' (using the common cultural definition i.e. "viewing erotica") found:

- Forty-seven per cent of US families self-reported that pornography was a problem in their home.
- Pornography use increases marital infidelity rate by more than 300 percent.
- Fifty-six per cent of divorces in the US involve one party having an "obsessive interest" in porn
- The average child is first exposed to porn at eleven and 94 percent will view it by the time they are fourteen
- Sixty-eight per cent of church-going men and over 50 percent of pastors regularly view porn
- Seventy-six per cent of young Christian adults 18-24 years old actively search for porn.
- Thirty-three percent of women aged twenty-five and under search for porn at least once per month.
- Only 13 percent of self-identified Christian women say they never watch porn.
- Only 7 percent of pastors say their church has a program to help people struggling with pornography.[1]

In its 2016 study 'The Porn Phenomenon', the Barna Group found that, fortunately, attitudes towards sex have shifted dramatically within the last couple of decades. People are more open to talking about it than ever before. "It does not have the same social taboo it once did. When respondents were allowed to "opt-out" of questions of a personal nature, more than 90% continued through the survey questions, indicating data reliability." Here are some of their findings regarding viewing porn:

- Seventy-one percent of young adults and 50 percent of teens come across what they consider to be porn at least once a month, whether they are seeking it or not.
- People who identified as Christians were the most likely to feel guilty about viewing pornography.
- More people considered "not recycling" a worse problem than viewing pornography.
- Despite the awareness of the problem, most churches do not have programs specifically designed to assist those struggling with porn use.[2]

This is unfortunate because religious communities are to be a safe haven for the ailing. Clergy are "among the most trusted professionals in society" and churches have tight social networks in place to help prevent substance abuse and addictive behavior, as well as to aid in recovery.[3]

Writer Steve Gallagher profiles the typical Christian man that a counselor will help. He "has been involved in illicit sexual activities for years...almost entirely in secret." While the average counselee will be a man who is simply addicted to erotica, addicts will also indulge in other forms of pornography including:

- adultery (this includes dwelling on extramarital sexual fantasies)
- fornication
- masturbation
- adult bookstores
- strip clubs
- massage parlors
- prostitutes
- peeking in windows
- exposing himself
- obscene phone calls
- sexual assaults
- bestiality
- teen and adult promiscuity

- homosexuality
- orgies
- incest[4]

We live in a day and age when our culture is encouraging sexiness in younger and younger girls. We are setting them, and our young men, up for sensuality, a serious problem we will discuss in a later chapter. Provocative clothing, attitudes, and behaviors are the norm even in grade school. Children are exposed to more and more explicit material at younger and younger ages and in more venues than ever before.

Our mainstream media is increasingly hypersexualized. We are grooming our young men and women for addiction and providing the long-term customer-base that traffickers can sell to. While this industry is dominated by men, no pun intended, there are more and more women working as pimps as well as using the services provided by trafficking. Further, thanks to our "liberated" status today, women are increasingly exposed to, and more brazen in flirting with men who are not their husbands. Many women harbor a regular crush, secret or not, towards other men and women.

There are numerous other areas of idolatry that are more innocuous but no less effective in their capacity to turn our hearts away from God. Dr. Neil Anderson's Steps to Freedom in Christ lists things or people that we easily elevate above Jesus Christ in our lives. I have modified and added to it:

- Ambition/Achievement/Talents
- Appearance/Image/Fashion/Being organized
- Boyfriend/Girlfriend
- Busyness/Activity
- Celebrities
- Children
- A Church/Minister
- Church activities/Ministry
- Cultural heritage

- Drugs (any mood-altering substance including caffeine, alcohol, cigarettes, inappropriately used prescription drugs, etc.)
- Electronics/Gaming/ TV/Movies/ Music/Other media
- Food/Diet
- Friends
- Fun/Pleasure/Carousing
- Group affiliations (including religious)
- Health/Exercise/Diet
- Hobbies
- Knowledge/Being right
- Money/Possessions
- Parents
- Popularity/Opinion of others
- Power/Control
- Security/Finances/Future
- Sports
- Spouse
- Work
- Yourself

More people consider "not recycling" a
worse problem than viewing pornography.
Barna Group

Chapter 11

The Physiology of Addiction—Part 1

I praise you because I am fearfully
and wonderfully made;
your works are wonderful,
I know that full well
(Psalm 139:14).

Please indulge my left brain here.

Every part of our body consists of cells. Brain cells are called *neurons*. A human brain has about 100 million neurons.[1] They are some of the longest living cells in the body.[2] Neurons help us perform complex cognitive functions and integrate ourselves in our environment through the senses of sight, hearing, tasting, smelling, feeling, and the equally important but frequently overlooked one, the sense of movement (e.g. kinesthesia and proprioception.) This sensory input is processed in various brain parts.

It was long believed that adults had all the brain cells they'd have for life. In 1962 American Biologist Joseph Altman presented the first evidence of *neurogenesis* ("neuro" meaning brain and "genesis" meaning birth).[3] This portends that adults can memorize and learn new habits, and that they can heal after neural (brain and spinal cord) damage such as from strokes and addiction.

Neuroplasticity ("plasticity" meaning changeability) is the capacity of the brain to change concretely over time with use. *In utero*, all humans have relatively similar neural circuitry. There and throughout life, neuroplasticity takes place as the person interacts (or not) with his or her environment. Thousands of cells die every day and new ones are made. At any given time, brain function is as fluid and enthralling as a murmuration of starlings in the air, flying as one organism, changing directions in a mesmerizing fashion.

Brains change so that learning can happen. These alterations happen regularly just by going through normal life. They can also change suddenly and drastically, such as when we have intense new experiences e.g. falling in love or incurring a stroke. These amazing brains also ebb from lack of engagement in meaningful activities. Think of children in orphanages who sit in their cribs all day long, or of elderly folks cooped up in wheelchairs with no activities or interaction. These suffer awful occupational injustice that negatively affects their physical, emotional, and spiritual health and well-being.

Along with electricity, the brain uses neurotransmitters to function. Neurotransmitters are natural chemicals that communicate information from one neuron to the next at astonishing speed. The neurotransmitter is released into the space between the neurons called a *synapse*. Think of the process of learning anything (habit, skill, way of thinking, etc.) as a massive construction site. The synapses form the foundation of this building process with much traffic (electrical and neurochemical) coming to and from the site. Just like a construction site, changes take place at these synapses. In the brain, the astounding changes facilitate thought and behavior patterns. These synaptic changes either become engrained as we focus on and invest in them, or they wane if we ignore them.

Physical architecture influences our use of physical spaces and, in turn, our use of the space influences architecture. This is a feedback loop that has evolved over millennia. In the same way, our experiences shape our neural circuitry. With time, the circuitry exerts an influence on experiences. Each influences the other. As materials (neurochemicals) are dropped off at the synapses, behavioral and thought patterns are built, remodeled, and/or demolished. The construction site then changes in response to experiences throughout life by becoming more or less concrete.

Though tremendous gains have been made in understanding the brain, it remains a vast, mysterious realm. Let's home in on just one of its countless aspects as it pertains to this book—desire. Addiction is merely a runaway, intense desire that has kidnapped a life. *Dopamine* is the name of the neurotransmitter that is the brain's General Foreman (GF) in the matter of learning and desire. Dopamine plays an important role in the modulation of behavior and cognition, voluntary movement, motivation and drive, punishment and reward, inhibition of prolactin production, sleep, dreaming, mood, attention, working memory, and learning.[4] It also controls heart rate, blood vessel function, kidney function and pain processing.

Mammals are born with what's called a "reward pathway" which helps us stay alive or create a life by rewarding us when we engage in acts that promote life (e.g. eating, relaxation, leisure, sex, etc.) and/or avoid pain. Desire is founded upon this "reward pathway," which GF Dopamine oversees.

Reward pathways see to the pursuit of pleasure and safety while avoiding risk or pain. The tightly regulated reward pathway entails the release of neurotransmitters, particularly our friendly foreman Mr. Dopamine. Dopamine provides *temporary* pleasure. When we have achievements or are at peace, the reward pathway reinforces us positively with a hit of dopamine. When we do things we enjoy or value like hanging out with loved ones or enjoying a rigorous time of exercise, getting to the next level on a video game or reading a great book, we get rewarded with dopamine.

While dopamine is motivating your brain to do (or avoid) things and rewarding it for doing so, a protein called Δ*FosB* (pronounced, delta Fos B) is quietly leaving trail markers in your brain, creating a pathway to help you get back to the pleasurable experience. Think of Δ*FosB* as the construction crew blasting new pathways and laying a highway to ensure future access to the source of pleasure. We've learned that in time, the pathway (the building project) becomes increasingly concrete. The associated behavior becomes more automatic.

"DeltaFosB may accumulate in response to many types of compulsive behaviors."[5] "The brain is certainly built to make any action, repeated enough times, into a compulsion. But the emotional heart of addiction—in a word, *desire*—makes a compulsion inevitable, because unslaked desire is the springboard to repetition, and repetition is the springboard to compulsion." This is why "addiction belongs to a subset of habits: those that are most difficult to extinguish."[6]

By way of analogy, where the brain is the world, picture the landmass of Canada, the USA, and Central America as three main parts that form the reward pathway. It is also known as the *dopaminergic system*.

Diagram of Brain's Reward Pathway[7]

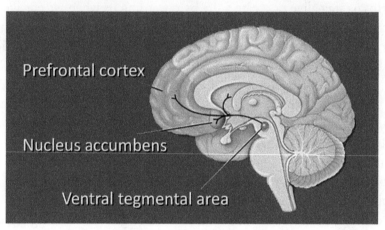

Dopamine is secreted from the ventral tegmental area (VTA), a part of the midbrain. Let's call that Central America. While dopamine is being released, there are hundreds upon hundreds of related and unrelated processes going on in the incredible brain, just like we're having certain experiences in our country, while there are countless related and unrelated things going on around the world.

Dopamine's target area is the striatum (a part of which is the nucleus accumbens in the diagram). Let's call that the USA. This area is concerned with rewards, movement, motivation and drive. It is overseen by the Prefrontal Cortex (PFC). The PFC constitutes a whopping two-thirds of the human brain.[8] We will call this area Canada. It oversees what is called executive function including alertness, problem-solving, learning, empathy, comprehension, memory, judgement (foresight, insight, and hindsight), planning, self-control and all other aspects of cognition. It is the control center of the brain.

Dr. Marc Lewis states that "new neuronal pathways, and corresponding patterns of thought and behavior, start off tentative and fluctuating. But after they've been activated repeatedly, fledgling pathways get more entrenched, more concretized, and eventually carved in stone, or at least in flesh."[9] As we continue to have experiences, construction material is laid down in the brain as with wet cement. The resulting behavior is pretty awkward and mechanical at first (think of a toddler stiffly teetering along as he or she learns how to walk) and may seem insignificant.

Think of the behavior or way of thinking as the building. This can be a habit such as cooking or learning how to weld; or thought responses such as 'they're smiling at me, they must be friendly,' or 'they're smiling at me, they must want something from me.' Learning the thoughts or behavior is reinforced by repetition. With each life experience, our GF Dopamine sees to it that more materials are swiftly, repetitively dropped off for continued construction and the cement becomes increasingly set. The more we practice a thought or behavior, the more graceful, adept, and automatic it becomes. The building blocks are getting concretized in place—learning is happening. Habits are developing.

With this in mind, consider the importance of our senses and what we expose ourselves to, as well as what we choose to dwell on in our thought life. The Apostle Paul's words are spot on neuro-scientifically when he says,

> *Finally, brothers and sisters, whatever is*
> *true, whatever is noble, whatever is right,*
> *whatever is pure, whatever is lovely, whatever*
> *is admirable—if anything is excellent or*
> *praiseworthy—**think** about such things.*
> *Whatever you have **learned** or **received** or*

__heard__ from me, or __seen__ in me—put it into
__practice__. And the God of peace will be with you
(Philippians 4:8-9, emphases added).

Where there's little motivation (a function of the striatum), the foreman takes a chill pill. The infrastructure there is like a deserted, bumpy, little country road. Activity at the construction site (synapse) can grind to a halt. Minimal, if any, building materials are deposited, and pretty soon the site may even be abandoned. Use it or lose it. Some materials may be hauled off as they are no longer being used. Of course, dilapidated foundation can remain in place and a construction site be reactivated years or even decades later, if motivation or need arises in that area. For example, running into an old lover can reactivate a building site in no time if the foreman sees it as important. Another example is hopping back on a bike after years of not using one. This may entail a momentary wobble then off we go as pathways that haven't been used fire away in recognition.

Dopamine release from the midbrain or VTA to the striatum is triggered by arousal, novelty/surprise, and shock. These facilitate learning for children and adults. Playing peek-a-boo with a baby is a fascinating way to watch this in play. The human face is a jungle gym to a baby. Its appearance from behind a cover evokes peals of laughter and delight. Soon though, one needs to change it up from time to time otherwise boredom sets in, i.e. novelty wears off and arousal levels drop. Just showing up from a different side of the cover, or varying your timing is enough of a surprise to keep the child engaged, not to mention the variety in the combination of noises, contortions, and silliness that emanate from the eyes, nose, mouth, and other body parts.

Just as the world has different countries that interact with each other, other parts of the brain such as the limbic system interact with the midbrain and are affected by the foreman. The limbic system

NAPPING IN DELILAH'S LAP

connects memories and emotions, playing an active role in habit formation. The highway to our building can be a country road or an
international highway. The more numerous and trafficked the pathways are, the easier it is for the user to go back, whether they want to
or not. The more ΔFosB, the greater the drive to engage in the habit,
whether one likes it or not.

What does this look like in practice? Through repeated exposure to trials, the Apostle Paul learned that God is faithful and that he
would see Paul through any circumstance. As a result of the practice
he had, he trained his mind to be content. He learned contentment
which goes against the flesh when we are not getting our way. He
invested in pathways of contentment versus pathways of indulging
the flesh and grumbling. He retrained his brain to get a dopamine
hit from things of the Lord.

> *I hope in the Lord Jesus to send Timothy*
> *to you soon, that I also may be cheered*
> *when I receive news about you*
> (Philippians 2:19).

Paul had originally treasured and invested in the same things
that give us a lot of us a dopamine hit. That is, until an encounter
with Jesus catapulted him off his high horse. A brain transformation
took place with the power of a lightning bolt as the Lord blinded him
and radically rewired his neural pathways. He was temporarily shut
down for an upgrade. Thereafter what used to provide his dopamine
hits—his identity and pedigree, was hauled off the construction site
in garbage truck after garbage truck.

> *My beloved ones, don't ever limit your*
> *joy or fail to rejoice in the wonderful*
> *experience of knowing our Lord Jesus!*
> *I don't mind repeating what I've already written*
> *to you because it protects you—beware of those*
> *religious hypocrites who teach that you should be*
> *circumcised to please God. For we have already*

*experienced "heart-circumcision," and we worship
God in the power and freedom of the Holy Spirit,
not in laws and religious duties. We are those who
boast in what Jesus Christ has done, and not in
what we can accomplish in our own strength.
It's true that I once relied on all that I had
become. I had a reason to boast and impress
people with my accomplishments—more than
others—for my pedigree was impeccable.
I was born a true Hebrew of the heritage of
Israel as the son of a Jewish man from the tribe
of Benjamin. I was circumcised eight days after
my birth and was raised in the strict tradition
of Orthodox Judaism, living a separated and
devout life as a Pharisee. And concerning the
righteousness of the Torah, no one surpassed
me; I was without a peer. Furthermore, as a
fiery defender of the truth, I persecuted the
messianic believers with religious zeal.
Yet all of the accomplishments that I once
took credit for, I've now forsaken them and I
regard it all as nothing compared to the delight
of experiencing Jesus Christ as my Lord! To
truly know him meant letting go of everything
from my past and throwing all my boasting
on the garbage heap. It's all like a pile of
manure to me now, so that I may be enriched
in the reality of knowing Jesus Christ and
embrace him as Lord in all of his greatness.
My passion is to be consumed with him and
not clinging to my own "righteousness" based in
keeping the written Law. My "righteousness" will
be his, based on the faithfulness of Jesus Christ—
the very righteousness that comes from God. And
I continually long to know the wonders of Jesus
more fully and to experience the overflowing*

power of his resurrection working in me. I will
be one with him in his sufferings and I will be
one with him in his death. Only then will I be
able to experience complete oneness with him
in his resurrection from the realm of death.
I admit that I haven't yet acquired the absolute
fullness that I'm pursuing, but I run with
passion into his abundance so that I may
reach the purpose that Jesus Christ has called
me to fulfill and wants me to discover.
(Philippians 3:1-12, TPT).

Notice the terms he uses in Philippians 3 above and how they tie in to the concept of desire: "my passion," "to be consumed," "continually long to know," "to experience the overflowing power," "experience complete oneness," "I'm pursuing," "I run with passion." The passage also speaks to a heightened state of living versus boredom and the tedium that marks the lives of so many: "the wonders," "absolute fullness," "abundance," "reach the purpose that Jesus has called me to fulfill and wants me to discover."

So first we perceive with the senses—we hear, see, and receive what is modeled to us as we were taught in Philippians 4:8. Then we choose what to dwell on/think about. We then practice that (verse 9). With practice, we increasingly relate to Paul in learning and knowing.

*I **know** what it is to be in need, and I know*
*what it is to have plenty. I **have learned***
the secret of being content in any and every
situation, whether well fed or hungry,
whether living in plenty or in want
(Philippians 4:12, emphases added).

Finally, we reach our goal:

> *I can **do** all things through him*
> *who gives me strength*
> (Philippians 4:13, emphasis added).

What a magnificent example of brain rewiring. Imagine the investment in time and resources that Paul had put in from childhood. Imagine the kudos he received every time he walked on the streets, his learned robes swishing behind him in the wake of status and importance. People stepped aside for him. Dopamine hit upon dopamine hit. He was passionate, purposeful, motivated, driven, brilliant, well-studied. With astounding prowess, he engaged in heated mental wrestling and repeatedly flipped his opponents on their backs in submission. Dopamine hit after dopamine hit. Then he met his maker and all that changed instantly. His construction sites were demolished immediately and he began a whole new construction process.

> *Therefore, if anyone is in Christ, he is a new*
> *creation. The old has gone, the new has come*
> (2 Corinthians 5:17).

The brain is certainly built to make any action, repeated enough times, into a compulsion. But the emotional heart of addiction—in a word, *desire*—makes a compulsion inevitable, because unslaked desire is the springboard to repetition, and repetition is the springboard to compulsion.

Marc Lewis

Chapter 12

The Physiology of Addiction—Part 2

In all the matters discussed herein, "addiction" and "dependence" are factors that bear defining. "Dependence" used to refer to a *physical dependence* on a substance or habit as is characterized by the symptoms of tolerance and withdrawal. While one can have a physical dependence without being addicted, addiction is usually right around the corner.

"Addiction" is *mental* and *physical* reliance on a substance or habit. It leads to a change in behavior caused by the biochemical changes in the brain after continued use. Engaging in the addiction becomes the main priority of the addict regardless of negative consequences to themselves or others. An addiction causes people to act irrationally when they can't engage in the habit they are addicted to.

In the Western world, addiction is categorized as a mental health disorder. Two main entities in the medical realm tackle the nosological issue of addiction-related matters:

1. American Psychological Association's (APA) current Diagnostic and Statistical Manual of Mental Disorders (DSM) which exists to provide common research and clinical language for mental health problems
2. The World Health Organization's current International Classification of Disease (ICD-11) whose goal is clinical utility in a broad range of settings, global applicability, and scientific validity.

Drs. Grant and Chamberlain explain the defining features of a mental health disorder as:

- a behavioral or psychological syndrome or pattern that occurs in an individual,
- causing clinically significant distress or disability,
- not an expectable response to common stressors and losses,
- reflecting an underlying psychobiological dysfunction,
- not solely a result of social deviance or conflicts with society,
- having diagnostic validity using one or more sets of diagnostic validators, and
- having clinical utility.[1]

In 2013, the APA released the updated DSM-V and changed the definitions relating to addiction. The APA dropped both "substance abuse" and "substance dependence" in favor of "substance use disorder" (SUD). SUD is now the medical term for addiction. Formerly, *abuse* was considered a mild form of addiction, and *dependence* was a moderate or severe form of addiction. Translate and think of these with regard to habits (including innocuous-seeming ones such as hobbies) and gauge your dependence on them, as they fill your needs for comfort and/or identity.

The DSM-V identifies nine categories of addictive substances. I remember these by the non-sense acronym COCASHISHAT: caffeine; opioids; cannabis; alcohol; stimulants; hallucinogens; inhalants; sedatives, hypnotics, and anxiolytics; and tobacco. These are characterized by their impact on the brain's reward circuitry, and because their co-occurrence is common (i.e., they are used together; e.g., drinking and smoking).

The category of "Substance-Related Disorders" is now called "Substance-Related and Addictive Disorders" to encompass *behaviors*, and not just *substances*, as addictive. In the medical field, the concept of putative "behavioral addictions" is generally rejected, though it is clear that debilitating behaviors—such as gambling, intermittent explosive anger (IED), compulsive sexual behavior, compulsive stealing, compulsive buying, and problem internet use—

have phenomenological and neurobiological parallels with psychoactive substances.[2]

At this time, the only behavioral disorder that has been added to the DSM-V category of "Substance-Related and Addictive Disorders" is gambling disorder. It was formerly "pathological gambling" under the section on impulse control disorders, not elsewhere classified. Gambling is listed because of its high co-occurrence with addictive substances, unlike other behaviors listed. Drs. Grant and Chamberlain report that "evidence from neuroimaging studies supports a shared neuro-circuitry of gambling disorder and substance use disorders."[3] Unlike other behavioral disorders, gambling disorder appears to respond positively to certain opioid medications. Furthermore, there is insufficient evidence to list these other behaviors as addictive.

Kleptomania, pyromania, IED, oppositional-defiance disorder, and conduct disorder are categorized under disruptive, impulse-control, and conduct disorders. These are disorders which cause anger or aggression toward people and/or property. Grant and Chamberlain report that problematic internet use, compulsive buying, and compulsive sexual behavior "were deemed to have insufficient evidence for their inclusion as a disorder…"[4] at this time. Note that many countries around the world categorize and treat compulsive electronics use as a disorder.

I lean toward the (ICD-11) which has, instead of all the above categories, "proposed that the category of impulse-control disorders should be retained and should broadly define these disorders by the repeated failure to resist an impulse, drive, or urge to perform an act that is rewarding to the person (at least in the short-term), despite longer term harm either to the individual or to others."[5] The ICD-11 places gambling under impulse control disorders.

SUD has eleven characteristics according to the DSM-V. Impulse-control disorders share many of these characteristics. According to the DSM-V, two or three symptoms indicate a mild disorder; four to five symptoms indicate a moderate disorder; and six or more symptoms indicate a severe disorder.

Consider these characteristics in Table ii. below with regard to substances and/or habits (including your innocuous-seeming ones). Where do you see your reflection looking back at you? Gauge your dependence on substances and habits as they fill your needs for comfort and/or identity. Knowing who we are as Christians, I came up with this mnemonic to remind myself of the characteristics: **He Raised Powerful Warriors That Lost Control to Chasing Guilty Pleasures.** I have emboldened the letters that represent each characteristic.

Table ii. Characteristics of Addiction

He	1. Using/engaging in ways that are **hazardous** to you or others (e.g. gaming to the point of neglecting your children, using drugs till you pass out, driving drunk)
Raised	2. Failure to fulfill major **role** obligations—family (e.g. spouse, parent, etc.) occupational (e.g. employee, student, etc.)
Powerful	3. Causing social or interpersonal **problems**—e.g. causing conflict at home, legal problems, financial problems, etc.
Warriors	4. **Withdrawal** symptoms—(includes using the substance or habit to avoid withdrawal) physical and emotional symptoms such as anxiety, headaches, sadness, irritability, shakes, nausea
That	5. **Tolerance**—need for increased amounts in order to achieve a desired effect. The same amount no longer produces the same intensity of desired effect.
Lost	6. Using **larger** amounts over a **longer** period than intended

Control	7. Unsuccessful efforts to **cut down** or **control** the use—including using/engaging even when the person doesn't want to; regretting use/engagement; repeated failed efforts to cease
To	8. Great deal of **time** committed to the habit/behavior—contemplating, obtaining, using/engaging, concealing/minimizing, planning, or recovering from the habit. Includes lying, hiding, etc.
Chasing	9. **Craving** the substance/activity
Guilty	10. **Giving up** or minimizing important social, occupational, or recreational activities
Pleasures	11. Use/engagement seriously impacts **physical** or **psychological** health (e.g. depression, cancer, cirrhosis)

Steve McVey and Mike Quarles who run an addiction recovery ministry holistically view a human being as being comprised of body, soul, and spirit. Addiction affects all these aspects of a man and various approaches target each as they excellently outline in Table iii. below.

Table iii. The Problem of Addiction[6]

Area	Nature	Cure	Issue	Result
BODY	Physical addiction	Abstain	Actions	Behavior change
SOUL	Emotional habituation	[Healthy] coping	Feelings	Improve self
SPIRIT	Spiritual bondage	The Cross	Identity	New person

The way we meet our basic
needs for love and worth
is where we find our identity[7]

Chapter 13

Adverse Childhood Events (ACES)

Yet man is born to trouble
as surely as sparks fly upwards
(Job 5:7).

I shared my childhood story and some resultant choices to illustrate an important point that physicians around the world are starting to recognize and attend to. From 1995 to 1997 the Center for Disease Control and Kaiser Permanente conducted the original Adverse Childhood Experiences (ACE) Study, with over seventeen thousand Kaiser Permanente members participating. This ACE study is one of the largest investigations of childhood abuse (psychological, physical, and sexual); neglect (emotional and physical); and household dysfunction (mental illness in the home, violence against a mother, separation/divorce, incarceration, and substance abuse) as they relate to health and wellbeing later in life.

There is no question that childhood trauma has far-reaching impact. Childhood trauma leaves children's brains and bodies marinating in toxic stress hormones such as adrenaline, during their most formative years. I hope that studying the brain and its workings, as we just did, provides a deeper appreciation of this. These children live in a constant state of fight, flight, or fright. These hormones may be helpful in the short-term to help the children cope with the stressor. To remain in long-term circulation is akin to driving 60mph in 2nd gear. It's just not sustainable without doing damage. As a result, toxic stress impedes brain development and predictably leads to chronic diseases in adulthood, along with a host of social and emotional problems. Moreover, ACES have genetic effects that can be passed on to the next generation (epigenetics).

This invaluable study has changed the lives of thousands of people and has massive potential to address people in their brokenness. The Lord used it as an eye-opener in my life. Author Jackie Hill Perry might as well be describing ACES when she says, "Pain being bigger than me can't naturally fit inside my body or stay put for too long before it starts seeping out in various ways."[1] John Piper puts it this way, "Alien affections and passions move in where there's emptiness."[2]

Dr. Neil Anderson claims, "Sexual addiction is frequently bundled up with "early childhood experiences…"[3] Van Cleave et al. quote Dr. Conway Hunter, Jr., saying, "You show me your child of an alcoholic and I'll show you a sick child."[4] The same holds true for children of any addict. Science is just now catching up and revealing how much and for how long people's sins can affect us.

Moreover, we don't have to have traumatic experiences to set us up to sin. Habits can get a foothold in us just through our prevailing experiences, which are our regular everyday experiences in our homes, schools, neighborhoods, churches, the media, and what we are or aren't exposed to there.

This makes me think of a wonderful story about Jesus. He was walking along with his disciples one day when they saw a man born blind. John chapter 9 recounts this event. The disciples asked an interesting question,

> *"Rabbi, who sinned, this man or his*
> *parents, that he was born blind?"*
> *"Neither this man nor his parents sinned," said*
> *Jesus, "but this happened so that the works of*
> *God might be displayed in him. As long as it is*
> *day, we must do the works of him who sent me.*
> *Night is coming, when no one can work. While*
> *I am in the world, I am the light of the world."*
> (John 9:3).

The prevalent culture believed that sins had consequences that would be revisited upon future generations (Exodus 20:5, Exodus 34:7, Numbers 14:18). We have a God who delights and specializes in twists in the stories of our lives. In this man's case, neither he nor his parents sinned. In our case, sometimes both we and our parents have sinned—and we suffer the terrible consequences. I believe that current approaches to addictive disorders are spending a lot of time asking and answering the same question as the disciples. Yet, I'm hearing that at some level, it doesn't matter whether there is sin or not. If there is sin, I'm also hearing that it doesn't matter whose it is. Jesus echoes Job's words at the start of this chapter and assures us,

> *In this world you will have trouble*
> (John 16:33).

Dr. Daniel Sumrock, director of the Center for Addiction Sciences at the University of Tennessee Health Science Center, says addictions should not be called "addiction" but *ritualized compulsive comfort-seeking*. "Ritualized compulsive comfort-seeking (what traditionalists used to call addiction—now referred to Substance Use Disorder and addictive disorders, as we saw in the chapter titled *The Physiology of Addiction—Part 2*) is a normal response to the adversity experienced in childhood, just like bleeding is a normal response to being stabbed."[5] His description of the things or habits we flee to as ritualized compulsive comfort-seeking, resonates deeply with me.

Fortunately for us, our plight in this fallen world, runs blindly, smack into him who is the light. So. That. The. Works. Of. God. Might. Be. Displayed. In. Us! Jesus can then finish the verse above by saying,

> *But be of good cheer, I have overcome the world!*

Jesus says His work is to do the works of His Father. What is that work? Each person of the Trinity has an extensive job description. One role that the three have in common is comforting. Did you know that God is our true ACE? He is our Advanced Comfort Executor!

1.   God the Father

I even I, am he who comforts you
(Isaiah 51:12a).

Praise be to the God and Father of our Lord Jesus
Christ, the Father of compassion and the God of
all comfort, who comforts us in all our troubles
(2 Corinthians 1:3-4a).

2.   God the Son

For the Lamb at the center of the
throne will be their shepherd...
'And he will wipe away every tear from their eyes'
(Revelation 7:17).

3.   God the Holy Spirit.

Jesus said, "And I will ask the Father, and
he will give you another comforter
[Gk.—parakletos] to help you
and be with you forever"
(John 14:16).

The Father, our Comforter. Jesus, our Comforter. The Holy Spirit, our Comforter. Three Comforters in one. This tells us that this is prevalent and supremely important work! Moreover, the Comforter doesn't come and just rock us in our brokenness, stroking us in endless pity, shushing, "You poor thing." No matter the source of our pain, God hugs us long and tenderly, acknowledges the pain, wipes our tears, then stands us up. The Greek word *parakletos* also means an advocate, a helper, a counselor. We are to accept that healing, abandon our worthless ritualized compulsive comfort-seeking behaviors, and run into the arms of our Comforter. He walks us to a place of healing then gently says, as he did to the ill-fated woman caught in adultery,

> *Neither do I condemn you; go and sin no more*
> (John 8:11b).

As though that's not enough, as only he can do, God will use the adversity that the enemy meant for evil and turn it around for good. Nothing is wasted in his economy. He upcycles everything! He used my ACES to turn me into a person I might not be otherwise. To this day, I am a highly sensitive person. I'm constantly detangling my propensity to read deeply into people and hear what they're not saying or to lend words to what they can't. I am amazed at my capacity to sense and evaluate the mood in a room. As I expose my sin and merely one aspect of my difficult past, I feel some troubled people heave a sigh of relief, as though invited to peel off their asphyxiating masks. He poured into me from the flowing river of life, and now I get to pour out into others.

> *Praise be to the God and Father of our Lord Jesus*
> *Christ, the Father of compassion and the God of*
> *all comfort, who comforts us in all our troubles,*
> *so that we can comfort those in any trouble with*
> *the comfort we ourselves receive from God*
> (2 Corinthians 1:4).

But counterfeits abound from time immemorial. When God used Moses to miraculously deliver the children of Israel from Egypt, God personally led them through the wilderness on their way to the Promised Land. In their unrest and disquiet, while Moses was meeting with God on Mt. Sinai, the crowd began to grumble against God and against Moses. Aaron, who'd been left in command, appeased the restless crowd by creating a golden calf for them to worship.

Christian, beware of the sin of grumbling. It is a sure precursor to idolatry. For some, grumbling is such a way of life that it is no longer recognizable. I guarantee that by the time you give verbal vent to your frustration by grumbling, you are already hip-deep in trouble and seriously flirting with idolatry, if not already engaged in it. Notice the lie in the declaration upon the calf being presented to them:

> *These are your gods, O Israel, who*
> *brought you up out of Egypt*
> (Exodus 32:8).

After the nation of Israel split into two kingdoms, King Jeroboam of the Northern tribe of Israel doubted God's promise to sustain his position of victory. Christian, doubting is another landmine. In a moment of anxiety and insecurity, his mind concocted lies and he chose to run with them. Beware of that in your life.

> *Jeroboam thought to himself, "The kingdom will*
> *now likely revert to the house of David. If these*
> *people go up to offer sacrifices at the temple of*
> *the Lord in Jerusalem, they will again give their*
> *allegiance to their lord, Rehoboam king of Judah.*
> *They will kill me and return to King Rehoboam."*
> *After seeking advice, the king made two golden*
> *calves. He said to the people, "It is too much for you*
> *to go up to Jerusalem. Here are your gods, Israel,*
> *who brought you up out of Egypt." One he set up*
> *in Bethel, and the other in Dan. And this thing*

became a sin; the people came to worship the one at
Bethel and went as far as Dan to worship the other
(1 Kings 12:26-29).

Our addictions and compulsions are as these golden calves. What a slap to Jehovah's face! We commit these exact atrocities when we fall before our golden calves for deliverance, for hope, for security, for pleasure, for comfort. Our substances and habits are as capable of delivering us from the brutal sting of the Egyptian's whip in our lives, as this cold, impotent, lifeless calf was. Our indulgences are as able to part the Red Seas in our lives as these calves were.

The case of Jeroboam was not true worship. It was the appearance of worship, which is easy to specialize in. This was a religion of convenience, one to pacify a troubled conscience and to people-please. Whatever we go to for gratification, far or near, is as able to comfort us and provide for our needs in the wilderness of life, as these calves were. Note how Jeroboam cloaked this offer in apparent concern, speaking for his people and saying, "it is too much for you to go all the way to Jerusalem." Moreover, isn't it interesting that we sometimes exert ourselves tirelessly to get to our idols, when it would be much simpler to worship the living God. In the same way, we'll spend hours on TV, movies, news, YouTube and Facebook, memes and gifs, till our shoulders are stiff and our eyes crossed, but find it too much work to spend 30 minutes in God's word.

I recently learned something that thrilled me that pertains to this. In the 1930's, Nobel laureate Nikolaas Tinbergen coined the term *supernormal stimuli.* He found that "birds that lay small, pale blue eggs speckled with grey preferred to sit on giant, bright blue plaster dummies with black polka dots. A male silver washed fritillary butterfly was more sexually aroused by a butterfly-sized rotating cylinder with horizontal brown stripes than it is by a real, live female of its own kind. Tinbergen coined the term "supernormal stimuli" to describe these imitations, which appeal to primitive instincts and, oddly, exert a stronger attraction than real things."[6] These organisms chose to stick with the fakes, even when they didn't deliver. Some might say, well, maybe we're just built that way.

Do not be like the horse or the mule,
which have no understanding
but must be controlled by bit and
bridle or they will not come to you
(Psalm 32:9).

These idols guarantee a Promised Land they are impotent to deliver. Moreover, they cause us to despise what God calls the *pleasant land* as we shall see in a later section. Remember how the Apostle Paul participated in Christ's job of rewiring his brain, I challenge you to engage in some spiritual Cognitive Brain Therapy and replace the lie with the truth:

This is what the Lord says—Israel's King and
Redeemer, the Lord of Heaven's Armies:
"I am the First and the Last; there is no other
God. Who is like me? Let him step forward
and prove to you his power. Let him do
as I have done since ancient times when I
established a people and explained its future.
Do not tremble; do not be afraid. Did I not
proclaim my purposes for you long ago? You
are my witnesses—is there any other God?
No! There is no other Rock—not one!"
How foolish are those who manufacture idols.
These prized objects are really worthless. The people
who worship idols don't know this, so they are all
put to shame. Who but a fool would make his
own god—an idol that cannot help him one bit?
All who worship idols will be disgraced along
with all these craftsmen—mere humans—who
claim they can make a god. They may all stand
together, but they will stand in terror and shame.
The blacksmith stands at his forge to make a
sharp tool, pounding and shaping it with all his
might. His work makes him hungry and weak.

It makes him thirsty and faint. Then the wood-carver measures a block of wood and draws a pattern on it. He works with chisel and plane and carves it into a human figure. He gives it human beauty and puts it in a little shrine. He cuts down cedars; he selects the cypress and the oak; he plants the pine in the forest to be nourished by the rain. Then he uses part of the wood to make a fire. With it he warms himself and bakes his bread. Then—yes, it's true—he takes the rest of it and makes himself a god to worship! He makes an idol and bows down in front of it! He burns part of the tree to roast his meat and to keep himself warm. He says, "Ah, that fire feels good." Then he takes what's left and makes his god: a carved idol! He falls down in front of it, worshiping and praying to it. "Rescue me!" he says. "You are my god!" Such stupidity and ignorance! Their eyes are closed, and they cannot see. Their minds are shut, and they cannot think. The person who made the idol never stops to reflect, "Why, it's just a block of wood! I burned half of it for heat and used it to bake my bread and roast my meat. How can the rest of it be a god? Should I bow down to worship a piece of wood?" The poor, deluded fool feeds on ashes. He trusts something that can't help him at all. Yet he cannot bring himself to ask, "Is this idol that I'm holding in my hand a lie?" (Isaiah 44:6-20, NLT).

The field of ACES is becoming increasingly popular in mainstream healthcare, as it should. Friends, explore and prayerfully revisit your ACES. They have to do with abuse (physical, emotional, or sexual); neglect (physical or emotional); and household dysfunction (mental illness, incarceration, violence, substance abuse, and divorce). Each of these categories is as a knife in your heart. As we saw earlier, the heart is the center of our being. Spiritually, the heart corresponds to the mind and is tightly interwoven with our soul and spirit. One of the functions of the heart entails an important list. I remember it by the acronym PAPDATE: the heart is the wellspring of our **p**urposes, **a**ffections, **p**assions, **d**esires, **a**ppetites, **t**houghts, and **e**ndeavors. (Remember you're a gynecologist and the heart comes in on its PAPDATE. Those are the checkpoints you must assess.) If sticking out of your heart is a knife or two- or more—from ACES, all these areas are deeply impaired. That is why we must do the hard work required for emotional healing.

One imperative aspect that should emerge from that exercise is forgiveness of those that caused hurt. Hurt hearts lead to solid brain pathways of bitterness and pain. This harm leads to adverse health conditions that seriously impact life. It crops up at every turn. Whether you realize it or not, it's affecting your relationships—today! Why? Because the hurt is like a knife impaling your heart. Beloved, we cannot heal if a knife is sticking out of our heart. The blade sticking out of it catches on the darndest stuff. You can nurse and manage the wound all you want but it's a futile pursuit. Most importantly, Christian, let your ritualized compulsive comfort-seeking take you to the Comforter, all other ground is sinking sand! He is the master healer of hearts as we will see in the chapter entitled *The State of the Heart*. Take the time now to look up an ACE scoring protocol online.

No matter what your ACES, God is your true ACE—your Advanced Comfort Executor. That's your identity. Your trauma doesn't define you. You are not what you used to do or what was done to you. Shed the labels as you would a coat. As writer Perry admonishes, "I don't believe it is wise or truthful to the power of the gospel to identify oneself by the sins of one's past or the temptations of one's present but rather to only be defined by the Christ who overcame both for those He calls His own."[8] Learn what he says of you and wear that instead.

Bible teacher Beth Moore has a powerful "Five-Statement Pledge of Faith" that states:

- God is who He says He is.
- God can do what He says He can do.
- I am who God says I am.
- I can do all things in Christ.
- God's word is alive and active in me.[7]

Memorize that and repeat it to yourself frequently, on and off the battlefield. Build a portable arsenal in your heart. Include powerful weapons of warfare such as memorized truths like these, hymns, scripture, etc. Think of David, the man after God's own heart who spoke the words of this fantastic Psalm—despite his behavioral track record:

> *The Lord has dealt with me*
> *according to my righteousness;*
> *according to the cleanness of my*
> *hands he has rewarded me.*
> *For I have kept the ways of the Lord;*
> *I am not guilty of turning from my God.*
> *All his laws are before me;*
> *I have not turned away from his decrees.*
> *I have been blameless before him*
> *and have kept myself from sin.*
> *The Lord has rewarded me according*
> *to my righteousness,*
> *according to the cleanness of my hands in his sight*
> (Psalm 18:20-24).

> *You are a chosen people, a royal priesthood, a*
> *holy nation, God's special possession, that you*
> *may declare the praises of him who called you*
> *out of darkness into his wonderful light*
> (1 Peter 2:9).

Jesus loved children and wanted them to come to him. Have you ever wondered what he said to them when they came to him? Surely, he didn't just pile them on his lap and absently pat their backs while he talked to the adults. He didn't just have a giant tickle pile and laugh till he cried. I believe he addressed some ACES. I can see him holding Little David's face, staring into his big brown eyes and saying, "You are brave and smart. Don't believe what those bullies tell you. You are a mighty leader, David, and you are a special friend of God." I see him holding little Rahab's hands to his face and saying, "You are gifted and compassionate. You will do amazing things for the kingdom of God. And God is your friend, Rahab." To Martha, "You are beautiful and strong and dignified, Martha. God is pleased to call you his friend."

To me, a trembling, whimpering little girl with snot and tears on my face, peering from behind the brown velvet sofa at those I loved the most as they spewed venomous molten lava at each other, he said, "You are precious to me, Hannah. You are mine. You *will* overcome this. I *will* give you beauty for ashes. I *will* give you your voice and you *will* proclaim healing to the nations. I am God Almighty and you are my special friend." That brings tears to my eyes to this day!

What did he say to you, Christian?

Suffering not only makes you like
Jesus, but it also sends you out into the
suffering world to minister like Jesus. Your
experiences, lessons learned, and empathy
gained through suffering are the very
things that make you a better minister.

Rick Warren

Chapter 14

God's SWAT Team Comes for You

For you have been my hope, Sovereign
Lord, my confidence since my youth.
From birth I have relied on you; you brought
me forth from my mother's womb.
I will ever praise you.
I have become a sign to many;
you are my strong refuge.
My mouth is filled with your praise,
declaring your splendor all day long.
In you, Lord, I have taken refuge;
let me never be put to shame.
In your righteousness, rescue me and deliver
me; turn your ear to me and save me
(Psalm 71:5-8, 1).

Why did you survive the adversity you lived through? How did you do it? Psalm 124 peels back the curtain and shows you a classified behind-the-scenes look. Be warned that this is a sensitive chapter that may evoke visceral reactions in the reader by revisiting trauma. I'll hold your hand through it but it is imperative that you read through this prayerfully. In the scripture below, we will dig through the meaning of words that may astound you. Take a deep breath and come with me.

A song of ascents. Of David.
If it had not been the Lord who was
on our side," Let Israel now say—
"If it had not been the Lord who was on
our side, when men rose up against us,
Then they would have swallowed us alive,
when their wrath was kindled against us;
Then the waters would have overwhelmed us,
the stream would have gone over our soul;
Then the swollen waters would
have gone over our soul."

Blessed be the Lord, who has not
given us as prey to their teeth.
Our soul has escaped as a bird from
the snare of the fowlers;
The snare is broken, and we have escaped.
Our help is in the name of the Lord,
who made heaven and earth
(Psalm 124).

There are fifteen songs of ascent—Psalms 120-134. They are a collection of short, pithy psalms, fraught with repeated formulaic phrases that make them rhythmic and memorable. They employ a literary technic called *anaphora* whereby phrases are repeated, as we shall study. They were sung or recited during an ascension and indicate a change in elevation, a journey to a higher place. They may have been used by pilgrims ascending to Jerusalem or may have been chanted by worshippers ascending the fifteen steps to the Temple in Jerusalem. Biblically, the number fifteen is symbolic of healing, rest, and restoration after deliverance. "This number symbolizes acts wrought by the energy of divine grace."[1]

The subjects of Psalm 124 had survived a significant assault. They were commiserating about it and marveling at God's role in their survival. Jehovah was *at* their side through their experience. In your case, it may be childhood or adulthood trauma. It may be past or ongoing. As he was with them, Jehovah was and is *at* your side during every moment of your traumatic experience. Moreover, not only was he *at* their side, he was *on* their side. He had to choose sides and he sided with them. In the same way, God was not only at your side, be he chose to be *on* your side. Jehovah was with them and today he is Emmanuel, God with us.

Verse two identifies some entity who "rose up" against you. That term paints a scenario of someone coming on the scene, and making a stand against you. This may have been someone who should have stood up *for* you and defended you. Yet he or she chose to satisfy his or her selfish desires before considering you and your needs. This person or system gained and maintained power over you in an imposing way. In the previous chapter we studied Adverse Childhood Experiences (ACEs) which include neglect (emotional and physical); abuse (psychological, physical, and sexual); and household dysfunction (children growing up in a home where there is mental illness, violence against the mother, separation/divorce, incarceration, and substance abuse).

We will explore several lies that traumatic experiences can cement in the victim's mind. One has to do with time. Verse one above says, "Let Israel *now* say," whereas verses three, four, and five begin with the word *then,* a classic example of *anaphora.* Here, scripture makes a distinction in time. We know that in the spirit realm time and space are immaterial. Nevertheless, adverse experiences occur in real space and in real time. Many victims of trauma get stuck in the place and time of their trauma. No matter how much time has passed, their current speech, demeanor, outlook, and behavior betray that they are still very present in the moment of assault.

Note that as long as one remains ensnared in past trauma, the perpetrator remains successful in his or her goals. Three times, Emmanuel is inviting you to distinguish between *then* and *now,* Christian. Ask for his help in moving forward away from that space and time. Healing entails experiencing a separation between the *then* and the *now.* It entails a change in elevation from that miry bog to the solid ground of a sound, restored mind. May your life resonate with the songs of ascension as you ascend to a place that is higher than that valley of death.

A second lie the enemy tells is that the intentions of the offender became our reality. It is imperative that we identify and distinguish between two important factors: the intention of the offender versus what actually happened. Failure to do so results in muddying the waters of our thinking and also results in one remaining stuck in the trauma. See Table iv. below.

Table iv. Intentions vs. Reality

Intentions	Reality
1. To "swallow you alive" 2. For the waters to overwhelm you/ For the stream or proud/ swollen waters to "go over" our soul	1. They "rose up" against you 2. Their "wrath" was "kindled" against you

Let's break down the intentions of the enemy. To "swallow one alive" (Hebrew *bala*)[2] is to eat up, to devour, to destroy them. It is to spend, to squander, and to use them up. The devil's intention is that when this offender (whether an individual, an institution, or a way of thinking) was done with you, you would only be good for garbage pickup. The psalm says the "waters" would have "overwhelmed" you. This scene is pumping with adrenaline and rife with real threats.

"Waters" (Hebrew *mayim*) are symbolic of danger and violence. They refer to a body of water that bursts its banks and causes destruction. Note the tie in with the entity which "rose up" against you—they overflowed their prescribed capacity. They overstepped their bounds. They did not confine themselves to their defined path but instead used their power inappropriately, to your detriment. The "proud" (Hebrew *zeydon*) waters indicate churning, raging, turbulence, and insolence. They are out of control and wreaking havoc in their wake. To bring it home painfully for some of you, precious readers, biblically, "waters" also refer to the bodily fluids of urine or semen.

To "overwhelm" (Hebrew *shataph*) means to engulf, overflow, wash off, gush, or inundate. By analogy, they aimed to gallop over you, to conquer you, drown you, aiming to wash you away. In order for them to "rise up," they had to have come from a place lower in elevation. They come up, snatch you, and take you back down to the depths with them. The goal would be to suck you under and cause you to disappear from the face of the earth. The stream would have "gone over" (Hebrew *abar*) meaning to pass over or through you, engulfing you. The theme of abuse in general, and sexual abuse in particular, continues here as, figuratively, this term means to cover in copulation, to impregnate.

Your offender came at you with his or her wrath kindled against you to consume you. The word "wrath" (Hebrew a*ph)* is a picture of impassioned, rapid breathing. "Kindled" (Heb. *charah*) means to be hot, furious, incensed, burning. Figuratively, it entails blazing or flaring up against you. Visualize flames rising and licking the meat on your BBQ. These flames can impregnate the meat with a charred taste and even ruin the cut. You were to be charred, disfigured, ruined, left as a pile of ashes.

My heart goes out in anguish to every single person that has had the body of another smother them sexually in the graphic ways described by these words. Please hear and believe that this horrific act was not your fault. There is absolutely no reason for a human being to impose him or herself on another in this way. This also applies to you being forced to do perform sexual acts against your will, even if the person did not touch you physically. God carefully chose the graphic words used here to describe the atrocities done because that's how seriously he sees them. He doesn't downplay what happened to you.

The psalm identifies where the punch is taken—the soul. The impact of these forms of adversity can span the spectrum from, at the very least, slightly charring the soul, as a flame-licked piece of meat; to, at the worst, destroying it. Your soul (Hebrew *nephesh*) is the core of who you are, your living, breathing self. It is your inner being. I remember it by the acronym A.M.P.E.D with a W thrown in at the beginning—WAMPED. It is the center of, or entails the activity of your: Will, Appetites, Mind, Passions, Emotions, and Desires. Note how closely intertwined it is with the heart, as we studied in the previous chapter. Needless to say, different people emerge from the storm in various stages of damage to these six aspects that comprise the soul—some just wet, and others a moldy, damaged mess.

The Psalm calls us to bless (Hebrew *barak*) Jehovah. This is an invitation to acknowledge him. We are to thank and praise him because had he not risen up *for* us, the enemy's intentions would have become our reality. Many people ask, "Where was God when *xyz* happened to me?" He was right there. Had he not been *on* our side, you and I would have been utterly destroyed. Had he not been *at* your side, we would not be here having this conversation. He has not "given us" (Hebrew *Nathan*) over to the intentions of the enemy. He didn't deliver us up or permit the destroyer to have his way with us, despite how far the latter went. The enemy did not have permission to do what he did and his intentions were cut short.

Have you any idea how many snares have been set for your soul that you weren't even aware of? I attended Catholic school and was taught that in heaven we will review our lives as on a video. I hope that's true. If so, it'll blow our minds to see what we were saved from when the fowler (Hebrew *yaqosh)* lured, set a snare or devised plans against us! As for the traps and plots that we did get caught in, because Jehovah was on our side, we escaped (Hebrew *malat).* That simple word means that we slipped away and were delivered, saved, released, rescued. We got to leap out and be preserved speedily and surely. Here is the exciting part, this wasn't a quiet, simple escape.

The psalmist says the snare has been broken (Hebrew *shabar).* Hear this—anyone coming upon the snare would be gob-smacked and gasp, "What happened here?" That's because that mangled mess was unidentifiable. This reminds me of an exciting day in our boys' lives when a microwave we owned finally died and they asked permission to beat it up. To my dismay and their utter surprise, my husband allowed them to. They looked at each other in slow motion with huge eyes and jaws dropping in testosterone-driven anticipation. They were allowed to use whatever they wanted on it. By the time I walked up to its sorry remains at the end of their barrage, all I could say was, "What happened here?" What *Shabar* actually means is that your God went ballistic on that trap. He rent it violently. He wrecked, crushed, and maimed it. He shattered it in pieces and destroyed it beyond recognition. Hallelujah!

> *"They have greatly oppressed me from my youth,"*
> *let Israel say;*
> *"they have greatly oppressed me from my youth,*
> **but they have not gained the victory over me"**
> (Psalm 129:1,2, emphasis added).

Indeed, you are victorious because God is your help (Hebrew *ezer*). He is your aid and your succor. Remember the word beset which means to enfold? *Ezer* is synonymous. It means he surrounds you. Earlier, I explained that the number fifteen symbolizes acts wrought by the energy of divine grace. His grace is a SWAT team that hems you in as it comes to rescue you. SWAT stands for Special Weapons and Tactics. This branch of law enforcement is unleashed to combat critical incidents that pose a threat to safety and that supersede the capacity of regular police forces. They are specially trained and equipped to use high-powered armor and other specialized equipment my boys would like to get their hands on and use against a dead microwave.

> *You have hedged me behind and before,*
> *And laid your hand upon me.*
> *Such knowledge is too wonderful for me;*
> *It is high, I cannot attain it*
> (Psalm 139:5, NKJV).

Because of what God has done, I can sing a song of ascents as I journey to a higher place.

Arise, my soul, and sing his praises!
(Psalm 108:2, TPT)

Take new joy in the words of the hymn Amazing Grace and bless him as you sing,

Through many dangers, toils, and snares,
I have already come.
'Tis grace hath brought me safe thus far,
And grace will lead me home.[3]

Chapter 15

Of "Holey" Rugs and Filthy Carpets

My husband and I hadn't been married long. We loved our first home, an upscale shack that he had scrimped and saved for. It was our pride and joy. The carpet in it was about four hundred years old. I could never come to the end of getting dirt out of it. I would have been wiser to try and compact the dirt in it, instead of the endless, fruitless extraction of layers of it. It was disgusting beyond words.

One Fall, someone gave us a much more powerful stove insert than the one that came with the house and we couldn't wait to install it. On a Saturday morning that September, my husband was pulling away the carpet around the old fireplace.

"Wife," he called urgently. "You've got to see this."

I came running. "What is it?"

"I think we have wood under this carpet."

"What?" I exclaimed. How could that be? We had dreamed of installing wood floors someday but knew it would be years down the road before we could afford it. And now, here we stood with wood floors! Sure enough, by the end of the day, we had torn off gross carpet and outdated linoleum to expose those beauties. We were ecstatically dancing on wood floors!

———————————

The old man—the flesh with its sinful tendencies—works in the members of our body to bear fruit for death (Romans 7:5). Pastor Harrell says, "So long as we are in this life, we drag around with us the dead remains of what we once were apart from Christ."[1] That's the part of me that's a dirt-bag! There is no end of dirt to be extracted from it. Christ calls us *and* empowers us to crucify the flesh, to put off the old man, and to put it to death. Paul teaches,

> *Those who live according to the flesh have their minds set on what the flesh desires; but those who live in accordance with the Spirit have their minds set on what the Spirit desires. The mind governed by the flesh is death, but the mind governed by the Spirit is life and peace. The mind governed by the flesh is hostile to God; it does not submit to God's law, nor can it do so. Those who are in the realm of the flesh cannot please God. You, however, are not in the realm of the flesh but are in the realm of the Spirit, if indeed the Spirit of God lives in you. And if anyone does not have the Spirit of Christ, they do not belong to Christ. But if Christ is in you, then even though your body is subject to death because of sin, the Spirit gives life because of righteousness.*
> [See chapter titled *Sin Leading to Death.*]
> *And if the Spirit of him who raised Jesus from the dead is living in you, he who raised Christ from the dead will also give life to your mortal bodies because of his Spirit who lives in you. Therefore, brothers and sisters, we have an obligation—but it is not to the flesh, to live according to it. For if you live according to the flesh, you will die; but if by the Spirit you put to death the misdeeds of the body, you will live*
> (Romans 8:5–13).

Christian, don't keep vacuuming and fruitlessly trying to fix up the old carpet and its holes that you carefully sit on by facade management. The supply of dirt is bottomless; the task-master brutal and tireless. Instead, pull out the sharp blades and tear it out! You have wood floors! Your sin does not define you; your past does not define you. You are a new person. Teach that very valuable to your brain!

Christian, here are five unshakable truths I need to remind you about *you*:

1. Salvation.

     a.   God chose you. Your salvation wasn't your idea. Your salvation was his idea. Jesus assures you,

     You did not choose Me, but I chose you
     (John 15:16).

     Knowing full well that this writer would sin in numerous ways and repeatedly drag his name in the mud, God chose her, created her, loved her, saved her, delivered her, and is using her for his glory as he makes her more and more like himself. Amazingly,

     Even before he made the world, God loved us
     and chose us in Christ to be holy and without
     fault in his eyes. Then, when the time was
     right for us to be saved, He called us
     (Ephesians 1:4 NLT).

b. God sustains you. This is God's job. Your salvation doesn't depend on you.

> *And I am certain that God, who began*
> *the good work within you, will continue*
> *his work until it is finally finished on*
> *the day when Christ Jesus returns*
> (Philippians 1:6 NLT).

2. Eternal Security. You in your salvation are forever safe and secure in His hands—no matter what you do! No one can steal you from His hands, no one can separate you from his love, not even yourself. Rest assured of that for several reasons:

a. His love and grace are eternal.

> *I have loved you with an eternal love*
> (Jeremiah 31:3).

> *He who did not spare his own Son, but gave*
> *him up for us all—how will he not also, along*
> *with him, graciously give us all things? Who*
> *will bring any charge against those whom*
> *God has chosen? It is God who justifies. Who*
> *then is the one who condemns? No one. Christ*
> *Jesus who died—more than that, who was*
> *raised to life—is at the right hand of God and*
> *is also interceding for us. Who shall separate*
> *us from the love of Christ? Shall trouble or*
> *hardship or persecution or famine or nakedness*
> *or danger or sword? As it is written:*

> *"For your sake we face death all day long;*
> *we are considered as sheep to be slaughtered."*

No, in all these things we are more than
conquerors through him who loved us. For
I am convinced that neither death nor life,
neither angels nor demons, neither the present
nor the future, nor any powers, neither height
nor depth, nor anything else in all creation,
will be able to separate us from the love
of God that is in Christ Jesus our Lord
(Romans 8:32-39).

b.   You didn't earn it.

For God's gifts and his call are irrevocable
(Romans 11:29).

He saved you by his grace, not by your works
(2 Timothy 1:9, NLT).

c.   You are adopted into his forever family.

He predestined us for adoption to sonship
through Jesus Christ, in accordance
with his pleasure and will
(Ephesians 1:5).

But when the set time had fully come, God sent
his Son, born of a woman, born under the law,
to redeem those under the law, that we might
receive adoption to sonship. Because you are his
sons, God sent the Spirit of his Son into our hearts,
the Spirit who calls out, "Abba, Father." So you
are no longer a slave, but God's child; and since
you are his child, God has made you also an heir
(Galatians 4:4-7).

    d.   God is the strongest force and no one can overpower Him.

> *I give them eternal life, and they shall never*
> *perish; no one will snatch them out of my hand*
> (John 10:28).

3.   Freedom & Victory.

> *It is for freedom that Christ has set us free.*
> *Stand firm, then, and do not let yourselves*
> *be burdened again by a yoke of slavery*
> (Galatians 5:1).

Freedom is yearning for and working to grow in the knowledge and love of God, and actively submitting to and obeying Him. On the one hand, our eternal security is guaranteed. On the flip side, on a day to day basis, we can easily relinquish our victory and freedom by letting ourselves be shackled. Are you consciously and actively surrendered to his will and ways—daily, moment by moment—or do you not even pay heed to His presence and working in your day?

The Apostle Paul states,

> *Beloved ones, God has called us to live a life*
> *of freedom in the Holy Spirit. But don't view*
> *this wonderful freedom as an opportunity to set*
> *up a base of operations in the natural realm.*
> *Freedom means that we become so completely*
> *free of self-indulgence that we become servants*
> *of one another, expressing love in all we do*
> (Galatians 5:14, TPT).

People go to various idols to get specific desires met, e.g. in the old testament, Molech granted financial prosperity. This worship has a self-centered, self-serving approach. On the contrary, worship of Jehovah primarily asks us to give to him, not just going to him for favors. Victory doesn't mean amassing wealth. It doesn't mean defeating your enemies. It doesn't mean having a beautiful spouse and successful children. It doesn't mean climbing the corporate ladder.

In his clip on working out, comedian Jim Gaffigan questions the presence of mirrors in the gym, then mocks the typical gym-user: "If I'm going to be working out, I want to look at something, like myself. I wanna look a' myself while I work a' myself…as I leaf through Myself Magazine, read how myself can improve myself… *Yo soy muy importante*!"[2] Christians, we can be steeped in idolatry and the worship of self while still verbally proclaiming Jesus as Lord. Is he Lord over your life or are *you* on the front cover of Myself Magazine? This makes the difference between living a victorious Spirit-filled, Spirit-led life, versus living a defeated fleshly life which may appear successful in the eyes of the world.

4. Power and Authority—Writer Tony Evans makes an astute and apt observation. "In a football game, the players tower over the referees. The players are bigger, stronger and more powerful than the older, smaller and, often, out-of-shape referees. In a game, the players can use their power to knock you down, but the referees can use their authority to put you out of the game!" Then he warns us to never confuse power with authority.[3]

As we shall see in the chapter titled *Temptation*, you have authority in Christ. Satan has no authority over you unless you hold out your hands in front of you like a prisoner, so he can cuff you. *You* have authority over you. Only when you have allowed him to bind you, have you abdicated authority to him. You become his fool, his court jester. Like Samson, your mighty muscles grind the Philistine's grain at the millstone. He uses you to make sport of Jesus.

Fortunately for you, at any given time, you are *one* decision away from busting those cuffs—for good! Realize and declare the authority you have over Satan. God commands us to different actions against the devil based on the situation: cast his authority away, resist him, or flee from him. In so doing, you stand firm in your authority and freedom in Jesus.

> *For the Spirit God gave us does not*
> *make us timid, but gives us power,*
> *love, and self-discipline*
> (2 Timothy 1:7).

Believer, you have power! Power is the ability or capacity to perform, conveying the idea of effective, productive energy. You get to face temptation and fight sin with power. Fortunately, it is not your own power. You have the power of the Maker of the universe who promises to fight this battle for you, with you. I love the truths embodied in the song "Defender":

> You go before I know
> That You've even gone to win my war
> You come back with the head of my enemy
> You come back and You call it my victory,
> You go before I know
> That You've even gone to win my war
> Your love becomes my greatest defense
> It leads me from the dry wilderness…
> Hallelujah, you have saved me
> So much better Your way
> Hallelujah, great Defender
> So much better Your way.[4]

> *You give me your shield of victory,*
> *and your right hand sustains me;*
> *your stoop down to make me great*
> (Psalm 18:35).

I carry the verse below like a Swiss-army knife in my pocket and use it several times a day, every day. It comforts me, sets me straight, and galvanizes my faith when I feel weak. I share it with others frequently.

I am with you like a mighty warrior
(Jeremiah 20:11).

John MacArthur is quoted as saying "resources we have from our heavenly Father are *power* and love and discipline, when we are vacillating and apprehensive, we can be sure it is because our focus is on ourselves and our own human resources rather than on the Lord and His available divine resources." If God has told us to do something this verse takes away the excuse "I can't do it, it's too hard".[5]

The Apostle Paul paints a festive scene:

For He [Christ] is the complete fullness of deity living in human form. And our own completeness is now found in him. We are completely filled with God as Christ's fullness overflows within us. He is the Head of every kingdom and authority in the universe!

Through our union with him we have experienced circumcision of heart. All of the guilt and power of sin has been cut away and is now extinct because of what Christ, the Anointed One, has accomplished for us.

For we've been buried with him into his death. Our "baptism into death" also means we were raised with him when we believed in God's resurrection power, the power that raised him from death's realm. This "realm of death" describes our former state, for we were held in sin's grasp. But now, we've been resurrected out

of that "realm of death" never to return, for we
are forever alive and forgiven of all our sins!
He canceled out every legal violation we had
on our record and the old arrest warrant that
stood to indict us. He erased it all—our sins, our
stained soul—he deleted it all and they cannot be
retrieved! Everything we once were in Adam has
been placed onto his cross and nailed permanently
there as a public display of cancellation.

Then Jesus made a public spectacle of all the
powers and principalities of darkness, stripping
away from them every weapon and all their
*spiritual **authority and power** to accuse us.*
And by the power of the cross, Jesus led them
around as prisoners in a procession of triumph.
He was not their prisoner; they were His!
(Colossians 2:9-14, TPT, emphasis added).

What graphic language Paul uses—circumcision, ouch! If you are circumcised, you cannot become uncircumcised again. The old foreskin is shriveled, dead, and long disposed of in a biohazard container that can't be reopened. As a teenager I read a quote that's stuck with me, "Sin has many tools but a lie is the handle that fits them all." Christian, it is imperative to Satan that you believe his lies. Dr. Anderson announces, "The only way he can have authority over you is if you believe his lies... The only power Satan has over you is the power of the lie." [6]

June Hunt identifies many lies that the saint struggling with harmful habits believes and tells. These may include negative self-talk and excuses which play an important role in cementing these habits e.g. "I can't control this," "I don't have what it takes to beat this," "I can't help it," "God can't help someone like me," "I've gone too far," "This is just who I am now," "I'll do it just one more time," "I don't have time to focus on this right now," "I can control this any time," "I deserve this," "everyone's doing it." [7]

Jesus lambasted the Jewish leaders and declared,

> *You belong to your father, the devil, and you*
> *want to carry out your father's desires. He was*
> *a murderer from the beginning, not holding*
> *to the truth, for there is no truth in him.*
> *When he lies, he speaks his native language,*
> *for he is a liar and the father of lies*
> (John 8:44).

This type of thinking must be replaced with the truth of Scripture *every single time* it occurs so as to form new neural pathways and renew the mind. As we learned, because of their nature, habits and patterns are deeply engrained in the brain due to the repetition and the reward. This is what makes them difficult (but not impossible!) to break. Hunt says, "New patterns of behavior can be learned, which, in turn, will alter your brain. Eventually the connections between the brain neurons are slowly modified, thus making it more difficult for you to make different choices."[8]

That is biblical wisdom, which is to know, to believe, and to obey the truth. Take the time to identify the lie and replace it with truth. Then doggedly practice the truth.

> *For you were once darkness, but now you are*
> *light in the Lord. Live as children of light (for*
> *the fruit of the light consists in all goodness,*
> *righteousness and truth) and find out what pleases*
> *the Lord. Have nothing to do with the fruitless*
> *deeds of darkness, but rather expose them*
> (Ephesians 5:8-11).

I love that as soon as you expose the lie, its power is shattered. While there may work left to do after exposing the lie, that act alone fractures the grip of your snare. Anticipating the exposure and the actual exposure may also hurt like Confession makes a big impact in brain neuro-circuitry because the brain avoids it as a self-preservation measure. It is a powerful force for good insofar as disrupting established patterns and laying groundwork for new pathways.

Saint, you don't get to kick back and do nothing. There is work for *you*. No one can turn from darkness to light for you. No one can believe for you, no one can confess your sins for you, no one can renounce Satan for you, no one can forgive others for you. You have to show up for this. The Bible calls it working out your salvation. Yet even that he avails all his resources to help you.

> *Therefore, my dear friends, as you have*
> *always obeyed…continue to work out your*
> *salvation with fear and trembling, for it*
> *is God who works in you to will and to*
> *act in order to fulfill his good purpose*
> (Philippians 2:12-13).

For the latter section, The Passion Translation says,

> *God will continually revitalize you, implanting*
> *within you the passion to do what pleases him.*

And that's our great calling as Paul prayed in a piece of Scripture I call my life anchor.

> *For this reason, since the day we heard about*
> *you, we have not stopped praying for you.*
> *We continually ask God to fill you with the*
> *knowledge of his will through all the wisdom*
> *and understanding that the Spirit gives,*
> ***so that you may live a life***
> ***worthy of the Lord** and*
> ***please him in every way**:*
> *bearing fruit in every good work, growing in*
> *the knowledge of God, being strengthened with*
> *all power according to his glorious might so that*
> *you may have great endurance and patience,*

and giving joyful thanks to the Father, who has
qualified you to share in the inheritance of his
holy people in the kingdom of light. For he has
rescued us from the dominion of darkness and
brought us into the kingdom of the Son he loves, in
whom we have redemption, the forgiveness of sins
(Colossians 1:9-13, emphasis added).

Saint, do not think for a moment that this is a cakewalk. God had to fortify even his own Son to see obedience through to the end. He repeatedly sent strength and provision to prophets such as Elijah in the old testament. It will be no easier for us. Indeed, it will get crazy tough before it ever gets easier. But we do hard things. When the going gets tough, the tough kick butt! We are more than conquerors. The glory to be awarded for endurance will be worth every temporary glory you give up.

So do not throw away your confidence;
it will be richly rewarded.
You need to persevere so that when
you have done the will of God,
you will receive what he has promised
(Hebrews 10:35-36).

If this book becomes an impetus for you to identify and expose areas of darkness in your life, my goal will be accomplished. If you turn from idolizing them to exalting Christ as the zenith of your life, Christ's work will be powerfully accomplished in you! Plug in to the power of the Holy Spirit to transform your very being; to renew your mind. From there you can exercise the power *and* the authority to know and obey the Truth. That is the definition of wisdom. You get to share in his calling, his power, and authority to walk in freedom, to make disciples, and to set the captives free.

The Spirit of the Lord is on me, because
he has anointed me to proclaim good news

to the poor. He has sent me to proclaim
freedom for the prisoners and recovery of
sight for the blind, to set the oppressed free
(Luke 4:18).

Wisdom = Skill gained from Knowing Truth
+ Belief in the Truth + Obeying the Truth

Chapter 16

What's So Wonderful about Sex?

Therefore, brothers and sisters, since we have confidence to enter the Most Holy Place by the blood of Jesus... let us draw near to God with a sincere heart and with the full assurance that faith brings, having our hearts sprinkled to cleanse us from a guilty conscience and having our bodies washed with pure water. Let us hold unswervingly to the hope we profess, for he who promised is faithful. And let us consider how we may spur one another on toward love and good deeds... If we deliberately keep on sinning after we have received the knowledge of the truth, no sacrifice for sins is left, but only a fearful expectation of judgment and of raging fire that will consume the enemies of God (Hebrews 10:19, 21–24, 26).

Someone has said that "go forth and multiply" is the only one of God's commands that mankind has taken seriously—and that's only because a ridiculously pleasurable experience is attached to it! "Sexuality is at the heart of our humanity,"[1] claims popular counselor and writer, Dr. Gary Chapman. According to writer Tony Reinke,

God has an "astonishing but unblushing design for human sexuality and procreation."[2]

God is all about complete intimacy. He is all about complete *unity*. This plays out in the Trinity between the Father, the Son, and the Holy Spirit.

Jesus taught:

I and the Father are one
(John 10:29).

[K]now and understand that the Father
is in me, and I in the Father
(John 10 38b).

Now the Lord is the Spirit, and where the Spirit
of the Lord is, there is freedom. And we, who with
unveiled faces all reflect the Lord's glory, are being
transformed into his likeness with ever-increasing
glory, which comes from the Lord, who is the Spirit
(2 Corinthians 3:17, 18).

Some who do not believe in the Trinity use the scripture above to say that Jesus and the Spirit are the same entity. This is erroneous and instead lends to how closely intimate they are. Scripture distinguishes them clearly and then goes a step further and ties us into the intimacy circle. Before Jesus left earth he said,

And I will ask the Father, and he will give you
another helper to be with you forever, the Spirit
of truth. The world cannot accept him, because
it neither sees him nor knows him. But you know
him, for he lives with you and will be in you. I
will not leave you as orphans; I will come to you.
Before long, the world will not see me anymore,
but you will see me. Because I live, you will also

will live. On that day you will realize that I am in
my Father, and you are in me and I am in you.
(John 14:15-20).

As intimacy plays out between God and man, it then spills over and binds brothers and sisters in Christ, past and present:

There is one body and one Spirit, just as you were
called to one hope when you were called; one Lord,
one faith, one baptism; one God and Father of
all, who is over all and through all and in all.
(Ephesians 4:4-6).

My prayer is not for them alone [his followers
at the time]. I pray also for those who will
believe in me [you and I] through their message,
that all of them may be one, Father, just as
you are in me and I am in you. May they also
be in us so that the world may believe that
you have sent me. I have given them the glory
that you gave me, that they may be one as we
are one—I in them and you in me—so that
they may be brought to complete unity. Then
the world will know that you sent me and
have loved them even as you have loved me.

"Father, I want those you have given me to
be with me where I am, and to see my glory,
the glory you have given me because you
loved me before the creation of the world.

"Righteous Father, though the world does not
know you, I know you, and they know that
you have sent me. I have made you known to
them, and will continue to make you known

in order that the love you have for me may be
in them and that I myself may be in them
(John 17:20-26).

In Genesis 2:24, God strategically institutes marriage: the man leaves his parents and cleaves to his wife till death parts them. Through sex, "the two become one," each ceding their body to please the other. Marriage is supposed to be all about *unity*. Sex is all about *unity*. God gives them sex as a physical gift and as a powerful metaphor to showcase his desire for unity and intimacy with us, with a focus on pleasing and worshiping him. The result is an exclusive love relationship—enjoying glorious pleasure in a state of sensitivity to each other and to him. That's what's so wonderful about sex!

Tony Reinke adds, "In Christ, we see through the showers of gifts to behold the glory of the Giver as we wait for an eternity in the matchless delights of God's presence. He is the supreme gift of all—the gift toward which all the other gifts have been pointing and leading us all along!"[3]

Mankind has twisted this truth ever so slightly and chosen to focus mainly on the personal pleasure one can derive from sexual experiences. Dr. Kim Kimberling wrote an excellent devotional highlighting lust as one of The Seven Deadly Sins. In describing the Hebrew word *dod* for godly sexual intercourse, he says it is loosely translated as "a mingling of souls." Pause a moment, take a deep breath, and visualize that tantalizing, ethereal concept. Can you hear the wind-chimes tinkling in the background? He contrasts that with the crude concept of lusty, mechanistic sex as merely "bodies banging against each other."[4]

Dannah Gresh expounds on this. The book of Genesis claims that Adam and Eve *yada*—"lay" together. *Yada* is another Hebrew word for sex. This one means "known, recognized, understood, respected."[5] Wow! Isn't this a fantastic picture of how God relates to us? Isn't this the crux of spiritual intercourse? "Ultimately, this intimate relationship with God must become our greatest motivation for purity, greater than a fear of getting caught or a fear of consequences,"[6] encourages Bible commentator David Guzik. Jesus taught that the first and greatest commandment is to love the Lord our God with all our heart, and all our mind, and all our soul. The second is to love our neighbor as ourselves. Everything else hangs on these two.[7]

What about the repugnant account in Genesis 19:33 whereby Lot's daughter had sexual intercourse with her father? The word there is *sakab*. It means "to exchange bodily emissions." Could it be more mechanical? Contemplate these definitions then rate your sexual experience and/or understanding of this magnanimous gift. Now place yourself on the continuum below:

<--->

Mingling souls/
Known, recognized,
understood, respected/
Pleasing another person

Banging bodies/
Mingling bodily emissions/
Personal pleasure

God wants to be intimately united to our hearts, which, according to Dr. Shaw are our spiritual bodies. He doesn't want just part of it. He wants the whole of it. May he say of us as he did of Caleb and David,

*...my servant Caleb has a different spirit
and follows me wholeheartedly*
(Numbers 14:24a).

*David kept my commandments and followed me
wholeheartedly by doing only what I approve*
(1 Kings 14:8b).

In Christ, we see through the showers of
gifts to behold the glory of the Giver as we
wait for an eternity in the matchless delights
of God's presence. He is the supreme gift of
all—the gift toward which all the other gifts
have been pointing and leading us all along!

Tony Reinke

Chapter 17

God's Goals vs. Satan's Goals—
The Doctrine of Balaam

In true devil fashion, through pornography, Satan perverts the gift and metaphor of sex. He turns the focus from experiencing and glorifying God to self-gratification—from serving and pleasing a spouse, to self-absorption. This results in a state of desensitization to God and to our spouse. Sadly, what God intended as an object lesson of his love for us becomes a means that separates and distances us from Him. We saw this in Samson's case. He abandoned God's call on his life and was absorbed with foreign women who effectively turned his heart away from God. Let's consider wise King Solomon.

> *Was it not because of marriages like these that Solomon king of Israel sinned? Among the many nations there was no king like him. He was loved by his God, and God made him king over all Israel, but even he was led into sin by foreign women. Must we hear now that you too are doing all this terrible wickedness and are being unfaithful to our God by marrying foreign women?"*
> (Nehemiah 13:26-27).

This concept is called the "teaching or doctrine of Balaam." In the book of Numbers, we meet Balaam, a non-Israelite sorcerer in land known as Shittim. King Balak of Moab wanted Balaam to curse the Israelites, God's blessed people. Balaam said,

> *How can I curse*
> *those whom God has not cursed?*
> *How can I denounce*
> *those whom the Lord has not denounced?*
> (Numbers 23:8).

Balak tried to have Balaam curse the Israelites a second time. But God's people were powerfully shielded by Yahweh. Hear Balaam's report to Balak delivered in several messages:

> *God is not human, that he should lie,*
> *not a human being, that he*
> *should change his mind.*
> *Does he speak and then not act? Does*
> *he promise and not fulfill?*
> *I have received a command to bless; he*
> *has blessed, and I cannot change it.*
>
> *"No misfortune is seen in Jacob, no*
> *misery observed in Israel.*
> *The Lord their God is with them;*
> *the shout of the King is among them.*
> *God brought them out of Egypt; they*
> *have the strength of a wild ox.*
> *There is no divination against Jacob,*
> *no evil omens against Israel.*
> *It will now be said of Jacob*
> *and of Israel, 'See what God has done!'*
> *The people rise like a lioness; they*
> *rouse themselves like a lion*
> *that does not rest till it devours its prey*
> *and drinks the blood of its victims*
> (Numbers 23:19-24).

It was impossible to destroy the Israelites with curses. Because of God's shield around them, they were impenetrable from the outside. Balaam knew it. Any breaching of the shield would have to be an inside job. Balaam knew that too. The Apostle John refers to this when God is addressing the church at Pergamos. Here again, we see the close relationship the Bible weaves between idolatry and sexual immorality. They are two horns on the same goat.

> *Nevertheless, I have a few things against you:*
> *There are some among you who hold to the*
> *teaching of Balaam, who taught Balak to entice*
> *the Israelites to sin so that they ate food sacrificed*
> *to idols and committed sexual immorality*
> (Revelation 2:14).

Bam! Balaam knew that it was impossible to destroy the Israelites with curses. But there was a trick in his lure-box that worked every time. It worked in dusty olden Shittim and it works in sophisticated 2020: good old pornography!

> *While Israel was staying in Shittim, the men*
> *began to indulge in sexual immorality with*
> *Moabite women, who invited them to the*
> *sacrifices to their gods. The people ate the*
> *sacrificial meal and bowed down before these*
> *gods. So Israel yoked themselves to the Baal of*
> *Peor. And the Lord's anger burned against them*
> (Numbers 24:1-3).

In the world today, "my body, my choice" is a common mantra. This godless attitude has snuck into the back row of the church and permeated it. It violates an indispensable truth—(bristle alert!) *my body isn't mine alone!* First off, my body belongs to God. You may buck at the thought of being owned. It may trigger a great or small visceral reaction within you. Here's what scripture says,

> *Know that the Lord is God.* **It is He**
> **who made us, and we are His,** *we are*
> *His people, the sheep of His pasture*
> (Psalm 100:3, emphasis added).

> *The body, however, is not meant for sexual*
> *immorality but for the Lord, and the Lord for*
> *the body. Do you not know that* **your bodies**
> **are members of Christ himself?** *Shall I then*
> *take the members of Christ and unite them*
> *with a prostitute? Never! Do you not know*
> *that he who unites himself with a prostitute is*
> *one with her in body? For it is said, "The two*
> *will become one flesh." But whoever is united*
> *with the Lord is one with Him in spirit.*
> *Flee from sexual immorality. All other sins*
> *a person commits are outside the body, but*
> *whoever sins sexually, sins against their own*
> *body. Do you not know that your bodies are*
> *temples of the Holy Spirit, who is in you, whom*
> *you have received from God?* **You are not**
> **your own; you were bought with a price.**
> **Therefore, honor God with your bodies**
> (1 Corinthians 6:13b-20, emphases added).

Secondly, my body is my spouse's. Biblical sex is a voluntary, sometimes sacrificial, gesture of physical and emotional sensitivity *intended to please a spouse.* Reinforcing the matter of unity, Paul teaches:

> *The wife does not have authority over her own*
> *body but yields it to her husband. In the same*

way, the husband does not have authority
over his own body but yields it to his wife
(1 Corinthians 7:4).

A married man is concerned about...how he can
please his wife... A married woman is concerned
about...how she can please her husband.
(1 Corinthians 7:32b, 34b).

The main things we get to do with the body are to crucify it, to put off its fleshly passions and desires, to present it as a living sacrifice to God, to steward it because it is God's temple, and pretty much other such things that aren't meant to idolize it. Please do not hear me say that we are not to enjoy our bodies. I am not preaching asceticism. I am saying that the amazing designer of our phenomenal bodies knows the parameters within which sublime pleasures abound. Flying in the face of God's plan, pornography is activity *intended solely for self-gratification*—this insatiable, sensual self-indulgence unfailingly becomes a downward spiral of deep despair. The Bible is replete with clear instructions in the matter of sexual conduct.

Christian, your body belongs to God and your spouse, if you have one. As I stated earlier, there are times when sex will be an act of sacrifice to God and to your spouse. At those times may it be a fragrant offering, an act of worship. Paul challenges us to,

Follow God's example, therefore, as dearly loved
children and walk in the way of love, just as
Christ loved us and gave himself up for us as
a fragrant offering and sacrifice to God
(Ephesians 5:1–2).

[Y]ou must no longer live as the Gentiles do, in
the futility of their thinking. They are darkened
in their understanding and separated from
the life of God because of the ignorance that is
in them due to the hardening of their hearts.

*Having lost all sensitivity, they have given
themselves over to sensuality so as to indulge
in every kind of impurity, with a continual
lust for more… But among you there must
not even be a hint of sexual immorality*
(Ephesians 4:17-19 and 5:3a).

*For you were called to freedom, brothers. Only
do not use your freedom as an opportunity for
the flesh, but through love serve one another.*
(Galatians 5:13).

Submit to one another out of reverence for Christ
(Ephesians 5:21).

*For to this you have been called, because
Christ also suffered for you, leaving you an
example, so that you might follow in his steps*
(1 Peter 2:21).

We have learned that the goal of the doctrine of Balaam is to separate people from God. It is the exact opposite of the unity and intimacy that God desires. Because sex is so intensely sensual, I believe extra-marital sex/pornography is a perfect tool the enemy uses to introduce a barrier between us and the Lover of our Souls. Jackie Hill Perry states "that every person, place, or thing that I loved more than Him could not keep its promise to love me eternally. Nor was my heart created for them to hold. But they would instead do to me what all sin does, separate me from God, and thus true love, forever. It would be the death of me."[1]

We learned that pornography is a heart or spirit of idolatry, that is frequently, but not strictly, manifested by sexual immorality. Table v. below summarizes the issues at hand.

Table v. What God Wants vs. What the Devil Wants from Us

What God Wants for/from Us	What the Devil Wants for/from Us	References
Have life, and have it to the full	Kill, steal, and destroy	John 10:10
Please God	Grieve God	1 Thessalonians 4:1 Eph. 4:30
Be sanctified (set apart to/for God)	Be separated from God (The Doctrine of Balaam)	1 Thessalonians 4:3
Avoid sexual immorality	Sexual indulgence	1 Thessalonians 4:3
Approval	Punishment	1 Thessalonians 4:6
Holy lives	Impure lives	1 Thessalonians 4:7
Accept God	Reject God	1 Thessalonians 4:8
Learn to control your own body in a way that is holy and honorable	Passionate lust like the pagans, who do not know God	1 Thessalonians 4:4-5
No one should wrong or take advantage of a brother or sister	Use freedom to devour each other	1 Thessalonians 4:6 Galatians 5:15
Take up our cross/ Self-denial	Physical sensuality = self-gratification	Matthew 10:38 Ephesians 4:19
Sensitivity—soft, tender hearts that are responsive to God	Insensitivity—hard hearts that are desensitized or callous to God	Ephesians 4:19

HANNAH THUKU KOLEHMAINEN, PHD.

Despite having been in conservative churches for over thirty years, I held the commonly misconceived definition of pornography as merely viewing erotica. I also held a rather worldly mindset regarding some aspects of pornography, by the biblical definition. To begin with, I had neither been taught nor had I taken the time to study and learn God's definition of pornography. I knew sex was important to God, and I held it in high esteem. I got married a "technical virgin" despite much pressure, having resolved early in my walk to save myself for my future husband in the context of marriage. I learned to go "so far" and then stop so as to appease my conscience.

That resolve didn't stop me from engaging in what I now know to be utter sexual immorality—mentally and physically. Despite being very strict in some aspects, I carried very liberal thinking about what was acceptable behavior before and into my marriage and therefore the marriage bed. Some of my behavior, I didn't even consider to be bondage—but that doesn't mean that it wasn't. Some had started willfully, but before I knew it, the more I tried to extricate myself, the tighter the chains held, the snare sinking its cold, jagged, scabrous fangs, deeper, deeper. Its rust shot straight to my heart.

I am challenged by Paul's words about Timothy and aspire to be like him as I live my life before the Lord. Paul said of him,

> *I have no one else like him, who will show genuine*
> *concern for your welfare. For everyone looks out **for***
> ***their own interests, not those of Jesus Christ***
> (Philippians 2:19-20, emphasis added).

What a grand commendation! May God our Father say that of us as he transforms our ways and makes us more like some of our amazing spiritual ancestors. And isn't it astounding that even after we have messed up royally, as many of them did, we can say with David, despite his track record,

> *For I have kept the ways of the LORD; I have*
> *not done evil by **turning** from my God. All his*
> *laws are before me; I have not **turned away***

from his decrees. I have been blames before him and have kept myself from sin. The LORD has rewarded me according to my righteousness, according to the cleanness of my hands in his sight (Psalm 18:21;24, emphasis added).

Sexual immorality just might be
Satan's primary trusted go-to lures
in his tackle-box of temptation.

Chapter 18

Overindulging Does Not Mean Cherishing

Psst, don't look now, but check out Uncle Jedidiah over at the buffet. Everyone knows he wears suspenders and unbuttons his pants at the Thanksgiving table so he can eat till he's sick. He barely notices who's around him as he returns for mound after mound of helping after helping. His napkins pile high beside his plate. He talks incessantly, his blathering punctuated by belching. He claims that he "just loves food." Everything is "so good!"

I see now that I was a fat slob gorging myself at the table of sensuality. California-based therapist Alexandra Katehakis teaches that, "people can, and often do, engage in copious sexual activity while utterly repressing their core sexuality."[1] In another of her devotionals titled *Sexual Abandon* (which she defines as surrendering to carnal desire), she says, "[S]exual abandon, ironically, perpetuates the greatest of inhibitions because it's being used to *block* real experience and to *numb* our highest functions. So sexual abandon, while touted as the very symbol of emotional and sensual growth, can in fact *paralyze* our spiritual being and our sexual potential"[2] (emphasis added). It's no wonder that we're passed out—numb and paralyzed in Delilah's Lap. Remember John Piper's comment about affections and passions moving in where there's emptiness?

God has systematically helped me put on His *whole* armor, starting with the belt of truth. Before coming to my awakening, I was wearing the belt of truth—but it wasn't buckled! Over the years, as I marinade myself in his Word, God in his grace and mercy is constantly and systematically shining his light of conviction on thoughts and activities that my conscience has embraced as acceptable—and this, decades into my walk with him, *oy vey*!

Clearly, God unfolds and addresses matters in our lives systematically. He doesn't expect us to never sin again the moment we are saved, even though he instantly calls us holy. He raises us like the dear children of his that we are, constantly coaching us; teaching us new things and applying them to our lives as he renews our minds. Our identity is rooted in God's presence, in God's Word, and among God's people. That is why it is imperative to be actively immersed and involved in these 3 arenas. We must live and breathe the truth of our identity in God. That truth must replace the lies we've bought into.

My "Uncle Jedidiah" thinking was sloppy and short-sighted. It was clearly comfort-seeking, that came from an immature, indulgent heart. Indulgence says, "I can have all I want. Mine!" Or, it can be a little more sophisticated and say, "I'll have just a little more." Incidentally, the attitude of indulgence steals into numerous other aspects of my life such as my eating, sleeping, shopping, and many other forms of pampering the flesh that we've identified. Lack of discipline manifests itself in umpteen forms in one's life. Nobody deals with just one form of idolatry. We are brilliant at diversifying our pornography portfolio. We have back-ups of back-ups. The flesh demands to be catered to. Sometimes, dealing with my flesh feels like an interaction with a bratty three-year-old who wants what she wants, right now! Be the boss of that three-year-old or she will terrorize your spiritual walk!

The Mercy Corps board admitted in a letter to Tania Culver dated April 5th 1994, "As we explored your complaints, we looked for *similar* mistreatment of the organization and *as might be expected*, [emphasis added] a person who creates a dysfunctional family, will be a dysfunctional influence in an organization… It will take time to repair the problems that were more deep rooted than we were aware."[3]

Sometimes a person will be very strict in one area and totally undisciplined in another. Here's an example from my life. Have you ever sat with someone to have a conversation and they take a couple of minutes to check their phone before they settle in so they don't interrupt the visit? I appreciate that because I know that I'll have their undivided attention during our time together. What catches in my craw, even during a casual visit, is when someone checks their phone every two minutes. It's one thing if they've informed me they have a situation they're dealing with and need to attend to, but another very rude matter if not. I don't like it when people do that to me and I work very hard not to do that to others.

Yet I turn around and do exactly that to God. My goal when I wake up in the morning is to spend quality time with the Lord in His word and in prayer before I do anything else. After all, not only is He the most important thing in my day and I want to honor Him as such, but also, I am his maidservant and want to catch His directive for my day. I want my mind to be saturated with Him before my feet hit the floor.

I get my laptop and my phone along with my Bible and my journal. I open my phone to my reading outline. I notice a text from my dear friend, Dot who sends me a verse every day. It's a great one, and I let her know it and wish her a good day.

After that one is another from my employee seeking clarification on a medication procedure due in an hour. I answer it quickly to get it out of the way. Then I remember I have a document I need to submit to the insurance company to close up the claim from the car accident a few months ago. I shoot the agent a quick email to let her know I'll take care of it by the end of the day.

My Bible verse friend texts back, "Have a beautiful day too." I smile in appreciation. It's a good thing I glanced at that email in the sea of others, because I notice tomorrow is the last day to register my son for school. I think, "Thank you Lord for showing that to me. That would have been a disaster. Then comes my favorite part when it comes to emails: delete, delete, delete. I'm so glad I'm not shopping from this website any more. Seventy per cent off, wait, what? I wonder what it is…

Ugh! It's been over a week since I called Dad. He lives in a time zone twelve hours ahead. I keep remembering to call at all the wrong times. I'd better do that now or it'll never happen.

An hour later, I still haven't started my devotion time! By the time I get to it, my mind is a whirling dervish and I'm just doing the reading to check it off my extensive to-do list. God must feel like I do when I sit with someone to have a conversation and they keep checking their phone!

On the flip-side, please be informed that doing my devotion is not what it's all about. I can spend hours in devotion with a heart that's very far away from God. Indeed, my devotion time can become an idol in and of itself. What's important is constantly turning my mind and my heart Godward, catching his eye and keying into his heart a million times a day. This reorienting has to happen daily, moment by moment, whether you've known him one day or walked with him for 60 years. Then shall come true the words of Helen Howarth Lemmel's hymn:

> Turn your eyes upon Jesus
> Look full in His wonderful face
> And the things of earth will grow strangely dim
> In the light of His glory and grace.[4]

Nobody deals with just one form of
idolatry. We are brilliant at diversifying
our pornography/idolatry portfolios.
We have back-ups of back-ups.

Chapter 19

My Mission

After salvation, our spirit comes to life, and we become a new person. We still lug around the old dirt-bag—the flesh and its sinful tendencies. Walking in and living in sin, as God defines it, is akin to my husband and I living with the filthy old carpet described earlier. Attempting to appear perfect, which the music group, Casting Crowns, refers to as the *stained-glass masquerade*, is the same as sitting on the numerous holes in the carpet. The whole time, the Lord is telling us to rip it out and expose the gorgeous floors beneath. Meditate on these lyrics to one of my favorite songs.

> Is there anyone that falls?
> Am I the only one in church today, feeling so small?
> Cause when I take a look around
> Everybody seems so strong
> I know they'll soon discover
> That I don't belong
> So I tuck it all away
> Like everything's OK
> If I make em all believe it
> Maybe I'll believe it too
> So with a painted grin
> I'll play the part again
> So everyone will see me
> The way that I see them

Are we happy plastic people
Under shiny plastic steeples
With walls around our weakness
And smiles that hide our pain
But the invitation's open
To every heart that's been broken
Maybe then we close the curtain
On our stained glass masquerade

Is there anyone who's been there?
Are there any hands raised?
Am I the only one who's traded in
The altar for a stage?
The performance is convincing
And we know every line by heart
Only when no one is watching can we really fall
apart
But would it set me free
If I dared to let you see
The truth behind the person
You imagine me to be
Or would your eyes be opened
Or would you walk away
Would the love of Jesus
Be enough to make you stay?...[1]

Relish with me what I have adopted as my life-anchor Scripture:

*For this reason, since the day we heard about
you, we have not stopped praying for you.
We continually ask God to fill you with the
knowledge of his will through all the wisdom*

*and understanding that the Spirit gives, so
that you may live a life worthy of the Lord and
please him in every way: bearing fruit in every
good work, growing in the knowledge of God,
being strengthened with all power according to
his glorious might so that you may have great
endurance and patience, and giving joyful
thanks to the Father, who has qualified you
to share in the inheritance of his holy people
in the kingdom of light. For he has rescued us
from the dominion of darkness and brought us
into the kingdom of the Son he loves, in whom
we have redemption, the forgiveness of sins*
(Colossians 1:9–14).

As a result of God saving me and then repeatedly, powerfully rescuing me from The Temptress's various dens of death, I am a woman on a mission:

1. To live a vibrant life worthy of the Lord and to please him. I desire to live before him moment by moment, to actively turn from works of darkness to works of light, and to shirk the stained-glass masquerade,
2. To bear good fruit in my own life and to foster that in the lives of others
3. To grow in the knowledge of God and to spur others on to do the same
4. To come to some understanding of the mind-blowing fact that I am strengthened with *all* power according to his glorious might and have great endurance and patience, and
5. To give ecstatic thanks to this amazing Father who, to my eternal stupefaction, has chosen and qualified me by salvaging me from the dominion of darkness into his marvelous light through no effort or merit of my own.

Live a life worthy of the Lord
and please him in every way.

Chapter 20

7 Reasons Why We Engage in Porn

The obvious reason for engaging in porn in all its forms, is self-gratification. It feels good and swiftly becomes compulsive as we studied in the chapter on the brain. We learned that our senses are integral to life. This applies to sins, especially sex, which I'll use to illustrate the tie to the senses. You can relate this application to any habit.

We've all heard that men are aroused visually and by erotic sounds and movements a woman may make, whereas most women are primarily aroused by touch and verbal affirmation. The male physiology works such that most men can change gears and be ready for sex at the drop of a hat. They prep like a microwave. They are also spent just as fast. It has been said that most women warm up slowly, like a crockpot. Many women report they need all day to work up to being ready for sex. After sex, they could use more touch and verbal affirmation as a tapering off to the romancing. This doesn't happen if the microwave is already out cold and snoring. This sensual difference can cause all manner of disconnect between a couple and lead to dissatisfaction.

Why do we engage in sexual idolatry? I posit seven reasons.

1. Lack of discipline

    From a young age, a human being needs significant adults in their life to say the word "no" for the child's protection. Along the way, we attempt to and learn to get away with as much as

144

we can and become quite sophisticated at doing so. This fuels the spirit of Samson within us. Ideally, the individual grows in maturity and learns to tell themselves "no" in various facets of life. We call it self-control or self-discipline. If we have experience after experience of indulging ourselves, we grow to think we can have whatever we want, when we want it. The book of Proverbs speaks soberly about this serious matter of discipline, as well as the grave consequences of its lack.

If we don't learn to say no in small matters, we'll have no idea how to do so in important matters. As an example, ogling others sexually can become a sport among young men. Rochester says, "Prior to marriage a man has the pick of the litter. With many [women] to choose from, variety is a game in a man's mind."[1] Marriage should signal the end of that mindset but undisciplined men and women do not know how to turn off the roving eye. The neural circuitry is cemented and a habit has been formed. Rochester calls this the visual black book—"what a man observed in the street that caught his eyes and is filed in his soul or mind"[2] for regurgitation.

Sexual lack of discipline is not just a male problem. Women and children face it in thought, word, and deed. It doesn't take young girls long to realize the power they wield sexually. From an increasingly young age, flirting behavior (manifested in the extreme as sexting) is seen as innocuous and entails girls and women "putting themselves out there." It is not uncommon for women, including married women of all ages, to sit and chit chat about how hot some guy is, how easy he is on the eyes. This becomes our visual pink book of sin contacts. It is not a far step to go from this sin of thought and talk to action. We must remember that even at the thought stage, this behavior is full-blown sin.

2. Pleasure and Entertainment

A *Frontline* article points out that people view erotica to be entertained and to be distracted from work or other activities.[3] In an effort to unwind and de-stress, we can engage in excessive gaming, excessive exercise, or erotica. We binge-watch TV and overeat. Many women indulge in "soft porn" as read in romance novels, popular over-the-counter magazines, or viewed on regular TV shows. As Rebecca Bender notes, today, soft-porn is mainstream.[4] The material consumed therein is added to the woman's visual pink book—what she can recall to fill her mind in place of or during sex, especially if her sex life is unsatisfactory.

Remember that the brain and its reward pathways are excited and cemented by novelty. This is made all the more intense by adding violence because additional neurotransmitters are added to the dopamine cocktail, turning the regular cement into a quick-set formula. Gallagher emphasizes that

> Pornography and illicit sexual activities are merely extreme forms of pleasure. Therefore, it follows that the person who becomes addicted to pleasure and entertainment is himself very vulnerable to sexual temptation. People who increasingly fill their lives with "innocuous" pleasures find the step required to cross over into sinful pleasures getting progressively smaller.[5]

3. Escape (Emotional Pain Relief)

We engage in compulsive habits to combat low self-esteem, depression, despair, guilt, loneliness, sadness, frustration, and other painful emotions. Dr. Shaw teaches that "avoiding pain at all costs is called the "escape" of emotional pain relief. Addiction means that we are being driven by our feelings. Sometimes these feelings have been stuffed so deep that an addict may have no idea what I'm talking about and deny there are any feelings associated with their habit. It is imperative that we grow in the discipline of managing our emotions instead of being controlled by them, which is like holding a tiger by the tail. We must acknowledge them, feel them, experience them, process them, and evaluate them so we benefit from the gift that they are. We then expose them to our thinker (PFC) and make decisions on what our resulting actions, if any, will be.

Escaping to a pleasurable activity comes in many forms: alcohol, drugs, food, sex, sleep, work, vacations, shopping."[6] We flee to various types of idolatry for comfort. It's the easy way out and the brain, in its efficiency, takes the wide road. Instead of working to resolve difficult situations, many walk out on their spouses literally or figuratively by engaging in any of numerous forms of pornography. As we learned, we seek comfort for a variety of reasons but reach for it in all the wrong places. God is our true Comforter to whom we must flee in our time of need. It is to him we must go when we hurt, are lonely, dejected, and sad.

Momentary or systemic boredom is another culprit. We've all heard of reports that a person cheated on their spouse because a new person they met makes them feel young or alive or great about themselves. Of course an underlying spirit of selfishness and entitlement undergirds this thinking. Remember the novelty factor in brain science? What we fail to remember is that novelty wears off all too soon. We've been in situations where we were the novelty in a relationship. Years in, if that, we were replaced by yet another novelty.

Saints, solitude is a gift of God. Very few people in today's world are comfortable being alone either in private or in public. We can't bear to be alone with our own thoughts. Worse yet, like the Israelites, we are afraid to run the risk of encountering God.

When the people saw the thunder and
lightning and heard the trumpet and saw the
mountain in smoke, they trembled with fear.
They stayed at a distance and said to Moses,
"Speak to us yourself and we will listen. But
do not have God speak to us or we will die."
Moses said to the people, "Do not be afraid.
God has come to test you, so that the fear of God
will be with you to keep you from sinning."

The people remained at a distance, while Moses
approached the thick darkness where God was
(Exodus 20:18-21).

And what was God's first instruction to Moses after that?

Do not make any gods to be alongside me
(Exodus 20:23a).

Do we have a theme here? We flee to the cacophony of *any* distraction. We turn on the radio, or some other form of noise. Much of this is mindless, just to fill the void. How much better if we can couple this escape with self-gratification? Friend, try the disciplines of quietness and solitude in your life, even for short bursts at a time.

4.   Education

Young people watch erotica to learn about sex while adults report watching it to get new ideas.

5.   Peer pressure and rites of passage

Teens and young adults pressure each other to experiment sexually or with other compulsive habits. Adults influence a partner to try erotica or other sexual experiences such as spouse swapping. People may vow to engage in certain behaviors by a certain point e.g. to try drugs or lose their virginity by the time they graduate high school.

6.   Insomnia

Children, teens, and adults use orgasms and the resulting dopamine salvo to help them fall asleep. May God be our refuge in the watches of the night at which time we are vulnerable to the enemy of our souls. Indeed, may this be a time to connect with the Lover of our Soul who may be awakening us to intimately reveal himself to us in the quiet of the night. He calls this the *secret counsel* as described on my blogsite in a fascinating post by the same name.[7] In the same way, gamers will claim they can't fall asleep without a gadget in bed; and addicts that they can't sleep till they've had alcohol or other drugs. And should they awake in the middle of the night, guess what the first thought is.

7.   Vengeance

Because they know the excruciating pain associated with betrayal, a hurt person will go out and cheat on their spouse as a way to get even for pain caused.

Dr. Shaw discloses that, often, these momentary reasons belie a more serious problem of the heart that needs to be addressed quickly before it metastasizes! Our issues may look different on the outside "but they are all the result of the same inward problem of the heart: idolatry."[8] We must discipline our thinking, which is sometimes like herding turtles. Thank God for the great power we have over this wild herd. Ultimately, our battle is not against flesh and blood—including our own.

> *Our battle is against the rulers, against*
> *the authorities, against the powers of this*
> *dark world, and against the spiritual*
> *forces of evil in the heavenly realms*
> (Ephesians 6:12).

It behooves us to be mindful of all the influences which serve the Doctrine of Balaam—to turn us away from God—our true joy and comfort; to detract from our mission and from our task; to distract us from the one true Lover of our Souls; to disengage us from sensitivity to God and His ways so that we indulge in sensuality.

Author June Hunt teaches that we use harmful habits to meet our inner need for:

- *unconditional love* through sensual pleasure (porn, overeating, drugs, etc.)
- *significance* through achievement (power, position, performance, popularity, etc.)
- *security* through acquisitions (possessions, money, people, etc.)

Destructive habits are caused by misplaced dependencies. Our deepest longing is for intimacy with God. He made us with a desire to seek him. He alone can fulfill us—all other ground is sinking sand because everything and everyone else "is subject to death, or decay, destruction or dissipation."[9]

Addiction is the outward manifestation
of the inward problem of the lack of
intimate relationship with your Heavenly
Father... God graciously wants to have
an intimate relationship with you.[10]

Mark Shaw

Chapter 21

13 Problems with Porn

There is no wisdom, no insight, no plan
that can succeed against the LORD
(Proverbs 21:30).

If you are a Christian, the Jewish people in the Bible are your spiritual ancestors. You are one of the children of faith, foretold to Abraham when he was a young man. Their God, YAHWEH, is your God. The Bible characters are "your people." Their story is your story. Their rich legacy is your legacy. What fabulous wealth to own and embrace!

The Apostle Paul, our brother, tells a great story that has to do with you.

For I do not want you to be ignorant of the fact, brothers and sisters, that our ancestors were all under the cloud and that they all passed through the sea. They were all baptized into Moses in the cloud and in the sea. They all ate the same spiritual food and drank the same spiritual drink; for they drank from the spiritual rock that accompanied them, and that rock was Christ.

Nevertheless, God was not pleased with most of them; their bodies were scattered in the wilderness. Now these things occurred as examples to keep us from setting our hearts on evil things as they did. Do not be idolaters, as some of them were; as it is written: "The people sat down to eat and drink and got up to indulge in revelry." We should not commit sexual immorality, as some of them did—and in one day twenty-three thousand of them died. We should not test Christ, as some of them did—and were killed by snakes. And do not grumble, as some of them did—and were killed by the destroying angel.

These things happened to them as examples and were written down as warnings for us, on whom the culmination of the ages has come. *So, if you think you are standing firm, be careful that you don't fall! No temptation has overtaken you except what is common to mankind. And God is faithful; he will not let you be tempted beyond what you can bear. But when you are tempted, he will also provide a way out so that you can endure it* (1 Corinthians 10:1-13, emphasis added).

God wasn't fooling around with his children who were messing around then. Rest assured that He certainly isn't today. The Matthew Henry Commentary says,

> When we consider how much this sin [sexual immorality] abounds, how heinous adultery is in its own nature, of what evil consequence it is, and how certainly it destroys the spiritual life in the soul, we shall not wonder that the cautions against it are so often repeated.[1]

Some might be so bold as to ask, "What's the big deal with pornography?" The problems with pornography (here primarily meaning erotica but frequently applying to the various forms of sexual immorality) are numerous and grave. Many of these problems can be translated directly to whatever your idol of choice is:

1. Porn is an atrocious act of disobedience

    It grieves, displeases, *and* angers God, just as cheating on your spouse would grieve, displease, and anger them. It brazenly flies in the face of two mandates:

    > *Live a life worthy of the Lord and*
    > *please Him in every way*
    > (Colossians 1:10).

    > *And do not bring sorrow to God's Holy Spirit by*
    > *the way you live. Remember, He is the one who*
    > *has identified you as His own, guaranteeing that*
    > *you will be saved on the day of redemption*
    > (Ephesians 4:30).

2. Erotica is idolatry.

    Pornography is the epitome of sensuality and self-gratification. It is self-worship at its best. It turns us from sensitivity to God and places us in his place of prominence in our hearts, as we gratify ourselves. Psalm 106 is a magnificent chapter.

    > *In the desert they gave in to their craving; in*
    > *the wilderness they put God to the test.*
    > *They exchanged their glorious God for*
    > *an image of a bull, which eats grass.*
    > *They forgot the God who saved them,*
    > *who had done great things in Egypt,*

> *Then they **despised the pleasant land**;*
> *they did not believe his promise.*
> (Psalm 106:14, 20, 24).

In other words, when we indulge in pornography/idolatry we are holding God and his gifts to us in contempt. We are telling him we know better and that "the better" that we know is better than he is.

3.   Porn Steals Our True Glory

God promises us a future glory which is an exalted, splendid state.

> *I consider that our present sufferings*
> *are not worth comparing with the*
> *glory that will be revealed in us*
> (Romans 8:18).

> *To the elders among you, I appeal as a fellow*
> *elder and a witness of Christ's sufferings who*
> *also will share in the glory to be revealed*
> (1 Peter 5:1).

This is one of our great hopes as Christians. It is so powerful that it should motivate us to forego temporal worldly glory, such as praise of men, the high of a drug, immoral sexual pleasure, or other thrills. Yet, like Esau, we trade our birthright for a bowl of lentil soup. Even a five-year-old knows that is the worst trade on earth, yet we do it repeatedly in pornography. Satan is a liar. Just as he tempted Jesus, he offers us wondrous pleasures—now! Tony Reinke puts it beautifully, "If I don't grab this chance at glory now, sin tells me, it will be lost forever... We forget eternity. We so easily lose the faith to imagine that one day we will inherit the world and be more renowned...than [we] could ever imagine in this life. We want our share of glory now, instead of waiting for our "glory that is to be revealed.""[2]

4.   Pornography weakens, sickens, and kills people.

In the garden of Eden, God promised Adam and Eve,

On the day you eat of this fruit you shall surely die
(Genesis 2:17).

We are hidden and secure in Christ so we cannot die spiritually as we saw in the chapter titled *Sin Leading to Death*. When we consider our relationship to God, the state of death we are talking about here is characterized by broken fellowship with Him, separation from Him, and willful disobedience to Him. It can also mean physical death.

a.   God can allow the physical consequences of sinful behavior leading to sickness and death, as we just read in 1 Corinthians 10. Paul reinforces this harsh but fundamental truth.

Those who live according to the flesh have their minds set on what the flesh desires; but those who live in accordance with the Spirit have their minds set on what the Spirit desires. The mind governed by the flesh is death, but the mind governed by the Spirit is life and peace
(Romans 8:5-7).

She [Folly, the Temptress] sits at the door of her house, on a seat at the highest point of the city, calling out to those who pass by, who go straight on their way, "Let all who are simple come to my house!"

To those who have no sense she says,
"Stolen water is sweet;
food eaten in secret is delicious!"
But little do they know that the dead are there,
that her guests are deep in the realm of the dead
(Proverbs 9:14-18).

A man who strays from the path of understanding
comes to rest in the company of the dead
(Proverbs 21:16).

Though we are free in Christ, no man is a free agent.

Don't you know that when you offer
yourselves to someone as obedient slaves, you
are slaves of the one you obey—whether you
are slaves to sin, which leads to death, or to
obedience, which leads to righteousness?
(Romans 6:16).

When tempted, no one should say, "God is
tempting me." For God cannot be tempted by
evil, nor does he tempt anyone; but each person
is tempted when they are dragged away by their
own evil desire and enticed. Then, after desire
has conceived, it gives birth to sin; and sin,
when it is full-grown, gives birth to death
(James 1:13-15).

Needless to say, many have literally died in various ways while pursuing sexual pleasures. Today, sexually transmitted diseases (STDs) are a pandemic! Countless numbers have been murdered by a jilted lover. Behold this apt description:

> *For this command is a lamp, this teaching is a*
> *light, and correction and instruction are the way*
> *to life, keeping you from your neighbor's wife,*
> *from the smooth talk of a wayward woman.*
> *Do not lust in your heart after her beauty*
> *or let her captivate you with her eyes. For a*
> *prostitute can be had for a loaf of bread, but*
> *another man's wife preys on **your very life**.*
>
> *Can a man scoop fire into his lap without his*
> *clothes being burned? Can a man walk on*
> *hot coals without his feet being scorched? So*
> *is he who sleeps with another man's wife; no*
> *one who touches her will go unpunished.*
>
> *People do not despise a thief if he steals to satisfy*
> *his hunger when he is starving. Yet if he is caught,*
> *he must pay sevenfold, though it costs him all*
> *the wealth of his house. But a man who commits*
> *adultery [pornography] has no sense; whoever*
> *does so destroys himself. Blows and disgrace are*
> *his lot, and his shame will never be wiped away.*
>
> *For jealousy arouses a husband's fury, and he*
> *will show no mercy when he takes revenge.*
> *He will not accept any compensation; he*
> *will refuse a bribe, however great it is*
> (Proverbs 6:23-35, emphasis added).

b. While working in a maximum security psychiatric unit, I was stunned to note from my patient's chart reviews that approximately eighty per cent of them had been sexually abused as children. That selfish, atrocious act imposed on a child literally rewires their brain in damaging ways and opens the door to an array of mental health conditions that seriously impede their lives.

c. First Corinthians 11:27-34 outlines the importance of, and the proper state of heart to take communion in. Many believers are taking communion with sexual and other sin in their lives, which is a dangerous plight. The Apostle Paul said that there are many that are sickly and dead because they did not examine and judge themselves as guilty of sin. They desecrated the table of the Lord. This specific discipline is seriously downplayed in the Church today.

d. Innocent populations end up dead—think of the disturbing number of children who are aborted as a result of sexual immorality. Think of people living and dying in deplorable conditions as sex slaves. In the case of King David, four of his children ended up dead as a result of his secret sins of adultery and murder. Hear God's ruling on this matter:

> *This is what the Lord says: 'Out of your own household I am going to bring calamity on you. Before your very eyes I will take your wives and give them to one who is close to you, and he will sleep with your wives in broad daylight. You did it in secret, but I will do this thing in broad daylight before all Israel.'*
> (2 Samuel 12:11-12).

Yikes! His infant child from his affair with Bathsheba died. David's sons Amnon, whom Absalom killed for raping the latter's sister, Tamar; and both Absalom and Adonijah died in a coup attempt. As Dr. Anderson notes, all this happened because David "failed to turn away from the tempting sight of a woman bathing."[3] Let's not forget to add Bathsheba's faithful husband Uriah to that casualty list.

5.   Porn degrades and devalues you as a person.

    a.   We just read that

the prostitute reduces you to a loaf of bread
(KJV and NASB).

This paints a picture of making one worthless. Indeed, because of sexual immorality, we have seen how great men and women have lost places of prominence, impactful ministries, health, beautiful families, homes, opportunities, treasures and empires.

Porn steals your future. We have a generation of addicted gamers who aren't even showing up for the game of life. Interactions with young, smart men ensnared by gaming, have opened my eyes to two fundamental truths. First, when asked where they see themselves in 2 months or 2 years, they inevitably guffaw and say, "When you're addicted you don't think like that. You're just thinking of the next couple hours, if that." Secondly, as one stated confidently "no doubt about it, most gamers are seriously addicted to online porn. I'm talking hours and hours every day."

All this must cause the same heart break that would strike anyone watching big blind Samson, milling grain at the grind-stone with his bulky muscles, and, finally, being led by a small boy to the sad end of his life. Believers, those huge muscles were meant to cause tremors in the kingdom of darkness, not to grind grain for its citizens!

    b.   Psychologist Dr. Gary Brooks, who has worked with porn addicts for the last thirty years, states, "Any time a person spends much time with the usual pornography usage cycle, it can't help but be a *depressing, demeaning, self-loathing* [emphasis added] kind of experience."[4]

6.   Porn is futile and self-perpetuating

No idolatrous experience or thing benefits us in the long term. They can't love us back. They can't hear us, see us, or answer us. The more time we spend with them, the more like them we become.

> *The idols of the nations are silver and gold,*
> *made by human hands. They have mouths,*
> *but cannot speak,*
> *eyes, but cannot see. They have ears,*
> *but cannot hear,*
> *nor is there breath in their mouths. Those*
> *who make them will be like them,*
> *and so will all who trust in them*
> *[powerless and dead]*
> (Psalm 135:15-18).

The Passion Translation expounds on the first few verses, saying, "The unbelieving nations worship what they make. They worship their wealth and their work. They idolize what they own and what they do. Their possessions will never satisfy. Their lifeless and futile works cannot bring life to them!"

Dr. Anderson claims that "sexual sins, abuse, and addictions are the easiest to lie about."[5] That compounds the compulsion and makes it a very long and very lonely road.

> From a business perspective, the porn industry has a pretty clever racket going. Their product offers consumers temporary relief from anxiety, depression, and loneliness in exchange for making these same problems much worse in the long-term. That works out really well for pornographers [the producers of pornography], since the worse their customers' anxiety and isolation grow, the more reason they have to turn back to porn. But for the consumer, the end result isn't nearly so nice."[6]

7. Pornography can be a form of God's discipline. This is a tricky concept to which the pornographer might originally say, "Bring it on!" Unfortunately, intimacy with the Temptress is the last stop before the grave.

> *The mouth of an immoral woman is a deep pit;*
> *a man experiencing the LORD's wrath will fall into it*
> (Proverbs 22:14).

> *Because of this, God handed them over to*
> *the vile desires of their heart to disgrace*
> *their bodies among themselves*
> (Romans 1:24, Aramaic Bible in Plain English).

It has been said that divorce doesn't start in court. It starts long before that in the troubled marriage. In the same way, habitual sexual sin starts long before there is any acting out. God will sometimes give us over to our desires if we persist in unrepentance. Look at a fearsome account of this concept as it played out among the Israelites in the desert on the way to the Promised Land. (Egypt is symbolic of bondage while the Promised Land is symbolic of abundant living in intimacy with God.)

> *The rabble with them began to crave other*
> *food, and again the Israelites started wailing*
> *and said, "If only we had meat to eat! We*
> *remember the fish we ate in Egypt at no cost—*
> *also the cucumbers, melons, leeks, onions and*
> *garlic. But now we have lost our appetite; we*
> *never see anything but this manna!"...*
> *"Tell the people: 'Consecrate yourselves in*
> *preparation for tomorrow, when you will eat meat.*
> *The Lord heard you when you wailed, "If only*
> *we had meat to eat! We were better off in Egypt!"*
> *Now the Lord will give you meat, and you will*
> *eat it. You will not eat it for just one day, or two*

*days, or five, ten or twenty days, but for a whole
month—until it comes out of your nostrils **and
you loathe it**—because you have rejected the
Lord, who is among you, and have wailed before
him, saying, "Why did we ever leave Egypt?""*
(Numbers 11:4-6, 18-20).

8. Porn lies to and confuses the sinner.

    a.   I love the graphic way Proverbs describes any attempt at counterfeiting God's intimacy:

> *Food gained by fraud tastes sweet, but one
> ends up with a mouth full of gravel*
> (Proverbs 20:17).

Our idols start off as meeting a need in our lives. Note the references to food and water in the passages above. Our human needs don't get more basic than that. No one goes out in search of some good gravel to munch on. We want the good stuff. We think we found the good stuff. Insidiously, the idol presently becomes the need itself when we find we can't function without it. Remember the concept of withdrawal we learned in the chapter titled, *The Physiology of Addiction—Part 2.* Alcoholics and drug users can relate to this as can screen addicts. We start off using the substance or habit for pleasure or to relieve pain. Before we know it, the habit itself becomes the need and our bodies are miserable without it. We use/engage just to feel normal. Hunt says,

> The substance moves from being a need-meeter to becoming the need itself. Instead of using the substance to relieve stress, they end up using…because its mere absence causes stress.[7]

b. While many in the church, like the world, place a very high value on sex, Paul identifies singlehood as a gift and as preferred over marriage. If Paul were to stand at a modern-day pulpit and state, as he did in days of old, "It is good for a man *not* to have sexual relations with a woman," God's people would unanimously choke and sputter in disbelief, then say, "Are you kidding me?!"

We have it in our heads and culture that we *have to* have sex. Since people have trouble with self-control, he advises marriage,

> *as a concession, not as a command. I wish*
> *that all of you were as I am [single]*
> (1 Corinthians 7:6).

We "New Testamenters" are to marry because we can't control ourselves, not because we are human! Paul has two reasons for his teaching. First, because Christ's return is imminent, Paul desires for us to spend our time and energies single-mindedly doing Christ's bidding.

> *I would like you to be free from concern. An*
> *unmarried man is concerned about the Lord's*
> *affairs—how he can please the Lord. But a*
> *married man is concerned about the affairs of*
> *this world—how he can please his wife—and his*
> *interests are divided. An unmarried woman or*
> *virgin is concerned about the Lord's affairs: Her*
> *aim is to be devoted to the Lord in both body and*
> *spirit. But a married woman is concerned about*
> *the affairs of this world—how she can please her*
> *husband. I am saying this for your own good,*
> *not to restrict you, but that you may live in a*
> *right way in undivided devotion to the Lord*
> (1 Corinthians 7:32-35).

163

Remember, we are they upon whom the culmination of the ages has come. Time is short. Secondly,

Those who marry will face many troubles
in this life, and I want to spare you this
(1 Corinthians 7:28).

Paul acknowledges the difficult reality of committing your life to someone else for the rest of your life. It doesn't take a married couple long to realize that fairy tales and "happily ever after" are left at altar on the wedding day. Successfully married people will tell you that even a good marriage is arduous, unrelenting work. The guy that thinks marriage is a piece of cake won't be married long. Satan will tell us that singlehood is not healthy, not happy, not whole, and not of God. He'll tell us to lower our standards and just get married to whoever comes along, all in effort to conform to societal expectations. He'll even tell us not to wait. He'll tell us, "Why buy the cow when the milk is free?"

c. Porn competes with godliness. Though its cheap, instant thrill cannot match God's Word or the joy he gives, it is scintillating and tantalizing. Moreover, it delivers on instant gratification, albeit less and less. Like a weed in a garden, sin grows easier and faster than godliness. It multiplies more rapidly and can swiftly choke the latter out. Unfortunately, sin doesn't take much to grow in us if we nurture, water, and meditate on it. Worse yet, it grows if we just ignore it. It requires no effort to grow sin, whereas growth in godliness takes time and effort.

d. Porn steals our common sense and can turn us into fools. A friend was married to a deacon we'll call Stan who was addicted to online erotica. He didn't understand why his wife had a problem with this. He claimed that it sometimes brought him closer to the Lord as he was very picky and specifically solicited Christians. His passwords were even Christian in nature, e.g. JesusisKing. He told his wife that when he had live chats with girls online, they sometimes even talked about the Lord. I hope you're gob-smacked right about now.

What a prime example of a hijacking of the reward pathway. As often happens, communication between the prefrontal cortex (PFC, in charge of executive thinking) is cut off from the midbrain and the accumbens. Stan illustrates serious impairment in the capacity to understand and react to the feelings of others; in impulse-control, judgement, decision-making, and other PFC functions. The frontal cortex is two thirds of the human brain and its control center. It is an atrocity when its powerful capacity blows a fuse. The user is literally not using their brain!

e. The pornographer is confused regarding what is of value and what isn't. Porn causes you as a sinner to betray yourself and what you cherish. Stan in the example above, would come home and head straight to his room. His beautiful wife and precious baby girl rarely saw him. He'd come out to grab dinner and eat alone behind locked doors. Woe was her if she tried to talk him into joining them or question his behavior. The pornographer considers those who are truly enemies as friends. Loved ones become the enemy should they try to get in the way of the pursuit of sin. What is worthwhile and valued undergoes instant deflation while what is vile and harmful is guarded and treasured. Once cherished family, work, values, and responsibilities are spurned and tossed aside.

f. Porn competes with God's work. Family, work, and ministry suffer as a result. Nothing destroys more marriages and ministries than sexual impurity. Pornography can so overrun our minds that we abandon our posts as soldiers of the cross. The prodigal can't run his father's estate from a far country whether he is living the "high life" or wallowing in the pigpen. Consider Samson napping in Delilah's lap day after day, week after week. He was a national leader. Who was doing his work? Because of porn he was so engrossed in himself that he was literally sleeping with the enemy, having abdicated his God-given role as ruler.

Porn steals from us as time, money, energies, common sense, our purpose, and other resources leave the kingdom of light and go to this work of darkness. Christian, our works will be tested and rewarded accordingly. Fortunately, we can't lose our salvation. But porneia may lead us to lose our rewards.

If what has been built survives, the builder will receive a reward. If it is burned up, the builder will suffer loss but yet will be saved—even though only as one escaping through the flames (Corinthians 3:14, 15).

g. God says,

My people have committed two sins: They have forsaken me, the spring of living water, and have dug their own cisterns, broken cisterns that cannot hold water (Jeremiah 2:13).

As we saw, success, loneliness, depression, boredom, and frustration among other reasons may drive a Christian to the broken cistern of pornography to drink its green, slimy, putrid waters instead of doing the work required to press into the presence of God to have our needs met there. We settle for Tenbergen's cardboard butterfly when true comfort can only be found in God, our treasure.

h.   Porn causes us to compare wrongly. God wants marriage commitment for life, while the enemy of our souls, the Liar (John 8:44), lies to us as he did to Eve, that God is holding out on us. His goal is to convince us that what we have is not satisfying enough, not beautiful enough, not worthy enough of us. He'll tell us we are not understood, not appreciated, and not valued by our spouse as much as someone else would.

i.   The literature reveals that although the sex acts viewed in pornographic material appear consensual, many border on rape. Participating in porn significantly contributes to what Gallagher refers to the "rape myth" which is a sick belief, that some have, that women actually want to be dominated and raped.[8]

j.   Sex created for viewer entertainment is unrealistic and staged. Rochester reveals, "The adult film industry is all acting. It is all scripted. In fact, there's a male standby in the event that the other is unable to complete the tasks." In it, superficial beauty, youth, and performance are held in high esteem. Sex acts last for an inordinate amount of time. We all know that most normal people experience limits on such performance. Most of these actors are young athletic people who work out for their "job." It's unfair and impractical to compare regular people with regular jobs and lives, and expect them to perform sexually at this level.[9] What's a normal person to do with flabby arms and cellulite?

k.   Dr. Anderson admonishes, "If you think living righteously is difficult, try living unrighteously."[10] The truth is that,

The blessing of the Lord brings wealth,
and he adds no trouble to it
(Proverbs 10:22).

Few people stop to think about that. God desires to protect us. Satan has other plans for us and, like Delilah with Samson, despite the present pleasure, the plans are not for our good.

9.   Pornography undercuts true love and intimacy.

    a.   A common characteristic among idolatrous individuals is the propensity to place their own needs above those of others. I call it "trampling" or "cadging." They are either unconscious or unmindful of the feelings, space, needs, resources, and time of others. They may verbally acknowledge that they love others, but their behavior shows wanton disregard for those they claim to love. Parents ignore the needs of children. Teens ignore their personal hygiene, their chores, the rules, and their grades. Adults are late to work or consistently keep others waiting. Addicts embarrass their family and spend all the family's income on drugs and friends. They are happy to be takers rather than givers. Worse, they may see themselves as the victim.

         Seattle reporter Eric Johnson produced a documentary called *Seattle is Dying*. It highlights the problem that whole cities such as Seattle and Portland, Oregon, are experiencing. Once gorgeous and immaculate, they are now overrun with garbage (tents, mattresses, used needles, shopping carts, etc.), human excrement, and addicts strung out on sidewalks, cemeteries, and parks. The problem, he claims, isn't homelessness. The real homeless stay out of sight. The real problem is drugs and the problem of addiction that many leaders are afraid to point out.[11]

    b.   Pornography is betrayal of and unfaithfulness to your spouse if you are married. When you engage in this form of idolatry you are stealing something that is not yours. If you are not married, you are cheating on your prospective spouse, with someone else's spouse. What you see is not yours to see or touch. You are stealing from God, from the person you are violating, and from their spouse if they have or will have one. You are even stealing from yourself.

c.   Without fail, porn promotes loveless sexual relationships and promotes unhealthy attitudes about sexuality. I have multiple friends who have a "bed buddy." They have an agreement that their relationship is only sexual with no emotional ties. In shock, I ask, "In this day and age?" My children's doctor just informed me that fifty percent of young adults have STDs! Since one of my friends is only available to her bed buddy on weekends, I wondered how many other bed buddies he had and the ominous web created thereby. It would seem that everyone was sleeping with everyone.

Sexualization is a common phenomenon whereby one twistedly views others through sexual lenses. You get a rise out of a person and see them (actually, their body parts) for what pleasure they can give you. This is an easy trap to fall into and make a habit of. It promotes the consumer mentality of pornographers. When one has fallen into this trap, they twist regular interactions with others and turn them into sexualized encounters in their own minds. One habitually interprets an insipid look, a comment, or an action and sees it as sexually loaded. It results in a dopaminergic reward and can become addictive in itself.

Sex is a consensual act and you don't have the right or the person's permission to treat them this way. Here is a bristle alert because so many think, "But I'm not hurting anyone." Christian, their body is not yours to view or touch as you do in your mind. You are, in effect, violating the other person. Other sin or addiction can't be played out effectively in the mind through fantasy the way sex can. In sexual sin, one doesn't have to go out and perform physically. It can all happen in the confines of the mind. If you do not discipline yourself in this area, you may find yourself in the trap of duality whereby you are physically with one person, and mentally with another.

This points to the preeminence of sex as an act and even as an addiction. Jesus said,

> *Flee from sexual immorality [porneia]. All other*
> *sins a person commits are outside the body, but*
> *whoever sins sexually, sins against their own body.*
> (1 Corinthians 6:18).

Gallagher reports on the "dehumanization of women as sex toys,"[12] Sex becomes a common commodity as do the providers of it. There is little honor, little cherishing. If one doesn't get what they want from their spouse, an alternate experience is just a click away or more insidiously, just a thought away.

d. Porn can act as an escape for spouses when things get difficult in marriage. Instead of working on improving the marriage, porn becomes an acceptable sexual outlet. Many will even use the difficulty in the marriage as a reason why they engage in pornography. This spirals into further selfish indulgence and isolation in a relationship that is supposed to be marked by selfless intimacy.

10. Porn undercuts authenticity and solitude

Reinke states, "We need face-to-face time, and even then we are hardly prepared for the friction that God intends to use as we and our spouses are sharpened and shaped over the years into couples who reflect Christ and his bride. This is part of the genius (and the mystery) of marriage as a covenant bond between two people of differing genders and often differing ethnicities, talents, and interests… Friction is the path to genuine authenticity".[13]

God uses real people in our lives to bring about the constant necessary change we need in the journey towards Christlikeness.

Porn bypasses the person, much like literally cutting them out of a picture we have framed on a wall.

11. Porn swings the door open to demonic activity and influence in our lives.

Hosea 5:4 & 4:10 claims, "A spirit of prostitution [*zanah*—Hebrew word for fornication; figuratively, idolatry] is in their hearts" and "leads them astray." We learned that "spirit" is "a disposition or uncontrollable impulse." Rochester notes that porn "is an invasion of the Christian home of demonic doctrines designed to disrupt the peace of God in your heart and house." Further, it can transfer from generation to generation. "The sin cycle in families continues" e.g. with teen sex and babies.[14]

Because the Holy Spirit takes up residence in your heart at the moment of salvation, you cannot be possessed by a demon. However, you can be influenced by evil spirits, especially as you avail yourself to their agenda. In keeping with one of the DSM-V's (Diagnostic and Statistical Manual for Mental Disorders) criteria for substance use and addictive disorders, which is the lack of control, despite a desire to stop, notice that the spirit of *zanah* is by its nature, an uncontrollable impulse. We developed this further in the chapter titled *The Physiology of Addiction—Part 2*. Don't mess with it; you *cannot* control it on your own!

12. Pornography is a slippery slope.

a. Pornography is never enough. It never satisfies. Human nature stokes the fire of uncontrolled sexual urges, seeking novel experiences to extend the pleasure. "Just one more time" is a prevalent lie of the enemy. Beloved, here is a prime principle to take to heart: It is impossible to satisfy lust. Contrary to popular belief, indulging oneself does not satiate the appetites, it inflames them! C.S. Lewis muses,

> Everyone knows that the sexual appetite, like our other appetites, grows by indulgence. Starving men may think much about food, but so do gluttons; the gorged, as well as the famished, like titillations.[15]

Dr. Anderson states,

> The euphoric experiences of sexual and chemical highs wear off, and more stimulation is needed to get that same high. Every successive use or experience increases our tolerance to sex and chemicals… As lust grows, more stimulation is required to quench it. But it can't be satisfied. The more a fleshly desire is fed, the larger it grows. Normal sexual experiences don't seem to bring the euphoria that a simple touch once did. So other sexual experiences must be tried to get that same high. We want to have the first initial rush that felt so good, but greater levels of degradation take us further way, and our lifestyle has also moved far away from our baseline experience.[16]

This is one of the reasons why reconciliation after infidelity is so difficult. The spouse who was cheated on has trouble believing that the offender won't return to their old ways. It is the natural thing to do. That's why it is imperative that we not go there in the first place.

b. Porn contributes to lowering our standards and eroding our values.

Rochester asserts that in watching porn, one "will watch all types of sexual immorality…threesomes, orgies, and same-sex relationships,"[17] even though he or she may object to these. Repeated exposure raises our tolerance for various types of sexual sin that are an affront to us and effectively normalizes them. Note how well this lines up with the agenda of the world. Marshall Kirk and Hunter Madsen in their book *After the Ball—How America Will Conquer Its Fear and Hatred of Gays in The Nineties,* had one focus as making deviancy appear positive. Another was to display as normal that which had previously been viewed as abnormal.[18]

c. Many rapists and other sexual deviants confess to viewing porn at a young age. They swiftly moved to hardcore porn and/or perpetrated crime against others when simple self-gratification was not enough. Gallagher lists "aberrant and bizarre sex" as possible results of viewing porn.[19] Clearly, not all who watch porn end up as sexual criminals but all sexual criminals engage in viewing pornography.

13. Finances.

As C.S. Lewis discloses,

> There are people who want to keep our sex instinct inflamed in order to make money out of us. Because, of course, a man with an obsession is a man who has very little sales-resistance.[20]

Even when we don't pay for porn sites or magazines, we support the people and spiritual forces that promote, endorse, and host them. They make millions from advertisers from our participation. Every visit we make is a vote approving them and money in their pockets. We are endorsing not just this one activity but also others that are integral to upholding it. Any one sin networks with other sins and rarely works alone. The sin of pornography holds hands with many other revolting sins including adult films, brothels, sex-trafficking, prostitution, child abuse, drugs, and several other crimes across the globe.

Christian, a day of accountability for our works is coming.

For we must all appear before the judgment
seat of Christ, so that each of us may receive
what is due us for the things done while
in the body, whether good or bad
(2 Corinthians 5:10).

Look, I [Jesus] am coming soon! My reward
is with me, and I will give to each person
according to what they have done
(Rev 22:12).

Isolation + feeding on vanity =
soul-starving loneliness
Isolation + communion with God =
soul-feeding solitude

Tony Reinke

Chapter 22

20 Ways We Despise 'The Pleasant Land'

We know that idolatry lies to us. If we believe that God is truth, it is incumbent upon us to get on the same page as him in all matters. Bristle alert! He alone defines our reality; not the world, and not even our perceptions or understanding. Certainly not our feelings. Otherwise we fall for the same lie that Eve fell for when the enemy told her that she could be like God. He is God and I am not. My flesh begs to differ and therein lies the root of a brutal spiritual battle.

We want to be like God—to know everything and to be everything. His reaction to that is more of the stuff that chafes at the human sensibilities, causing many to walk away from him. The world holds that we are currently in a spiritual phase of evolution advancing into godhood. Jehovah begs to differ. He is very particular about order and hierarchy. He calls Top Dog and will not share his position with another. We aspire to godliness but not to godhood.

> *For who is God besides the LORD?*
> *Who is the Rock except our God?*
> (Psalm 18:31).

> *I am God, and there is no other;*
> *I am God, and there is none like me*
> (Isaiah 46:9b).

I am the Lord, and there is no other;
apart from me there is no God
(Isaiah 45:5a).

"For my thoughts are not your thoughts,
neither are your ways my ways,"
declares the Lord
(Is 55:8).

Woe to those who call evil good and good evil,
who put darkness for light and light for darkness,
who put bitter for sweet and sweet for bitter.
Woe to those who are wise in their own eyes
and clever in their own sight
(Isaiah 5:20-21).

As God, he gets to ordain and orchestrate our lives. The flesh doesn't like that. Like a horse or mule, we buck him and his plans because we have a grand idea about where we want to graze. We bloody ourselves kicking against the goads. We'll frequently pick an imitation over the original thing if the former strikes us as more appealing or makes us look good. Our primal instincts override an attraction to the real thing. Unfortunately, like Tenbergen's butterfly we fly to the cardboard mate, or more accurately, to the fire. Like his little bird, we stick our chests out in pride because we are sitting on a massive wooden egg. Like Samson, we demand,

get her for me, she pleases me
(Judges 14:3).

Remember writer Barrett's claims that supernormal stimuli are driving forces in many of today's most pressing problems, including obesity, our addiction to television and video games, and wars? "Manmade imitations have wreaked havoc on how we nurture our children, what food we put into our bodies, how we make love and war, and even our understanding of ourselves."[1] We dig our heels in, thoroughly committed to worldly ambition, stubbornness, and being quarrelsome. We are ravenous consumers in all ways versus being producers, we take offense easily, and compare ourselves to others.

In Psalm 106 God teases out a great concept he calls, "the pleasant land," He describes how we despise and oppose it and instead drool over cheap fakes.

We have sinned, even as our ancestors did;
we have done wrong and acted wickedly.
When our ancestors were in Egypt, they
gave no thought to your miracles;
they did not remember your many
kindnesses, and they rebelled by the sea,
the Red Sea.
Yet he saved them for his name's sake,
to make his mighty power known.
He rebuked the Red Sea, and it dried up;
he led them through the depths as through a desert.
He saved them from the hand of the foe;
from the hand of the enemy he redeemed them.
The waters covered their adversaries;
not one of them survived.
Then they believed his promises and sang his praise.

But they soon forgot what he had done and
did not wait for his plan to unfold.
*In the desert they gave in to their **craving**;*
in the wilderness they put God to the test.
So he gave them what they asked for, but
sent a wasting disease among them.

*In the camp they grew **envious***
of Moses and of Aaron,
who was consecrated to the Lord.

The earth opened up and swallowed Dathan;
it buried the company of Abiram.
Fire blazed among their followers; a
flame consumed the wicked.
At Horeb they made a calf and
worshiped an idol cast from metal.
They exchanged their glorious God for
an image of a bull, which eats grass.
They forgot the God who saved them,
who had done great things in Egypt,
miracles in the land of Ham and
awesome deeds by the Red Sea.
So he said he would destroy them—
had not Moses, his chosen one,
stood in the breach before him to keep
his wrath from destroying them.

*Then they **despised the pleasant land;***
they did not believe his promise.
*They **grumbled** in their tents*
and did not obey the Lord.
So he swore to them with uplifted hand
that he would make them fall in the wilderness,
make their descendants fall among
the nations and scatter
them throughout the lands.
They yoked themselves to the Baal of Peor and
*ate sacrifices offered to **lifeless gods**;*
they aroused the Lord's anger
*by their **wicked deeds**,*
and a plague broke out among them.
But Phinehas stood up and intervened,
and the plague was checked.
This was credited to him as righteousness
for endless generations to come.

By the waters of Meribah they angered the Lord,
and trouble came to Moses because of them;
*for they **rebelled** against the Spirit of God,*
and rash words came from Moses' lips.

They did not destroy the peoples as the
Lord had commanded them,
but they mingled with the nations
and adopted their customs.
*They **worshiped their idols**, which*
*became a **snare** to them.*
They sacrificed their sons and their
daughters to false gods.
They shed innocent blood, the blood
of their sons and daughters,
whom they sacrificed to the idols of Canaan,
and the land was desecrated by their blood.
They defiled themselves by what they did;
*by their deeds they **prostituted** themselves.*
the Lord was angry with his people
and abhorred his inheritance.
He gave them into the hands of the nations,
and their foes ruled over them.
Their enemies oppressed them and
subjected them to their power.
Many times he delivered them, but
*they were bent on **rebellion***
and they wasted away in their sin.
Yet he took note of their distress
when he heard their cry;
for their sake he remembered his covenant
and out of his great love he relented.
He caused all who held them
captive to show them mercy.

Save us, Lord our God, and
gather us from the nations,
that we may give thanks to your holy
name and glory in your praise.

Praise be to the Lord, the God of Israel,
from everlasting to everlasting.
Let all the people say, "Amen!"
Praise the Lord
(Psalm 106:6-48, emphases added).

Here's what this looks like in my life. My brain is an idea machine. At rest, my striatum (the part of the brain that has to do with drive and motivation) is busier than popcorn in a hot skillet. This can be a wonderful thing. I have great enthusiasm for life and delight in possibilities. I love a good challenge, thrive under pressure, and embrace change. I'm constantly thinking of multiple ideas at a time and processing possibilities. Some blossom and come to fruition, some integrate and meld into existing ones, and many lie latent.

I am blessed to have had many material possessions. I have pursued and benefited from amazing advanced educational opportunities. I have dreamt of and excelled at entrepreneurship. I am deeply grateful for and cognizant of God's lavish goodness to me. Be certain that many people the world over are much smarter and work much harder than I have. My accomplishments are not my doing. They are God's gift to me.

Along the ambition road, though, I have learned that no sooner do I attain one dream, then my heart has already moved on to the next one, and the newly attained one—so deeply desired, so hotly pursued, all too soon loses its luster. I have to keep an alert sentinel over my heart guarding against discontent, ingratitude, and constantly looking for the next new thing. My instincts are drawn to the cardboard butterfly. I have to override that draw. In Scripture the heart is the entity that oversees these things. Remember your PAPDATE checkpoints: passions, affections, purpose, desire, appetites, thoughts, and endeavors.

Above all, guard your heart, for
it is the wellspring of life
(Proverbs 4:22).

In your life, your drive may be for a spouse or a child; for your kids' success, a new car or home, a desired body weight or a position at work. It may be regarding a celebrity or the latest gadget. It may be how many likes you got on a post, or with manipulating circumstances to get what you want. Sometimes the sins of discontent and ingratitude can set in with a relationship, our station in life, our abilities, etc. especially if we compare ourselves to others, instead of living our lives before the Lord. We can find ourselves plagued with unfinished projects or hopping from one thing to the next (including from one church to the next). Today's concept of built-in obsolescence can creep into our hearts so we start to see blessings as disposable, leading us to constantly want to upgrade.

We then get in the habit of despising what God has already given us, what he calls pleasant, ample, and satisfactory. To despise (Hebrew *ma'as,*) is to spurn, reject, hate, contemn, or have little regard for.

What are the symptoms of that? The Psalm above outlined them for us:

1. We fail to rejoice
2. We fail to praise him
3. We do wrong. Some of us continue in our ancestral sins—do you know what those are for you?
4. We give no thought to his miracles in others' and our own lives, forgetting his kindness. We forget the seas he split for us, the deserts he led us through, the waters we, walked on and the enemies he slayed with a mighty hand and an outstretched arm
5. When we're in trouble to flee to him *after* we've tried all our idols and they've failed us. We then revert to them after the storm subsides

6. When we see his good works, we believe again and even sing his praises, then we forget what he has done
7. We fail to wait for his plan to unfold
8. We give in to our cravings
9. We demand what we want
10. We reject/despise what he gives us (including what we demanded)
11. We test/challenge God and other authority
12. We envy others (leaders, peers, etc.)
13. We worship idols, prostituting ourselves by our deeds
14. We don't believe his promises
15. We grumble in private, to a select few, or in public
16. We disobey and rebel against him
17. We fail to intercede for others
18. We do what we think is best over what he commands
19. We sacrifice our children to false gods. We sacrifice them to the fire by our provision of privileges and resources that end up being a trap.
20. We shed innocent blood including that of our children as we abdicate our responsibilities to them.

Today's concept of built-in obsolescence
can creep into our hearts so that we
start to see blessings as disposable,
leading us to constantly desire an upgrade.

Chapter 23

Temptation

Temptation is akin to a hunter's tactics. People take time off work and school during hunting season here in the Pacific Northwest, where hunting is a popular sport. Family members will be missing birthday parties. Their spot at the Thanksgiving table will be vacant. Everywhere I go, some people will be talking about what they got. Many will be talking about what they almost got and scheming what they will do differently next hunting season.

A hunter scouts his territory and is very familiar with what he is hunting. He knows the ways and the weaknesses of his prey. Hunters exchange tales of scouting for their prey for weeks, studying their habits and their routines. They'll set up camouflaged hunting shacks and go as far as spraying themselves with the urine of the prey in order to attract them or "call them in"! How much more intent do you think the enemy of our souls is in "calling us in"?

When we first dabble in idolatry, we think we are in control and safe. We think we can back out at any time. Like the curious deer or elk checking out the grain or hay set out by a hunter, we wouldn't go there if we knew our life was in peril. Knowing what we know now, we can well see that that is a lie. We would be wise to not only resist temptation, but also to *expect* it. Many a Christian is frequently caught unawares by temptation.

The other day, I was driving behind a car that had a bumper sticker that said, "The problem with trouble is that it starts out as fun." As Ravi Zaccharias said, the real problem is that sin will always take you further than you want to go—[way out of your way], keep

183

you longer than you want to stay, and cost you more than you want to pay! The pornographer is like the youth in Proverbs who lacks judgement and succumbs to the lure of the Temptress,

*He follows her on **impulse**, like an ox going to the slaughter, like a deer bounding into a trap, until an arrow pierces his liver, like a bird darting into a snare—not knowing it will cost him his life*
(Proverbs 7:22-23, emphasis added).

Underestimating Temptation

We must not underestimate temptation, especially sexual temptation. How powerful is it? How influential is the flesh? Rochester challenges us regarding David, the man after God's own heart. "How could a man who killed the biggest man on the planet, be anointed king of Israel, write the greatest songs ever, become so cold as to take a man's wife and kill her husband?"[1] If this mighty man, the one after God's own heart could fall so hard, how much more susceptible are we? Paul warns us to

have nothing to do with the fruitless deeds of darkness
(Ephesians 5:11).

These are a lure, a snare, "a calling in." Paul advises,

make no provision for the desires of the flesh
(Rom. 13:14b).

Making provision entails making arrangements. Think of Dr. Sumrock and his proposal that addiction is Ritualized Comfort-Seeking Behavior. Contemplate the rituals we set up and follow to facilitate our habits—we orchestrate the time of day, the way we set up the room just so, the people we surround ourselves with (or ensure that we are alone), the gadgets and paraphernalia, the stash; how we dream and fantasize about it, where and how we pick up the loot and how we dispose of evidence etc.

Opportunity to sin is as abundant as pimples on a teenager's face. And they keep coming. When we make provision, we are unwisely walking right into the path of a camouflaged hunting shack, occupied by an armed hunter. There is a time to take your stand, stand your ground, and fight, as Paul advises in Ephesians 6. But don't underestimate temptation, soldier. There is another time when we are to cut loose and run! Visualize handsome young Joseph, zits on his teenage face, fleeing from Potiphar's sex-crazed wife so fast that he came out of his coat and left it in her hands. Paul exhorts us to do a Joseph and

Flee from sexual immorality
(1 Corinthians 6:18).

Overestimating Temptation

My town used to do a small farmer's market in the summer. We close down the main drag for a few hours one day a week and many locals set up booths to sell their wares. I love the small town atmosphere and know I'll probably run into friends there. I love to walk up and down the road and see what the vendors have for sale. I can browse, buy an item or two, or nothing at all. I don't have to buy anything. I am not obligated. It is for that reason that I stay away from Tupperware parties. If you attend one of those, you are rather obligated to buy something, if not because you want it, then because you want to support your friend. The pressure to buy is very high. So I've learned to say a clear "no" to those invitations.

So it is with sexual temptation, or whatever your besetting sin is. Take a minute and name it now if you haven't already. Walking through life is like strolling through the market. You *will* be tempted to look at wares. I guarantee it. You might even see a friend or two there. Heck, it might be a friend selling the wares. Christian, you have zero obligation to any temptation, least of all sexual temptation. Keep walking! And certainly say no to the Tupperware party.

You may leave with the $200 Tupperware and a heart of regrets. The Blue-Collar Comedian said, "You might be a red-neck if all your dessert bowls match—and say Cool-Whip!"[2] Christian, keep your Cool-Whip containers. They serve you just as well and require much less maintenance.

> But each person is tempted when they are dragged
> away by their own evil desire and enticed. Then,
> after desire has conceived, it gives birth to sin; and
> sin, when it is full-grown, gives birth to death
> (James 1: 14, 15).

Temptation is the enemy on his bullhorn saying, "is anyone out there?" Have you ever seen an elk raise a hoof and say, "right here!"? Of course not. They might be smarter than us. Temptation is merely a suggestion. Your eyes send an image to your brain, your limbic system strokes its beard, analyzing it while it peruses associated memories. Your midbrain squirts dopamine towards your striatum, rousing interest, motivation, and drive in the direction of the shiny object.

If the temptation is an old timer for you, the superhighway has a slick, well-maintained layer of asphalt and all eight lanes are clear. The porn-mobile is revving like a song. All systems are go. You'd better have your battle gear on. Your striatum, flooded by dopamine, is flashing like a lightning storm, ignoring the prefrontal cortex—the executive thinking center, and all the warning bells going off there. God told Cain sin was crouching at his door. That goes for you too. Be *shomer*. Expect it. Don't be surprised or affronted. Tackle it at the threshold. Develop the maturity and discipline to say "no." This is the time to roar your war cry. Pray. Resist it. Call for back up. If you need to, do a Joseph—cut and run!

If this temptation is new for you, don't fall for the lure. Don't get taken in by Tinbergen's cardboard butterflies. Deviate the construction crew to a different site. Don't buy the Liar's story that the risk is worth the reward of self-gratification. It never is. Here's a great fact that you can use as a weapon: you can't think two thoughts at the same time. This is the time to flood your brain with Scripture.

Hopefully you have a verse or two (or ten) memorized to draw from. Stock up your arsenal. Use scriptures and songs I've quoted in this book as a starting point. Pull out that old hymn. Hopefully you've committed that to memory. Now is the time to armor up in these ways. When you're on the battle ground is not the time or place to be learning how to put on your armor and which end of the gun is the pointing end. Familiarize yourself with these during training. Now is the time of training.

> *The weapons we fight with are not the weapons*
> *of the world. On the contrary, they have divine*
> *power to demolish strongholds. We demolish*
> *arguments and every pretension that sets itself up*
> *against the knowledge of God, and we take captive*
> *every thought to make it obedient to Christ*
> (2 Corinthians 10:4-5).

> *[I]n truthful speech and in the power*
> *of God; with weapons of righteousness*
> *in the right hand and in the left*
> (2 Corinthians 6:7).

> *Since, then, you have been raised with Christ,*
> *set your hearts on things above, where Christ*
> *is, seated at the right hand of God. Set your*
> *minds on things above, not on earthly things*
> (Colossians 3:2).

If you fall for the temptation, don't be shocked by that either. Don't waste time beating yourself up. Be gracious to yourself and call on your God, your help in time of trouble. Your flesh will tell you to hid from him—let any shame you experience point you home to him. He is waiting to help you. He understands your frailty. Rise again. Reduce the amount of time it takes you to repent. Remember your forgiveness. Remember the strength and resources available to you. Ask for and accept help and get up a thousand times a day if that's what it takes. Again, pull out memory verses you have on the ready. A dear friend calls them her daggers in those moments of hand to hand combat.

Don't buy the lie that you're a screw up and there's no hope for you, or that some people just can't change, or that God must be tired of picking you up again. Are you still alive? Then the work of God in your life is not finished.

> *The steadfast love of the Lord never ceases;*
> *his mercies never come to an end;*
> *they are new every morning;*
> *great is your faithfulness.*
> (Lamentations 3:22-23, ESV).

Stay engaged in the battle, don't ever roll over and give up. Habits can take years to break. For me it's taken 2 years to really start owning new ways of thinking since my deliverance. I had ample opportunity months into the process to say, "you know, I don't think this is really working. I don't think it took." This is spiritual warfare. Satan's dominion over an area of your life is very important to him. You are precious territory and he won't give you up easily. Soldier up. This is you rewiring the neural circuitry in your brilliant brain. Actively put in the new highway in your brain.

Scripture emphasizes the *willfulness* of the Christian to this surrendering to temptation. When we submit, we are prostrating ourselves to sin's control and authority. Rochester adds,

> The enemy requires that you relinquish your rights and privileges as a child of God in order for sin to be accomplished. There's a quick...wrestling with your soul. It is because you have to make up your mind to sin or not to sin. *The spirit of God within your spirit man has already made the decision not to sin* (emphasis added).[3]

This is so empowering! Not only are you not at the mercy of your foe, but you have formidable supernatural aid on your side. Psalm 18 plays like a movie showing God coming to your aid, training and strengthening you to do battle, fighting alongside you, and utterly decimating the enemy. As though that's not enough, after wins the battle, he graciously hands you his shield of victory and calls it yours! Meditate on that priceless treasure trove.

Hide these missiles in your heart for use when in need. Share them with a struggling friend.

May the Lord answer you when you are in distress;
may the name of the God of Jacob protect you.
May he send you help from the sanctuary
and grant you support from Zion
(Psalm 20:1-2).

I am with you like a mighty warrior
(Jeremiah 20:11).

So do not fear, for I am with you;
do not be dismayed, for I am your God.
I will strengthen you and help you;
I will uphold you with my righteous right hand
(Isaiah 41:10).

When our conscience is healthy, a violent, bloody battle ensues when we surrender to temptation. Unfortunately, repeated consent atrophies our response and weakens our conscience making it less and less sensitive to God and more and more sensitive to what we want. The more we consent, the weaker and more ensnared we become. Remember the only power the enemy has over you is the power of the lie. Dig into your heart and find the lie that you have bought into that is disempowering you and leading you down this path. Ask God to show you what lie you have believed.

For the Lord searches every heart and
understands every desire and every thought.
If you seek him, he will be found by you
(1 Chronicles 28:9b).

You may say, "But I'm not an actual sinner. I don't go out there and actually do anything." There's another lie. There is no difference between this mental sin and practical sinning. As we saw, Jesus says,

But I tell you that anyone who looks at a
woman lustfully has already committed
adultery with her in his heart
(Matthew 5:8).

Further, I must not underestimate the influencing power of my freedom or my bondage. When I walk in freedom, I am influencing others. When I walk in bondage, I am also influencing others. My sin severely impacts others. "But I'm not hurting anyone else," is a common excuse and a lie. A sin that "doesn't hurt anyone else" is yet to be invented.

The Apostle Paul speaks like a neuroscientist when he sets himself up as a role model and says,

I press on toward the goal to win the prize
for which God has called me heavenward in
Christ Jesus. All of us, then, who are mature
should take such a view of things. And if on
some point you think differently, that too
God will make clear to you. Only let us live
up to what we have already attained.
Join together in following my example, brothers
and sisters, and just as you have us as a model,
keep your eyes on those who live as we do. For,
as I have often told you before and now tell you
again even with tears, many live as enemies of

the cross of Christ. Their destiny is destruction,
their god is their stomach, and their glory is in
their shame. Their mind is set on earthly things
(Philippians 3:14-19).

Whatever you have learned or received or heard
from me or seen in me—put it into practice...
(Philippians 4:9).

We are not lone rangers. We are soldiers of Christ. As in any military, we are to refrain from spiritual red light districts abroad for obvious reasons. We have no business there. It taints our image. Describing his military experience, Rochester says, "Criminal incidents of a sexual nature...by a single sailor could severely hamper relationships with hosting nations... It is the same in the church."[4] Moreover, sick sailors can't engage in their primary occupation—battle. Someone else has to pick up their slack and bear an unfair load. Believers, this is serious business!

Saint, God calls you a special possession in 1 Peter 2:9. That means you are a prized catch—a trophy. Let that sink in for a moment. A massive 7-point elk in the woods has not gotten that far by openly strutting his stuff to hunters. Hunters are boggled by the fact that before hunting season they saw that elk all over the place. Come hunting season, he becomes a ghost. You, my friend, are in open hunting season with temptation. Expect to be tempted. It is foolishness to be surprised when the enemy waylays us. That's his job. It's what he does. Don't be startled to see it. Don't open the door and get chummy with it. Paul admonishes believers,

Put to death, therefore, whatever belongs to your
earthly nature: sexual immorality, impurity,
lust, evil desires and greed, which is idolatry
(Colossians 3:5).

In the tragic story of Cain and Abel, God said to Cain,

Sin lies at the door. And its desire is
for you, but you must rule over it
(Genesis 4:6b).

So, if you think you are standing firm, be
careful that you don't fall! No temptation
has overtaken you except what is common
to mankind. And God is faithful; he will
not let you be tempted beyond what you can
bear. But when you are tempted, he will also
provide a way out so that you can endure it
(1 Corinthians 10:13).

What is more, God promises us great reward.

Blessed is the one who perseveres under trial
because, having stood the test, that person
will receive the crown of life that the Lord
has promised to those who love him
(James 1:12).

I want to receive that glorious crown and to lay it at Jesus' feet in adoration, and as the old hymn says, to "crown Him with many crowns."

How vulnerable are we? Consider King David. Despite one monumental success after another in ministry, David, the man after God's own heart, was headed straight for disaster. This was a blow to the kingdom that Gallagher laments "must have made angels sit down and weep."[5] How could that happen? The way you live your *daily* life will determine your susceptibility to falling for the snare of sin that Satan hides before you, no matter how spiritually successful you look right now.

Writer Cathy Goekler makes an observation as prickly as stinging nettle. "We don't really repent of some of our sins. We stop having sex outside marriage because we get married, not because we confronted the attitudes and *small daily choices* that inevitably led us to such a choice. We want something better for our children, but they observe those *small choices* we model and come to the same conclusion… We taught the rule apart from the discipline necessary to achieve it"[6] (emphases added). This statement shook me to my core as I observed the heart behind behavior in my children's lives. What a great wake-up call. The small things matter. Zechariah 4:10 tells us not to despise small things.

From his extensive experience counseling fallen ministers, Steve Gallagher warns that the way you live your daily life determines how vulnerable you are to the allurements of sin. He outlines five potential sexual pitfalls. These pitfalls apply to all Christians, of all ages regarding all kinds of sins:

Prayerlessness. After danger and spiritual hunger in a man's life, can come satisfaction and security which can allow the demands of ministry to erode personal time with God.

Pressure. Responsibility and stress swiftly follow success. "The crushing weight of high-intensity leadership tends to drain a person's spiritual vitality—often at a time when he needs it most," states Gallagher, adding that a pastime that starts off as a means to unwinding can lead to a quenching of God's Spirit. As Corrie Ten Boom once warned, "Beware of the barrenness of a busy life."

Prosperity. Wealth can diminish a person's dependence on God. It can avail a greater variety of leisure options. It makes one more attractive to others who may want to take them down.

Pleasure. Prosperity and prominence can foster self-indulgence. Paul warns that in the last days,

> *Many would be lovers of pleasure rather than*
> *lovers of God; holding to a form of godliness,*
> *although they have denied its power*
> (2 Timothy 3:4-5).

Power: Power can fan the flames of self-importance, then self-exaltation, which can result in a fall. A powerful servant can start to see himself as a master. Gallagher warns that a Christian leader can sin sexually as he loses "his sense of public responsibility to live above reproach."[7] Only the person walking in a consecrated, humble attitude will overcome temptation.

Sin will take you farther than you want to
go, keep you longer than you want to stay,
and cost you more than you want to pay.
Ravi Zaccharias

Chapter 24

The Purpose of Shame

The current worldview holds that shame is a bad thing. Many humanists shun shame and oppose it to its emotional cousin—guilt, claiming that guilt is okay because it tells us we have done something bad, whereas shame tells us we are bad for having done it.

I believe that shame is an emotional gift from God. Shame is a feedback emotion. It jolts me awake like a live current when I grab an exposed wire. It is embarrassment, the blush-factor, and the repulsive disgrace that tells me something is wrong. It warns me that I should not be indulging in works of darkness, because these are improper for me as God has called me holy. The Biblical characters Paul and Daniel taught the two truths below:

> *But among you there must not be even a*
> *hint of sexual immorality, or of any kind of*
> *impurity, or of greed, because these are improper*
> *for God's holy people. Nor should there be*
> *obscenity, foolish talk or coarse joking, which*
> *are out of place, but rather thanksgiving*
> (Ephesians 5:3-4).

> *We and our kings, our princes and our*
> *ancestors are covered with shame, Lord,*
> *because we have sinned against you.*
> (Daniel 9:8).

There is a place for shame and it is an important one. It can be a tool for growth. Psychotherapist Joseph Burgo distinguishes *toxic shame* from *productive shame*. I believe the former is what the world is referring to when it denounces shame. But we shouldn't throw out the baby with the bath water. Burgo holds that,

> Our feelings of shame tell us we've disappointed *reasonable* expectations we hold for ourselves. The function of shame is to prevent us from ruining relationships or to persuade us to repair them. Toxic shame brands you as unworthy and unlovable. By contrast, productive shame focuses on discrete traits or behaviors rather than the entire person. Instead of making global statements about someone as completely worthless and irredeemable, productive shame leaves room for her to feel good about herself as a whole while also suggesting changes that might help her feel even better[1] (emphasis added).

Toxic shame tells us that even perfection is not good enough. That is a lie from the lying Liar and too many people have bought into it. On the contrary, productive shame points out that we all have room for improvement. None of us is 'just fine.' Paul calls it pressing on toward the goal (Philippians 3:14). Because we all have work to do, we graciously realize we are imperfect and constantly in need of help to keep growing. Look at the beautiful result of productive shame as outlined in Scripture:

> *Cover their faces with shame, LORD,*
> *so that they will seek your name*
> (Psalm 83:16).

Contrast that with this vivid visual of shamelessness as personified by an adulterous woman:

> *She eats and wipes her mouth and*
> *says, 'I've done nothing wrong'*
> (Proverbs 30:20).

Christian, if you don't feel shame when you've done wrong, we have a problem. The Bible clearly shows there is a place for shame. Productive shame is the brain's stimulus pointing to a need for godly sorrow and repentance. Psychology professor Sam Vaknin teaches that shame is a threat and a challenge, forcing one,

> to "feel bad" about something she has said or done. The solution is usually facile and at hand: reverse the situation by apologizing or by making amends... So, while shame motivates normal people to conduct themselves pro-socially and realistically, it pushes the disordered patient in the exact opposite direction: to antisocial or delusional reactions. Shame is founded on empathy. The normal person empathizes with others. The disordered patient empathizes with himself.[2]

To be clear, to stay or live in guilt/shame is counter to the abundant life that God offers. If I were to go sight-seeing in California for two weeks, I'd be a fool to pitch my tent at a sign that pointed "California 50 miles" and to camp there for two weeks then return home and say I had quite a vacation in California. To dwell in shame is to camp at a forlorn sign post as though it's the destination. Further, shame does not have to come from external sources. It can be the internal work of our conscience. Your conscience sparks your shame. The more sensitive your conscience is to the Spirit, the more sensitive you are to productive shame. The gift of shame is meant to drive you to change, to point the way to repentance and restoration.

Therefore, since we have these promises, dear friends, let us purify ourselves from everything that contaminates body and spirit, perfecting holiness out of reverence for God… Yet now I am happy, not because you were made sorry, but because your sorrow led you to repentance. For you became sorrowful as God intended and so were not harmed in any way by us. Godly sorrow brings repentance that leads to salvation and leaves no regret, but worldly sorrow brings death. See what this godly sorrow has produced in you: what earnestness, what eagerness to clear yourselves, what indignation, what alarm, what longing, what concern, what readiness to see justice done. At every point you have proved yourselves to be innocent in this matter (2 Corinthians 7:1, 9-11).

I think this godly sorrow corresponds to productive shame. While reviewing my son's internet activity on his cell-phone, I came across an f-bomb he'd dropped during a chat. I groaned before I got a reality check and thanked God that that was the worst I'd found after perusing all his recent activity. I prayed about it then gently confronted him. Placing it in front of his face I said, "talk to me about this."

Instantly, his face dropped, the color drained from it, and his shoulders sagged. His breathing deepened, accelerated. Silence. Classic shame responses.

"What are you feeling?" I asked gently.

"I don't know." He averted his gaze. "Embarrassed."

"Why?" I asked.

"Because I know I shouldn't talk like that."

"That's right." I reached for that beautiful, now flushed face and whispered, with all the warmth I could muster, "That's not you my love. You are a man of God. You speak what is true, and right, and noble, and pure, and lovely, and admirable. You speak what is excellent and praiseworthy." I let that sink in for a long minute, then asked "How long should you be embarrassed?"

"I don't know."

"A week, a day?"

He looked at me quizzically. "I don't know."

"Not even a minute!" I declared, "What should we do?"

"Say sorry?"

"You know it! Tell him."

He confessed to his God and before he could say amen, I yelled, "That's it! You are forgiven. You know what Jesus would say now? "Go and sin no more." Isn't that great?" And we hugged. That was it. It might seem too simple for many. We are used to groveling, boot-licking, and flogging ourselves as penance. We drag ourselves and our cross down to a Golgotha of our own making, being ogled, spat on, slapped around, and mocked by others. Believer, Jesus did all that so you wouldn't need to. He bore your sin and shame so you don't have to. That's part of your freedom package!

I pray my son remembers that moment for the rest of his life. I jumped on the power of shame which zaps up our brain to high alert to imprint a critically important life lesson I was never taught—that shame is a sign post pointing us to repentance so we can get our forgiveness. We need not chain ourselves or others to it for flogging.

Ellsworth molesting his daughter from the time she was a little girl through high school is shameful. He was guilty and should have felt shame about it. His friends covering for him and allowing him to continue in ministry to women and children was shameful. They were guilty and should have felt shame. Now that the scandal is exposed, they are culpable and I suppose they feel shame. I would hope they feel shame!

A friend who's a great story teller tells a whopper about being invited by a professional fishing buddy. Though she was pretty green in the sport she determined that he wouldn't regret inviting her. He helped her catch and reel in a massive salmon. Her heart thumping, she was ready to avail her services to net the treasure. In its adrenaline rush, the giant leapt out of the net and onto the shore then straight into her startled arms. She couldn't believe it!

But that only lasted two seconds as he slithered away and started flopping back and forth on the ground. Before she could stop her impressive self, she flung her body onto the monster full-force, yelling, while still airborne, "I got it!"

"No you don't got it." replied Mr. Professional, swiftly trapping the fish about 5 feet away, much to the delight of onlookers.

"I was pretty sure I had it," my friend mumbled, brushing her bruised ribs and ego and wondering what had just happened.

Based on our families of origin, handling shame well can be as slippery as trying to grab a freshly caught fish. We need our parents and significant others to teach us to acknowledge shame, then quickly cross its road and get to godly sorrow and repentance. If we linger in it, we are in danger. I grew up in a shaming culture. All around me, I frequently heard, leveled at me and others around me, "Shame on you!" To this day, hearing that statement stabs my heart. Those words would be accompanied by a look of disapproval, disdain and disgust. It was also accompanied by statements such as, "Why can't you be like so-and-so." Linger on that busy road long enough and you will be creamed by the logging trucks of self-loathing, disappointment, comparison, people-pleasing, humiliation, depression, perfectionism, and dishonor. Those characteristics have a way of smearing themselves onto our very souls and tainting us.

I understand that that's what the world is talking about when it downplays shame. But we must not toss garbage can with the garbage. Feeling shame gives powerful emotional feedback. Camping there is what drives us to hide things we are ashamed of so we can bypass that stretch of road—i.e. getting in trouble, being dishonored, or disapproved of, by those who are most important to us. It creates a sense of rejection of who we are at our very core. Christian, there is a safe crossing. Walk to it. Let shame do its powerful work of getting you to restoration via the signpost and crosswalk of repentance.

Productive shame is the brain's stimulus
pointing the way to godly sorrow,
repentance, and restoration.

Chapter 25

We're All Pornographers

Therefore, confess your sins to each other
and pray for each other so that you may
be healed. The prayer of a righteous
person is powerful and effective
(James 5:16).

I deliberately bare my heart in this book at the risk of immense judgement. I am open to that. I am guilty as charged—and then some. I find comfort in several pieces of Scripture, not because they justify my behavior but because they unmask the enemy's lie to me that I'm the only one struggling. In reality, I find myself in good company. I have a dirt-bag (the flesh) and I live among people who have dirt-bags. The prophet Isaiah laments,

"Woe to me!" I cried. "I am ruined! For
I am a man of unclean lips, and I live
among a people of unclean lips, and my eyes
have seen the King, the Lord Almighty
(Isaiah 6:5).

For whoever keeps the whole law and yet stumbles
at just one point is guilty of breaking all of it.
Speak and act as those who are going to be judged

by the law that gives freedom, because judgment
without mercy will be shown to anyone who has
not been merciful. Mercy triumphs over judgment
(James 2:10, 12, 13).

[F]or all have sinned and fall
short of the glory of God
(Romans 8:23).

Richard Keyes says that "[a]n idol is something within creation that is inflated to function as a substitute for God."[1] Christian Union Teaching Fellow Nick Nowalk states:

> The persistent diagnosis of Scripture is that our main problem lies in the fact that we are not satisfied in God's beauty and goodness as the center of our existence. Rather, we illicitly horde the good gifts of creation over the Giver to whom they point, aiming to remind us along the way of why He is so outlandishly worthy to be loved with all of our heart and mind and soul and strength. We prefer the seductive allure of what God has created, and this spiritual disorientation then overflows into every other sphere of our existence—including our sexuality.[2]

We now know that pornography is a banner that covers sexual immorality and idolatry. I make that point to set the stage for the truth that we are all in need of a Savior, regardless of the sins we struggle with. Gallagher says, "Situated in the soul of every man is a spiritual altar, and seated on that altar is the most important object of his life."[3] The addict surrenders to and worships pleasure and self. Some are fighting this vicious monster with the dogged courage of wet cardboard. Some don't even struggle any more, they've laid themselves prostrate to the sin. Others don't realize there is any sin at all. The Apostle Paul begs to differ, and teaches,

> *You, therefore, have no excuse, you who pass*
> *judgment on someone else, for at whatever point*
> *you judge another, you are condemning yourself,*
> *because you who pass judgment do the same things*
> (Romans 2:1).

> *This is the message we have heard from him and*
> *declare to you: God is light; in him there is no*
> *darkness at all. If we claim to have fellowship*
> *with him and yet walk in the darkness, we*
> *lie and do not live out the truth. But if we*
> *walk in the light, as he is in the light, we have*
> *fellowship with one another, and the blood of*
> *Jesus, his Son, purifies us from all sin. If we*
> *claim to be without sin, we deceive ourselves*
> *and the truth is not in us. If we confess our sins,*
> *he is faithful and just and will forgive us our*
> *sins and purify us from all unrighteousness. If*
> *we claim we have not sinned, we make him*
> *out to be a liar and his word is not in us*
> (John 14:5-10).

"I don't do drugs," you may argue, "or steal or lie." Granted. Note, nevertheless, that a heart that is turned against God in self-righteousness is just as turned against God as a drugging one or a promiscuous one. Wise King Solomon stated plainly, "for there is no one who does not sin…" (1 Kings 8:46a). C. S. Lewis, in his book, Mere Christianity, writes about sexual morality, saying:

> If anyone thinks that Christians regard
> unchastity as the supreme vice, he is quite wrong.
> The sins of the flesh are bad, but they are the least
> bad of all sins. All the worst pleasures are purely

spiritual: the pleasure of putting other people in the wrong, of bossing and patronizing and spoiling sport, and back-biting; the pleasures of power, of hatred. For there are two things inside me, competing with the human self which I must try to become. They are the Animal self, and the Diabolical self. The Diabolical self is the worse of the two. That is why a cold, self-righteous prig who goes regularly to church may be far nearer to hell than a prostitute. But, of course, it is better to be neither. [4]

Solomon's sin led to his destruction. He married many foreign women who turned his heart away from God. When convicted of this, his response was to "hold fast to them in love" (1 Kings 11:2b). This was unlike his father David, the man after God's own heart. Believers, here is a mark of following after God wholeheartedly— David also sinned, but he did not allow even his sin to turn him away from God. When convicted of it he circled back in repentance and took care of business. His sin was thus a stumbling and not a fall beyond recovery, as Solomon's became. The only appropriate response to our sin is to become aware of it, experience a swift sense of shame and become like the tax collector in the temple who,

> *stood at a distance. He would not even*
> *look up to heaven, but beat his breast and*
> *said, 'God, have mercy on me, a sinner.'*
> (Luke 18:9-14).

> *Who can say, "I have kept my heart*
> *pure; I am clean and without sin"?*
> (Proverbs 20:9).

Every human being is an "idol factory."[6] We are like a Chinese sweatshop putting out and flooding the world market with piles of cheap imitations of our God. We aren't far above the insects and birds in the animal kingdom that Tenbergen studied. We are quite content to settle for sleazy fakes that don't satisfy.

Writer Barrett claims, "Supernormal stimuli are driving forces in many of today's most pressing problems, including obesity, our addiction to television and video games, and the past century's extraordinarily violent wars." She adds that awareness of this concept and its impact on our brains, "gives us the unique ability to exercise self-control, override instincts that lead us astray, and extricate ourselves from civilization's gaudy traps."[6]

Hear ye, hear ye: pornography in all its forms was not the primary problem in my life. It was a very secondary problem and a mere manifestation of my main problem. The main problem was my love of self. It was marked by a cute, miniscule view of my sin and a noble, amplified view of my capacity to save myself. The old man (the flesh) tugged at me from the realm of the dead. I would never have admitted this, but today I see it with fresh eyes and declare it boldly: my flesh is quite taken with myself, obsessed with myself, concerned with myself, tuned in to myself, about myself. *I* was on the front cover of every month's edition of Myself Magazine. *Yo soy muy importante*! I was steeped in idolatry, dutifully worshipping myself. My flesh is quite happy to be all about my pleasure, my comfort, my plans, my contribution to society, my prosperity, my life, my way, my fabulousness!

The daily grind finds us all guilty of one self-indulgence or another. Many of us are guilty of numerous forms of it. If you aren't, I commend you greatly, but be careful if you think you stand, lest you fall. Many who think that they aren't guilty may be ensnared by the idolatry of pride and Pharisaism. When I came to Christ, my old self was crucified with Him, in order that my body of sin might be done away with, so that I would no longer be a slave to sin, as Romans 6:6 instructs. Paul teaches me my position, my spiritual standing.

Now those who belong to Christ Jesus have
crucified the flesh with its passions and desires
(Galatians 5:24).

Yet Jesus taught,

> *Whoever wants to be my disciple*
> *must deny themselves and take up*
> *their cross daily and follow me*
> (Luke 9:23).

So daily, we are to bear our cross. No just perfunctorily kiss it and carry it around our neck. We're not talking about a pretty burnished one with our birthstone on it. We're talking a massive, rough-hewn beam with gnarly splinters on it. It is to rub a tough callous on our shoulders as we wrangle and crucify our flesh many times a day. Why? Because, as Paul teaches,

> *The cravings of the self-life are obvious: Sexual*
> *immorality, lustful thoughts, pornography, chasing*
> *after things instead of God, manipulating others,*
> *hatred of those who get in your way, senseless*
> *arguments, resentment when others are favored,*
> *temper tantrums, angry quarrels, only thinking*
> *of yourself, being in love with your own opinions,*
> *being envious of the blessings of others, murder*
> *[this includes anger], uncontrolled addictions,*
> *wild parties, and all other similar behavior*
> (Galatians 5:19-21, TPT).

These cravings do not raise their heads at predictable times. They don't contact you to schedule an opportune time. Indeed, each rears its ugly head when you expect it and three times when you don't. Each frequently brings a friend, or sends a relative. They beset you at every opportunity. So while you go about your busy day, they have nothing else to do but torment you and they take their job very seriously. The chapter titled *Temptation* taught us to actually expect them.

My point is, a heart that seeks sexual immorality is not the main problem. Uncontrolled shopping or overeating are not the problem.

Nor is lying, nor overworking, nor having a temper, nor smoking. It's not gambling or worrying or stealing, or controlling others. It's not gossiping or people-pleasing. The problem is not our propensity towards drama or negativity. It is not that we can't put electronics down, or how we keep checking in on social media. It is not the host of behaviors we could list if we went around the room. Those are merely indicators of an idolatrous heart. They point us back to our worship disorder.

> *So, my brothers and sisters, you also died to the law through the body of Christ, that you might belong to another, to him who was raised from the dead, in order that we might bear fruit for God. For when we were in the realm of the flesh, the sinful passions aroused by the law were at work in us, so that we bore fruit for death. But now, by dying to what once bound us, we have been released from the law so that we serve in the new way of the Spirit, and not in the old way of the written code* (Romans 7:4-6).

In practice, I still find my flesh, my Animal Self as C. S. Lewis calls it, drawn to numerous sins. It inclines to sin as the plant on the window-sill inclines towards the sun. I will battle that till I breathe my last breath. The important thing is that I engage my flesh in battle and not roll over and expose my underbelly to its control. I can well sympathize with Paul's cry:

> *So I find this law at work: Although I want to do good, evil is right there with me. For in my inner being I delight in God's law; but I see another law at work in me, waging war against the law of my mind and making me a prisoner of the law of sin at work within me. What a wretched man I am! Who will rescue me from this body*

that is subject to death? Thanks be to God, who
delivers me through Jesus Christ our Lord
(Romans 7:21-25a).

We could, with little or much effort, knock out a bad habit, but the issue would resurface elsewhere like a game of whack-a-mole. We often trade one form of idolatry for a "lesser" one. It's like telling your spouse you won't go out with prostitutes any more. You'll only keep one inexpensive one. If we were to hit our issues as they surface their ugly heads, we would be pounding away like a crazed drummer.

What we need is to be so in love with Jesus and to hold Him in higher esteem than we hold ourselves and our pleasures. We need to cherish Him more than we cherish our sin. We need to hurtle ourselves off the throne of our hearts and reinstate Him to His rightful place there. We need to learn to gain pleasure from our relationship with Jesus and our obedience to Him instead of chasing temporary thrills.

The Comforter (the Holy Spirit) convicts us "concerning sin and righteousness and judgement," John 16:8. This convicting entails bringing matters to light and comes with a suggestion of shame; to correct, reprove, to call to account, prove guilt with strong evidence, to chasten, to punish,[7] among other things. The only proper response to conviction is confession. Beloved, there is power in the discipline of confession. Look at the Berean Literal Translation of our opening Scripture.

Therefore, confess the sins to one another
and pray for one another, so that you may
be healed. The prayer of a righteous man
being made effective prevails much
(James 5:16)

Could we look at that last line as saying that confession is the prayer of a righteous man and that it prevails much? This discipline is like a surgeon's scalpel for stripping the self of the flesh. Confession thrusts a person's spirit light years ahead in growth and godliness by promoting humility, brokenness, and sincerity. We need to be divested of every sense of our own goodness outside of Christ. Spurgeon spoke of this when he said,

> If any man thinks ill of you, do not be angry with him. For you are worse than he thinks you to be. If he charges you falsely on some point, yet be satisfied, for if he knew you better he might change the accusation and you would be no gainer by the correction. If you have your moral portrait painted and it is ugly, be satisfied. For it only needs a few blacker touches and it would be still nearer the truth.[8]

What a refreshing thought the Father invites us to. This way of thinking liberates the soul and spirit. It frees us from having to defend ourselves and constantly guarding against who might be maligning us. It helps us be the first to laugh at ourselves and that should keep us amply entertained and occupied. I make it my ambition to call "dingbat alert" when I have goofed up. It's a great way to acknowledge my propensity to make mistakes. It's a great way to crucify the flesh. Where I would have sought to cover and hide mistakes and pretend I don't make any, I've learned that calling attention to it by saying "dingbat alert" diffuses and deflates it whereas covering up does the opposite. Covering up may help us avert shame in the short-term but it only defers it—with interest.

Is God big enough to replace our pleasures we die to? Is the Creator of the universe and of all these pleasures able to captivate and thrill our hearts beyond our wildest dreams? How does he rate on the "delight-scale" compared to the competition? Is he able to fill the holes in our hearts? Can he scintillate us? The answer is a resounding *yes!* We, along with the world, hold a common misconception that he is inadequate and outdated when it comes to fun or pleasure. Little do we know that in him we can rejoice with "joy unspeakable and full of glory" and all that with no regrets! He is engaging, thrilling, deep, rousing, enchanting.

> *In your presence is fullness of joy; At your*
> *right hand are pleasures forevermore*
> (Psalm 16:11, NKJV).

> *I said to the Lord, "You are my Lord; apart*
> *from you I have no good thing." The boundary*
> *lines have fallen for me in pleasant places;*
> *surely I have a delightful inheritance. You*
> *have made known to me the path of life*
> (Ps 16:2, 5, 6).

> *All my fountains are in you*

The CSB renders it

> *My whole source of joy is in you*
> (Psalm 87:7b).

As you enjoy your pleasures today, verbally elevate God. Extend kingdom thinking towards your daily blessings. For your delicious cup of coffee, say, "Lord, thank you for this fabulous cup. You are much more deeply satisfying than it is." Then search your heart. Do I need five cups? Do I even need one? "Lord, thank you for this elegant coat. You are more beautiful than it is." How many coats do I need, Lord? I have seven. Can they go to the kingdom? "Lord, thank you for the horsepower behind this engine. You are oh so much more powerful than it is. How can I use to serve your kingdom?"

Idolatrous Christian, what is your "beautiful woman?" Who's your "foreign woman?" Who's your "Temptress?" In what ways am I buying into the Doctrine of Balaam? Is it sugar, salt, or fat? Is it power or the company you're keeping? Is it alcohol, cigarettes, or electronics? Is it control or manipulation? Is it a cutting tongue or a grumbling spirit? Is it suicidality? Name it and confess to yourself, to your Father in heaven, and to a brother or sister that it's turning you away from the Lover of your Soul.

I have sins as vast as the sands on the seashore to confess at any given time. I'll let you in on a secret: when Satan reminds me of my sin, I completely agree with him. I even tell him there are many he forgot to bring up and others I don't even know about! My rap-sheet is tiresome. And then I remind him, that that is why I needed a Savior and why he bled out for me—to the last drop! I am saved, forgiven, covered, washed, justified, and victorious, thanks to the Master of the universe who is very much in love with me. So the devil can just keep telling me what I've done and what I've not, and what I am and what I'm not, because it all counts against him! "Shameless," you might say, to which I would respond with a definite "yes," because Jesus took away all my guilt and shame. He nailed it to the cross and disarmed it forever! Behold what Paul says about this:

> *Through our union with him we have*
> *experienced circumcision of heart.*
> *All of the guilt and power of sin has been cut*
> *away and is now extinct because of what Christ,*
> *the Anointed One, has accomplished for us.*
> *For we've been buried with him into his death.*
> *Our "baptism into death" also means we were*
> *raised with him when we believed in God's*
> *resurrection power, the power that raised him*
> *from death's realm. This "realm of death"*
> *describes our former state, for we were held in*
> *sin's grasp. But now, we've been resurrected out*
> *of that "realm of death" never to return, for we*
> *are forever alive and forgiven of all our sins!*
> *He canceled out every legal violation we had*
> *on our record and the old arrest warrant that*
> *stood to indict us. He erased it all—our sins, our*

*stained soul—he deleted it all and they cannot be
retrieved! Everything we once were in Adam has
been placed onto his cross and nailed permanently
there as a public display of cancellation.
Then Jesus made a public spectacle of all the
powers and principalities of darkness, stripping
away from them every weapon and all their
spiritual authority and power to accuse us.
And by the power of the cross, Jesus led them
around as prisoners in a procession of triumph.
He was not their prisoner; they were his!*
Colossian 2:11-15 (TPT).

[O]ur main problem lies in the fact that
we are not satisfied in God's beauty and
goodness as the center of our existence…
We prefer the seductive allure of what God
has created, and this spiritual disorientation
then overflows into every other sphere of
our existence—including our sexuality.

Richard Keyes

Chapter 26

Dr. Exposure

Have nothing to do with the fruitless deeds
of darkness, but rather expose them
(Ephesians 5:11).

When my friend shared her struggle that February afternoon, she couldn't begin to imagine the inferno she had sparked. The Lord used it to lead me to confess a secret sin to her, then swiftly wrought my deliverance from its grip. A revival triggered in my heart. Jesus and I started having increasingly intense times of intimate communion. My Nissan Rogue devotional time geared up like a Ferrari. My heart was on fire for his Word. I couldn't get enough of it. Day after day, he was showing me things I'd never seen before.

He awakened me at night, and we'd have extraordinary meditation sessions that lasted for hours and felt like minutes. He helped me memorize massive portions of Scripture in a way I've never been able to do. Then I'd bolt through my days with energy like I was on speed. I called them my midnight escapades with Jesus. It was unbelievable.

My eyes stay open through the watches of the night,
that I may meditate on your promises
(Psalm 119:148).

One day that Fall, he impressed upon my heart, with earnest, that I should share what he had done. Specific people immediately came to mind. I categorically silenced that voice in the name of Jesus! Why on Earth would anyone in their right mind do that? Surely no good could come of that! After all, I was delivered. I'd confessed to my friend and to you God. We had moved on. Remember, Jesus?

Then, nothing. Day after day and night after night, nothing! I prayed. My prayers hit the ceiling and plopped right back down. I dug into his Word. I might as well have been reading the World's Encyclopedia of Tires. It was awful. The spring had dried up. I knew full well exactly where the problem was. With a surrendered heart and a deep sigh, I prayed my favorite prayer, "Father, help!"

> *Blessed is the one whose transgressions are forgiven,*
> *whose sins are covered.*
> *Blessed is the one*
> *whose sin the Lord does not count against them*
> *and in whose spirit is no deceit.*
> *When I kept silent, my bones wasted away*
> *through my groaning all day long.*
> *For day and night your hand was heavy on me;*
> *my strength was sapped as in the heat of summer.*
>
> *Then I acknowledged my sin to you*
> *and did not cover up my iniquity.*
> *I said, "I will confess my*
> *transgressions to the Lord."*
> *And you forgave the guilt of my sin.*
> *Therefore, let all the faithful pray to you*
> *while you may be found;*
> *surely the rising of the mighty waters*
> *will not reach them.*
> *You are my hiding place;*
> *you will protect me from trouble*
> *and surround me with songs of deliverance.*
>
> *I will instruct you and teach you*
> *in the way you should go;*

I will counsel you with my loving eye on you.
Do not be like the horse or the mule,
which have no understanding
but must be controlled by bit and bridle
or they will not come to you.
Many are the woes of the wicked,
but the Lord's unfailing love
surrounds the one who trusts in him.

Rejoice in the Lord and be glad, you righteous;
sing, all you who are upright in heart!
(Psalm 32)

Instantly, the names of the people he'd laid on my heart came to mind—my sister, my church sisters from my accountability group, and my husband. My stomach bottomed out with a sickening thud. This was hands down, single-handedly *the* worst idea ever. My soul was deeply discouraged and disturbed. My heart was so downcast. I felt physically ill, drowning in dread.

Forlorn, I said, "I'll do it, Lord. But I need your help."

―――――――――――――――――――

The word of God is the blueprint and the standard for how we are to live our lives. Recall that in a healthy relationship, we are to love people the way they express they need to be loved, not the way we think they need to be loved. The Bible is God's expression of his desire for his preferred manner of intercourse with his creation. His Word is a clear communication of expectations so we're not left guessing or groping in the dark, like trying to please a difficult partner. Moreover, it provides a way back to intimacy after times of relational strain, which in our case, is caused by sin.

The unfolding of your words gives light;
it gives understanding to the simple
(Psalms 119:130).

Direct my footsteps according to your
word; let no sin rule over me
(Psalm 119:133).

Sin thrives in a warm, dark place. The light of exposure is deadly to sin. That is why Paul teaches,

Let us behave decently, as in the daytime…
not in sexual immorality and debauchery
(Romans 13:13,14).

Many pornographers work overtime not to leave a trail when they engage in behaviors they know to be taboo. Many have woven and manage complex undercover ploys and have different accounts, different cell-phones, undercover families, indeed a whole different underground life. That is part of their ritual. But with God, there is no incognito mode. Rochester states that no matter how well you may have erased your tracks, "there is a record in heaven that cannot be erased. When we continue to pursue porn, God has a way to recall the record to expose us."[1] This truth applies to all forms of idolatry: shop-lifting, embezzlement, being wily and under-cutting others, over-eating, hypocrisy, etc. God's mercy endures forever, but that does not mean that we will not get caught!

You have set our iniquities before you,
our secret sins in the light of your presence
(Psalm 90:8).

Infrared immunotherapy uses light to kill cancer cells but it spares healthy cells. God has a standing in-network contract with Dr. Total Exposure. This MD administers a similar light to malignant sin growths, decimating the beast within, while protecting all other organs. Christians, since Jesus's death, we know have access to a do-it-at-home-treatment protocol. We can self-administer the exposure by confessing our sins to one another before Dr. Exposure makes a house-call. We can even do a virtual call with him in this day and age of telehealth.

This makes me think of the current scandal with Mercy Corps. When Tania approached the board in the '90s, that was a perfect opportunity for these brothers to hold Culver accountable, difficult as that would have been for him and for them. Instead, the organization set a heavy piece of furniture with a vase of roses over the hole on their carpet—by moving him to a different position.

Successfully.

For decades!

When Tania and her husband again approached the organization in 2018, Mercy Corps had another chance to come clean. God provided another exit on the wide road that is the Sin Highway. They didn't take it. Instead, they danced around in legalese and again refreshed the vase of flowers. But God will not have it.

> Does he who fashioned the ear not hear?
> Does he who formed the eye not see?
> Does he who disciplines nations not punish?
> Does he who teaches mankind lack knowledge?
> The Lord knows all human plans;
> he knows that they are futile.
> Blessed is the one you discipline, Lord,
> the one you teach from your law
> (Psalm 94:9-12).

He will "out" us no matter how long we think we have been successful in hiding our sin. It has taken a scathing investigation by the world and produced a most embarrassing exposure of shameful practices in committing sin *and* in attempting to cover it up.

It is abominable that a young woman, *a child*, would take the excruciating step to come to powerful fellow believers for help; that some acknowledgement would be made of the problem, commending her courage in coming forward to expose the problem, and then they would stick a binkie in her mouth and slap some duct tape over it. It is atrocious that they would thank her, claiming that her complaint would help improve the organization, and that they'd take the redemptive approach to give her father and others an opportunity for growth. They claimed it would take time to repair the problems that were more deep rooted than they had realized, to which Tania must've wanted to say, "No ——!" The board knew there were some problems but admitted they didn't realize how deep the problems were till Tania came forward with her allegations. Then what did they do about it?

Tania's life has been devastated. How many more girls were molested by Culver? People in the organization lost their jobs. The name of Christ has been dragged through the mud. Mercy Corps was correct in telling Tania that, as might be expected, a person who creates a dysfunctional family will be a dysfunctional influence in an organization. And this about their own president! So they demoted him to vice president, and he continued to be their public face around the world.

The Lord is not slow in keeping his promise,
as some understand slowness. Instead he is
patient with you, not wanting anyone to
perish, but everyone to come to repentance
(2 Peter 3:9)

This verse unfailingly brings tears to my eyes.

When you did these things and I kept silent,
you thought I was exactly like you
(Psalms 50:21a).

Rochester reminds us that God has never tolerated secret sexual sins:

> For some reason, we have gotten this false notion that the Lord will overlook our secret sexual sins. He never does. From the moment we started to sin, he put our secret to a timetable. Just like trains operate on a timetable, your secret sexual sin has a last stop on God's timetable.[2]

The heart of the Bible message, in this regard, is underscored by Paul commanding us to

> *Have nothing to do with the fruitless deeds*
> *of darkness, but rather expose them*
> (Ephesians 5:11).

Jackie Hill Perry says, "Light has a way of welcoming in the truth and letting it put its feet up, which in turn means that everything not like it, though it may invite itself over, can't get comfortable enough to stay."[3] Blogger Greg Chandler relates sin to a scented trash bag. He says, "Perhaps it is time to take out the trash in our own lives. Though the devil may mask the stench of sin for a while, its true nature will ultimately be revealed."[4] While the tendency of the human heart is to sit on the sin-hole in the carpet, God teaches a very different approach, which is the heart-beat of my book. If you learn nothing else in reading this book, learn this:

> *For you were once darkness, but now you are light*
> *in the Lord. Live as children of light (for the fruit*
> *of the light consists in all goodness, righteousness*
> *and truth) and find out what pleases the Lord.*
> *Have nothing to do with the fruitless deeds of*
> *darkness, but rather **expose them**. It is shameful*
> *even to mention what the disobedient do in secret*
> (Ephesians 5:8–12, emphasis added)

Christian, you must tell someone your secret sin. The degree to which you cling in secrecy to your sin, instead of exposing it, is the degree to which you are bound up in slavery to it. Though it's the scariest thing, exposing your sin is the first step to walking back home, like the prodigal, from a distant land. You may ask, "What will people think of me?" You "live before God," as King David declared. This God chose you even though he knew all about your vileness. Spurgeon instructs us that the effect of living before him is "to set the Lord on high in the soul but to put human opinion in a lower place."[5] Those who really count in your life are too busy cleaning up their own business to focus on yours other than to pray.

By this powerful action on your part, the Lord will slay multiple dragons with one strike of the sword: your sin, your pride, people-pleasing, and many others besides. He will unshackle you, he will glorify himself, and he will free others. May this humble act of confession be as pleasing to your Lord as David's passionate dance was. I assure you people may think much and talk more, but it is inconsequential. People may look down their nose at you in contempt through their stained-glass window as Michal sneered at David when he danced before the Lord. Oh how she despised him in her heart. Oh how she let him know it, lip curled up, dripping with the venom of sarcasm.

> *When David returned home to bless his household, Michal daughter of Saul came out to meet him and said, "How the king of Israel has distinguished himself today, going around half-naked in full view of the slave girls of his servants as any vulgar fellow would!"*
> (2 Samuel 6:20).

His response thrills me,

> *It was before the Lord, who chose me*
> (2 Samuel 6:21).

I imagine that for years, David had applied the principle below to Michal's sarcasm,

> *Do not answer a fool according to his*
> *folly or you will become like him.*
> (Proverbs 26:4).

Then there comes a day when you've just had it and you put out fire with fire.

> *Answer a fool according to his folly,* or
> *he will be wise in his* own eyes
> (Proverbs 26:5).

He pretty much said, "You know what little lady, I do not perform for man. I don't aim to please your father The King—he rejected me repeatedly since I was a child despite my undying faithfulness to him. I could never please *him*. I certainly don't aim to please you, princess bride who reviles me. Heaven knows I've tried. It was before the Lord that I danced today and humiliated myself!" And he walked across her spotless floor with his dusty sandals.

In Ephesians 4:2 the Apostle Paul calls us to be "Completely humble and gentle." Nothing renders humility like confession of sin. If man derides you for it, know this,

> David would more and more abase himself
> before the Lord. He felt that whatever Michal's
> opinion of him might be, it could not be more
> humbling than his own view of himself.[6]

Because David trusted God, the true source of his calling and blessings, David could say with confidence,

> *I will celebrate before the Lord. I will become*
> *even more undignified than this, and I will be*

humiliated in my own eyes. But by these slave
girls you spoke of, I will be held in honor
(2 Samuel 6:21b-22).

Hear the heart of this same David who was so over himself that he sat before the Lord and said,

Who am I, Sovereign Lord, and what is my
family, that you have brought me this far?
And as if this were not enough in your sight,
Sovereign Lord, you have also spoken about the
future of the house of your servant—and this
decree, Sovereign Lord, is for a mere human!
What more can David say to you? For you
know your servant, Sovereign Lord. For
the sake of your word and according to
your will, you have done this great thing
and made it known to your servant.
How great you are, Sovereign Lord! There is
no one like you, and there is no God but you,
as we have heard with our own ears…
Sovereign Lord, you are God! Your covenant
is trustworthy, and you have promised these
good things to your servant. Now be pleased
to bless the house of your servant, that it may
continue forever in your sight; for you, Sovereign
Lord, have spoken, and with your blessing the
house of your servant will be blessed forever
(2 Samuel 7:18-22, 28-29).

I love this man! I also love how when we confess our sin, God sees to it that there are "slave girls" out there before whom he exalts you and who love you all the more for dancing with them before the Lord. These are the lowly and downtrodden. These are they who are openly struggling and reviled for it. God makes a soft spot in their heart for you and he uses you to bless them, and them you, as you strip yourself of your pretense.

Family, if you hear a dark word afoot about me, I want you hear it from me and not from another. Further, should Satan the Accuser point out a fault in me, I agree with him completely. I could point out many more besides. I then point at the cross and deal him a double upper-cut: there I am forgiven; there he is defeated!

An extremely powerful secondary principle is at work here. The very action of becoming vulnerable and exposing the works of darkness you have been involved in, causes massive quakes in the kingdom of darkness. Moreover, you can't begin to imagine the aftershocks that will cause.

> *But as it is written, "No eye has seen, no ear has heard, and no mind has imagined the things that God has prepared for those who love him"*
> (1 Corinthians 2:9).

> *But everything exposed by the light becomes visible—and everything that is illuminated becomes a light*
> (Ephesians 5:13-14a).

Everything? Everything. *Even your sin!* Only God can do that! He gives us a powerful privilege of partnering with him in breaking open the shackles that hold others captive. Astounding miracles ensue. Because God is so "resplendent with light," as Ps. 76:4a teaches, he lights up even your sin and, like the moon, it becomes a light for others in the dark! There's nothing like a floodlight for a rude awakening from sleep. God's floodlight will even raise the dead. And when they wake up, Christ will shine on them.

For it is light that makes everything
visible. This is why it is said,
"wake up, O sleeper, rise from the dead,
and Christ will shine on you"
(Ephesians 5:14).

For with you is the fountain of life;
in your light we see light
(Psalm 36:9).

So while everything within me winces and withers at the thought of the shame and disgrace associated with exposing just one of my sins (and I have many), his light quickened and compels me, under the cover and power of his grace, that formidable SWAT team. My Great Physician swiftly saws my chest open and performs a successful pericardiectomy as we saw in the chapter titled, *The State of The Heart—Sensitive or Sensual?* My once strangled, stifled, now-freed heart gasped desperately with searing pain, then violently exploded into new life. My life-blood pumps with the molten lava of truth and life.

Pour into me the brightness of your daybreak!
Pour into me your rays of revelation-truth!
Let them comfort and gently lead
me onto the shining path,
Showing the way into your burning presence,
Into your many sanctuaries of holiness.
Then I will come closer to your very altar
Until I come before you, the God of my ecstatic joy!
I will praise you with the harp
that plays in my heart,
To you, my God, my magnificent God!
Then I will say to my soul,
"Don't be discouraged; don't be disturbed,
For I fully expect my Savior-God
to break through for me.

Then I'll have plenty of reasons to
praise him all over again."
Yes, living before his face is my saving grace
(Psalm 43:3-5, TPT).

The Spirit of Michal

We learned that one definition of a spirit is an uncontrollable or unaccountable impulse. I'd like to take a moment to study the spirit of Michal. What does it look like?

1. Blessed. She is privileged and richly endowed with position or other gifting.
2. Isolationist. Michal insulates herself from people, especially if she isn't personally invited. She places and maintains barriers between herself and others. She doesn't put herself out. She's hard to reach and unavailable (at least emotionally) when you do reach her.
3. Pretentious. When invited, she may claim to have better things to do but will then spend her time looking at and pining after what others are doing.
4. Exclusive. She may view herself as better than others and may even have "legitimate" reasons for this. She stratifies people into classes and judges their worth as such. She does not mingle with certain types. If she must be associated with others, it'll be those with like pedigree or lack thereof. She idolizes people she values. Once she gets to know them, she quickly tears them down and devalues them. She is competitive and very few people, if any, are good enough. She wouldn't want to get "dirty" with relationships.

5. Insecure. She may have had a troubled parent who instilled fear and mistrust in her. She's guarded, secretive, superficial, and suspicious.

6. Cold. She has a cutting, critical tongue. Her speech is marked by scathing sarcasm and sneering put-downs. This may even be shrouded in humor and wit.

7. Overly sensitive. She is frequently vexed by people and easily annoyed. At any given time, her feelings are hurt. This leads her to isolate further. Her lip may be curled up in derision or pursed in pouting irritation—arms crossed and feet stomping to boot.

8. Calculated attacker. She corners her target when she senses their defenses are down and either they are in despair or in ecstasy.

9. Misinterprets or misrepresents facts. Her perceptions are exaggerated versions of reality or outright lies.

10. Barrenness. She is all show and tall, fluffed-up claims. She is dry, miserly, unproductive, unfruitful, lonely, hollow, and shallow.

Bristle alert! Yet again, a picture of someone may have hopped right into your mind. Pray for them. Then turn the lens around and ask the Holy Spirit to shine his light into parts of your heart where you have some Michal-like tendencies.

Sin thrives in a warm, dark place.

Chapter 27

Repentance

The law of the Lord is perfect, refreshing the soul.
The statutes of the Lord are trustworthy,
making wise the simple.
The precepts of the Lord are right,
giving joy to the heart.
The commands of the Lord are
radiant, giving light to the eyes.
The fear of the Lord is pure, enduring forever.
The decrees of the Lord are firm,
and all of them are righteous.

They are more precious than gold,
than much pure gold;
they are sweeter than honey, than
honey from the honeycomb.
By them your servant is warned; in
keeping them there is great reward.
But who can discern their own errors?
Forgive my hidden faults.
Keep your servant also from willful sins;
may they not rule over me.
Then I will be blameless,
innocent of great transgression.
May these words of my mouth and
this meditation of my heart

be pleasing in your sight,
Lord, my Rock and my Redeemer
(Psalm 19:7–14, emphasis added).

If we are wrong, we have to admit that we are wrong without attempting to justify ourselves and our actions. We need to take 100 percent responsibility for our actions. God, who does not want a single one of us to perish, gives us repentance as an escape hatch from the Den of Death.

We do not make requests of you because we are
righteous, but because of your great mercy
(Daniel 9:18b).

If you, Lord, kept a record of sins,
Lord, who could stand?
But with you there is forgiveness,
so that we can, with reverence, serve you.
I wait for the Lord, my whole being waits,
and in his word I put my hope.
I wait for the Lord
more than watchmen wait for the morning,
more than watchmen wait for the morning
(Psalm 130:3-6).

If my people, who are called by my name,
will humble themselves and pray and seek
*my face and **turn from their wicked ways**,*
then I will hear from heaven, and I will
forgive their sin and will heal their land
(2 Chronicles 7:14, emphasis added).

Repentance is the process of conviction leading to a turning away from our wicked ways. Dr. Neil Anderson describes how in the early church, believers would face west and declare, "I renounce you Satan, and all your works and ways." They'd then face east and affirm their faith in God.[1] I love this literal turning away and have been practicing it by facing one way for confession and then turning the other way and declaring or accepting forgiveness, then speaking God's truth as outlined in Scripture. By the way, you might want to take a moment to get your bearings, wherever you live. Identify where east is because that'll be the direction of his coming—not that you'll miss it if you don't know where east is. Keep glancing that way from time to time. You'll have a sweet surprise one fine day. But I digress.

Paul beckons excitedly,

> *Let us then approach the throne of grace with*
> *confidence, so that we may receive mercy and*
> *find grace to help us in our time of need*
> (Hebrews 4:16).

How deplorable that we serve a God who is eager to love and tend his flock, but the sheep won't go to him for help.

> *I long to redeem them; they do not*
> *cry out to me from their hearts. They*
> *do not turn to the Most High*
> (Hosea 7:12).

Hear this heart-rending lament of Jesus:

> *I gave her space to repent of her fornication*
> *[pornography], and she repented not*
> (Revelation 2:21).

> *"This is what the Lord says—your*
> *Redeemer, the Holy One of Israel:*
> *"I am the Lord your God,*
> *who teaches you what is best for you,*
> *who directs you in the way you should go.*
> *If only you had paid attention to my commands,*

your peace would have been like a river,
your well-being like the waves of the sea"
(Isaiah 48:17, 18).

Many struggling saints are entrenched in sorrow and shame about their behavior. Stopping there is a waste of time. We *should* feel shame, but not stop there.

Repentance is to turn 180 degrees from our old ways. It is to look at our wrong actions and say, "that's not me." We then turn towards God and seek a truth to adopt in place of our wrong actions. We must believe that God has forgiven us *all* our sins—past, present, and future. I frequently forget that, thinking he's mostly forgiven the ones from yesterday and before, and that today's are totally catching him by surprise. Repentance means I renounce my heart attitudes and their resultant behaviors. Too often we focus only on the behaviors. I must then turn around and own my new transformed heart which is to love and exalt Jesus above all else. This will result in me living in true freedom—submitted as a slave of Christ. How can submission and slavery mean freedom? God's kingdom is full of such paradoxes.

> "Freedom is doing what you love to do if what you love to do is what you ought to do. And transformation is the change of our heart so that what we love to do is what we ought to do."[2]

Confession is the second step. I can't say it enough: We are wretched. None of us is without sin! Every last one of us has a hole in our carpet. Don't own your sin by sitting on it—hiding and coddling it. Expose it and be rid of it. Light it up and turn it into a beacon for another entrapped soul. Beloved, when you come to realize that you have the capacity to commit any sin, you will be markedly closer to the truth. "I believe myself capable of every sin in the Bible—every one."[3] Under the right temperature and pressure, each of us really is capable of the worst atrocities. But for the grace of God, there go I.

This mindset also helps us not react with shock or disdain to other people's failures.

> *Therefore, confess your sins to each other*
> *and pray for each other so that you may*
> *be healed. The prayer of a righteous*
> *person is powerful and effective."*
> (James 5:16).

Mercy Corps finally did a wonderful job of this. The Oregonian reported, "Beth deHamel, interim chief executive officer for Mercy Corps, issued a separate statement: The external review makes it clear that Mercy Corps' handling of this case in 2018 added to a survivor's pain, and for that we are profoundly sorry. We take full responsibility for Mercy Corps' failings in this case. We have learned lessons from what happened and we are taking corrective action, including a significant increase in our investment in safeguarding, to ensure Mercy Corps provides survivors with the support they need and deserve."[4] In 2020 current Mercy Corps staff had a gathering in which Tanya addressed them.

The third step is to energetically make provision for righteousness, much like we did for sin. Out of love and devotion and a desire to live our lives before God, we press in to win the prize. This life is marked by non-stop praise, thanksgiving, and worship. An important aspect of making provision is making amends. Pray about, then talk to the people you hurt. Do *everything* in your power to make things right. Though effort this may not always be accepted by those you've hurt. Set your heart right before God by doing your part as he guides you. He will right the rest. Paul shows us how to live in the light,

> *To live like this is all the more urgent, for*
> *time is running out and you know it is a*
> *strategic hour in human history. It is time*
> *for us to wake up! For our full salvation is*
> *nearer now than when we first believed.*

*Night's darkness is dissolving away as a new
day of destiny dawns. So we must once and for
all strip away what is done in the shadows of
darkness, removing it like filthy clothes. And
once and for all we must clothe ourselves with
the radiance of **light as our weapon**. We must
live honorably, surrounded by the light of this
new day, not in the darkness of drunkenness
and debauchery, not in promiscuity and
sensuality, not being argumentative or jealous
of others. Instead fully immerse yourselves
into the Lord Jesus, the Anointed One, and
don't waste even a moment's thought on your
former identity to awaken its selfish desires*
(Romans 13:11-14 TPT, emphasis added).

How's that for letting shame do its work? Once shame does
its work, don't waste even a minute on it. God has credited you
with righteousness. David, the man after God's own heart, sinned
grievously in so many ways. He encourages you and I from personal
experience:

*Praise the Lord, O my soul, and forget not all
his benefits—who forgives all your sins and heals
all your diseases. who redeems your life from the
pit and crowns you with love and compassion,
who satisfies your desires with good things so that
your youth is renewed like the eagle's. The Lord
is compassionate and gracious, slow to anger,
abounding in love. He will not always accuse,
nor will he harbor his anger forever; he does not
treat us as our sins deserve or repay us according
to our iniquities. For as high as the heavens are
above the earth, so great is his love for those who
fear him; as far as the east is from the west, so
far has he removed our transgressions from us.*

As a father has compassion on his children, so the Lord has compassion on those who fear him; for he knows how we are formed, he remembers that we are dust. The life of mortals is like grass, they flourish like a flower of the field; the wind blows over it and it is gone, and its place remembers it no more. But from everlasting to everlasting the Lord's love is with those who fear him, and his righteousness with their children's children—with those who keep his covenant and remember to obey his precepts (Psalm 103:2-5, 8-18).

Let us tap into the power of the brain to learn and change. The brain in and of itself is amoral, it doesn't apply value judgements. It just does what it's trained to. Harmful pathways are formed in the exact way that useful ones are—exposure and repetition. You can thus train the mind for godliness or unrighteousness. In physical and mental therapy e.g. after brain damage such as is caused by strokes or other health conditions, we use the principle of neuroplasticity that we learned about earlier in a powerful modality called Cognitive Behavioral Therapy (CBT).

In therapy, the goal is to extinguish the established harmful or damaged pathways by barricading their use, and to facilitate the formation of new pathways for the desired habit. This is an ongoing process that takes time and intentionality. It takes a long time to establish bad habits and may take as long or longer to replace them and extinguish the drive towards the old well-worn ruts.

In Scripture, this principle is the brilliance of Paul's words,

*Therefore, I urge you, brothers and sisters, in view of God's mercy, to offer your bodies as a living sacrifice, holy and pleasing to God— this is your true and proper worship. Do not conform to the pattern of this world, but **be transformed by the renewing of your mind**.*

*Then you will be able to approve what God's
will is—his good, pleasing, and perfect will*
(Romans 12:2, emphasis added).

*You were taught, with regard to your former
way of life, to **put off your old self**, which
is being corrupted by its deceitful desires; to
be made new in the attitude of your minds;
and **to put on the new self**, created to be
like God in true righteousness and holiness*
(Ephesians 4:22-24, emphases added).

Repentance is the process of conviction, leading
to a surrendering of our wicked ways and being
transformed. The result is a godly walk of
faith characterized by the fruit of the Spirit.

Chapter 28

Standing Firm in the Battle

I am the LORD, your God, who takes hold
of your right hand and says to you,
Do not fear; I will help you
(Isaiah 41:13).

As we discussed, despite the believer being born again, and declared righteous and perfect, the flesh has tendencies that must repeatedly be put to death. Fortunately, in coming to Christ, we gain power over sin.

His divine power has given us everything
we need for life and godliness
(2 Peter 1:3)

But now that you have been set free from sin and
have become slaves of God, the benefit you reap
leads to holiness, and the result is eternal life
(Roman 6:22)

As a result, we can resolve with the Psalmist:

I'm trying my best to walk in the way of
integrity, especially in my own home. But I
need your help! I'm wondering, Lord, when
will you appear? I refuse to gaze on that which

is vulgar. I despise works of evil people and
anything that moves my heart away from
you. I will not let evil hold me in its grip
(Psalm 101:2–3 TPT)

Read these words imagining that the writer is wrangling with temptation and is determined to keep his heel on its neck, awaiting supernatural backup. Ephesians 6:10, 13, 14a teaches,

Finally, be strong in the Lord and in His mighty
power. Put on the full armor of God so that you
can take your stand against the devil's schemes...
So that when the day of evil comes, you may be
able to stand your ground, and after you have
done everything, to stand. Stand firm then!
(Ephesians 6:10-11).

If we don't stand, we fall. Isn't it interesting that, figuratively, we say one "fell into sexual sin"? Gallagher scoffs at this, claiming that we don't just fall into sexual sin as though we were innocently walking along and suddenly fell into a hole.[1] Getting into and knowingly remaining in sin is a deliberate, calculated prostrating of the self to it. Satan's strategy is simple but brilliant:

Smite the shepherd and the sheep will scatter
(Mark 14:27).

Rochester calls our spiritual leaders "high-value targets." Though any target will do—men, women, young, old, educated, uneducated, poor or rich; high-value targets are preferred, just as a hunter prefers a 7-point trophy to a 3-point one. He knows he can't get at God, but if he can convince us that our leaders are moral failures, it's a slippery slope to the belief that God and his Word are impotent. He adds, "There is a spirit and soul connection established between a leader and those who follow."[2]

Our communal or herd brain pathways are knit together and the shockwaves resulting from the fall of a leader rips through entire communities, leaving devastation in their wake. Humans mirror each other like herd animals. We reflect each other's mannerisms, words, and behavior. We especially do so with those we admire. When a pastor falls, many men and women may fall with him, either sexually or in disbelief, anger, gossip, or other sins. Such incidents shake us to our core as we realize how vulnerable we all are and how capable of sin. We are shocked that they would do such a thing and that we didn't see it coming.

In every struggle, we have two choices—to sin, or stand up to it; prostrate ourselves to it (which the devil banks on) or thrust a spear through it. You and I are fully culpable regarding the germination of the sin-seed in the womb of our hearts. Writer and counselor Robert Subby gives us a much-needed wake-up call, informing us that we are not victims, we are volunteers![3] We could abort the pregnancy at any point in its development.

> *It is for freedom that Christ has set us free.*
> *Stand firm, then, and do not let yourselves*
> *be burdened again by a yoke of slavery*
> (Galatians 5:1).

> *Beloved ones, God has called us to live a life*
> *of freedom in the Holy Spirit. But don't view*
> *this wonderful freedom as an opportunity to set*
> *up a base of operations in the natural realm.*
> *Freedom means that we become so completely*
> *free of self-indulgence that we become servants*
> *of one another, expressing love in all we do*
> (Galatians 5:13).

You are not a helpless victim,
You are a volunteer!

Rober Subby

Unfortunately, as we saw earlier, we over—or underestimate sin's power, and precious few of us choose to terminate the seed. We bow down at the altar of idolatry. We prostrate ourselves there and pledge allegiance to it. We generally nurture and coddle our pet sins, like soft bunnies, when we should treat them like a pile of feces. We treat them like cuddly kittens, when we should recoil from them as from a king cobra and impale them with a spear. God calls us to

> ***Put to death*** *the sinful, earthly*
> *things lurking within you.*
> ***Have nothing to do with*** *sexual immorality,*
> *impurity, lust, and evil desires*
> (Colossians 3:5 NLT, emphasis added).

The grace of God, by which you were saved, continues to work on your behalf, with your cooperation. Here's another of my favorite pieces of Scriptures:

> *For the grace of God has appeared that offers*
> *salvation to all people.* ***It teaches us to say***
> ***"No" to ungodliness and worldly passions,***
> ***and to live self-controlled, upright and***
> ***godly lives*** *in this present age, while we wait*
> *for the blessed hope—the appearing of the*
> *glory of our great God and Savior, Jesus Christ,*

who gave himself for us to redeem us from all
wickedness and to purify for himself a people
that are his very own, eager to do what is good
(Titus 2:11–14, emphasis added).

We don't say no to ourselves often enough. Not enough people walk around screaming "No!" to temptation. We should treat it like an enraged woman being followed by a stalker—kick it, scratch its eyes, spray it with mace, scream for your life! Instead we foolishly look the other way and hope he will leave us alone if we ignore him hard enough. That's foolishness. Friend, don't turn your back on him for a second. Keep in mind that these processes take a long time to establish and, short of a miracle, may take a long time to break. Be prepared for a long-term battle. Indeed, we will battle one thing or another till the day we die!

And if you find yourself ensnared, there is hope.

But we are a colony of heaven on earth as we
cling tightly to our life-giver, the Lord Jesus
Christ, who will transform our humble bodies
and transfigure us into the identical likeness of
his glorified body. And using his matchless power,
he continually subdues everything to himself
(Philippians 2:20–21, TPT)

Dr. Shaw points out, "Galatians 5:23 describes the final fruit of the Spirit which is self-control. Self is not the source of control. Self is the object that must be controlled. Self must continually remain under the control of the Holy Spirit, not itself."[4] This is contrary to what the world teaches about self, elevating it to a position of personal Savior.

Speaking of having nothing to do with these things, our belief about who we are and our speech about it is of great importance. God continues to use fallen mankind to bring about reconciliation to him. That is why I pour into Christians the truth of who they are in Christ. One of my life verses is,

*Paul, a servant of God and an apostle of Jesus Christ to **further the faith of God's elect and their knowledge of the truth that leads to godliness**—in the hope of eternal life, which God, who does not lie, promised before the beginning of time, and which now at his appointed season he has brought to light through the preaching entrusted to me by the command of God our Savior* (Titus 1:1-3, emphasis added).

Who we are determines what we do. Teachers teach, doctors doctor, and cooks cook. Addicts are addicted and junkies are hopeless. Believer, that's not your identity! You are a saint, you are loved, you are saved, you are cherished, you are made new, you are complete in Christ, you are empowered, you are victorious, you are perfected. Understanding and knowing this is what will transform you. Christ transplants your heart and the results of your next PAPDATE are outstanding. If not in practice, they can be, as you guard your heart and keep the bad guys out. Remember those checkpoints? Your heart is the fountain of your purpose, affections, passions, desires, appetites, thoughts, and endeavors. I am a witness and embodiment to this great truth! Let Jesus do this for you. You can't do it on your own. He alone is sufficient to meet your needs.

As Covenant Worship group says,

> Just one drop
> Would have been enough
> It would have been enough
> But You gave it all
> There upon the cross
> To demonstrate Your love.[5]

Think about it, without the shedding of blood there is no forgiveness of sin.[6] The Old Testament proved that rivers of blood from bulls and goats offered endlessly, every day, year after year could never make us perfect before God.[7] So Jesus became our High Priest, our ultimate sacrifice.

> *But when this priest had offered for all time one*
> *sacrifice for sins, he sat down at the right hand*
> *of God, for by one sacrifice **he has made perfect***
> ***forever those who are being made holy**.*
> *The Holy Spirit also testifies to us*
> *about this. First he says:*
> *"This is the covenant I will make with them*
> *after that time, says the Lord.*
> ***I will put my laws in their hearts,***
> ***and I will write them on their minds**."*
> *Then he adds:*
> *"Their sins and lawless acts I*
> *will remember no more."*
> *And where these have been forgiven,*
> *sacrifice for sin is no longer necessary*
> (Romans 10:12, 14-18).

I'm not making this stuff up; I'm just claiming it. I'm just owning it. Remember the Bible is your story, it's people are your people. Why wouldn't I take the only shot I have at perfection—and that already attained for me, signed, sealed, and delivered? A costly perfection handed to me with zero effort on my part. Anything I am and have is because of him. He says, "I started it, I'll finish it, you just sit by me for the ride of your life!"

> *"He reached down from on high*
> *and took hold of me;*
> *he drew me out of deep waters.*
> *He rescued me from my powerful enemy,*
> *from my foes, who were too strong for me…*
> *You, Lord, keep my lamp burning;*
> *my God turns my darkness into light.*
> *With your help I can advance against a troop;*

with my God I can scale a wall.
It is God who arms me with strength
and keeps my way secure.
He makes my feet like the feet of a deer;
he causes me to stand on the heights.
He trains my hands for battle;
my arms can bend a bow of bronze.
You give me your shield of victory
and your right hand sustains me;
you stoop down to make me great.
(Psalm 18: 16, 17, 28-29, 32-35).

The high priests never sat down. Their work was never done. But this one, my personal High Priest, said "It is finished,"[8] breathed his last and completed the work. Forever. That is why he sat down at the right hand of the Father. The job was finally done. Because of that, we have *great* hope and *great* power. We have been declared perfect forever. No matter how far, how long, or how deeply we have strayed! Christian, live in your freedom! You don't have to sin today even though you may have sinned every day for years. You are no longer a helpless victim in this matter, at this point you are a volunteer! If you are pregnant with sin, you can abort the monster at any trimester. Because your High Priest finished the work, because he sat down, you have firm footing. You are like a spiritual mountain goat on the cliffs of life. *Stand firm then!*

"He makes my feet like the feet of a deer;
he causes me to stand on the heights"
(Psalm 18:33).

Chapter 29

The Solution of Sanctification

*Listen to me, my sons, and pay attention
to my words. Don't let your hearts stray
away toward her [The Temptress]. Don't
wander down her wayward path*
(Proverbs 7:25).

God's Word is the only hope for deliverance from our besetting sin and must be the foundation for the Christian's course of action. It calls for genuine repentance and an aligning with God in regard to sin. *To restore* is the same term [Gk. *karartizo*] used to describe setting a broken bone. The church is to reset the struggling saint's fractured perspective "into a biblical mindset using correction from God's Word," under the guidance of the Holy Spirit, which often brings astounding results.[1]

As we have seen, lives are at stake. There is no question what the solution is. Wisdom yells urgently in the street corner regarding the seductress. If we are wise, we will heed her call. With the fire of an Old Testament prophet, I follow that up with a three-fold outcry.

1. Like a fence and sign on the edge of a cliff, I warn believers who are walking down the road to The Temptress's house,
2. Like an emergency crew at the bottom of the cliff, I burst into her den, as a firefighter into a burning building, and help evacuate the drowsy believers passed out on Delilah's bed or on her lap,

3. Like a hospital staff, I dutifully man the wound clinic to clean and set the bones broken by the brutal snare of pornography.

Believer, remember that it doesn't matter why one engages in pornography or any form of self-indulgence, there is no excuse for it. The only good thing that could come of it is us turning our sin over to Jesus. Like Jesus encountering the man born blind, may our deliverance be so that the works of God might be displayed in us (John 9:3).

When it comes to dealing with the sin, it doesn't really matter why a person is a pornographer! James places the onus squarely on our shoulders ultimately,

> *Each person is tempted when they are dragged away by **their own** evil desire and enticed. Then, after desire has conceived, it gives birth to sin; and sin, when it is full-grown, gives birth to death*
> (James 1:14–15, emphasis added)

Pornography doesn't have to end in death. The Great Physician prescribes a lethal birth control combined with a morning-after pill called sanctification. There is no place for gentleness toward this monster. The world and the flesh desire to understand the cause of the behavior. Many endorse sympathy, pity, time, and understanding toward it. Thankfully, that is not the approach that my dad's cardiologist took toward Dad's pericarditis. Dr. Njuguna said, "This thing is killing you. It needs to go. Catherine, find me an operating room and fit him on the schedule for tomorrow." He proceeded to *hurt* my father so as not to *harm* him. Believer, fit this business into your schedule, stat! Nothing else on your calendar is as important.

In almost every encounter that Jesus had with people, he called out sin. Unfortunately, unlike Jesus, we frequently don't want to hurt each other by doing the awkward business of calling out sin in each other's lives. In the process, we end up harming each other by turning the other way and ignoring it. Oregon-based writer Cathy Goekler teaches, "Your communication with each other needs to address the blindness we have toward ourselves. Develop the skill and discipline to lovingly call each other on inherent dishonesty and rebellion."[2] When we do call each other out, we must do this with humility and much love, fully cautious of our own capacity to fall. We must also be open and grateful to others who speak difficult truths into our lives.

> *Be completely humble and gentle*
> *What business is it of mine to judge those outside*
> *the church? Are you not to judge those inside?*
> (1 Corinthians 5:12).

We are saved by grace and remain saved through grace. We often think of grace as a sweet, gentle breeze that God wafts our way. In contrast, it is a typhoon force that blows down the caverns of our hearts and lives, like an invading SWAT team. Remember that SWAT stands for Special Weapons and Tactics and this spiritual campaign certainly calls for such a specialized, deliberate, and powerful counterattack.

> *And so now, I entrust you into God's hands*
> *and the message of his grace, which is all*
> *that you need to become strong. All of God's*
> *blessings are imparted through the message of*
> *his grace, which he provides as the spiritual*
> *inheritance given to all of his holy ones*
> (Acts 20:32, TPT).

> *For the grace of God has appeared that*
> *offers salvation to all people. It teaches us*
> *to say* **"No"** *to ungodliness and worldly*
> *passions, and to live self-controlled, upright*
> *and godly lives in this present age!*
> (Titus 2:11–12, emphasis added).

I must beat my body and make it my slave
(1 Corinthians 9:7).

We make provision for righteousness when we practice saying "no." It is also a mark of maturity. We've all been around a child that is not used to hearing their parents say, "no." It's not a beautiful thing. When you became a Christian, sanctification came with it. The power to immediately vanquish temptation is within you. When you believe and proclaim that you have been called and set apart for God, He immediately gives you grace to resist temptation.

And how about practicing the discipline of saying "no" to the flesh from time to time. That would take different forms for different people. For some, it would be saying, "I could sleep in till nine. How about I get up at eight, just because." "I could take a twenty-minute shower. How about a five-minute one today?" "That looks really good but I don't need a candy bar. No thanks." Find indulgences that you automatically go for and train yourself to cut back or say no altogether.

In all these situations, we must ask ourselves, "Who owns who?" Am I in firm control of these habits and possessions and do they have me by the tail? Am I in active combat against these desires or have I sold off and totally surrendered to their power over me without a fight? They all aim to separate me from God. They relate directly to the Doctrine of Balaam. Remember that in that doctrine, beautiful women turned the people's hearts away from God toward sensuality.

I write to you, young men, because you are
strong, and the word of God lives in you,
and you have overcome the evil one
(1 John 2:14c).

I see three types of deliverance at play in my life. He completely delivered me from some of my indulgences almost instantly, miraculously. I call that the "banana deliverance,"—it entails an easy peel job and it's ready to eat. The banana, *Musa acuminate*, may well be the cleanest fruit in the world to eat. Each bite is sanitary as you peel it, ready for each bite, and your hands never have to touch the actual fruit.

Other sins doggedly continue to stalk me, and I have to give them the stalker treatment described earlier. These come in two categories. The first is the "grapefruit deliverance." This one is more laborious than the banana deliverance. Most people I know can't very well ride a bike and eat a grapefruit, *Citrus paradisi*, at the same time. It may call for a tool or at least personal preparation such as handwashing. After the not very easy work of peeling it, you can then enjoy it by further dissecting back the wall of each segment to eat just the pulp. Don't miss that—just the pulp. The wall is acerbic as heck and is actually the culprit as to why ninety per cent of unsophisticated grapefruit consumers didn't enjoy the fruit when they tried it. Don't eat it any more than you would your banana peel, unless you're into that kind of fiber. Ugh!

An even more cryptic category is called the "pomegranate deliverance." It requires arduous work to actually find a pomegranate, at least where I live. In my life, eating a pomegranate is a grand family affair. The dining table becomes like a surgical table. One doesn't just hack into a pomegranate. It requires post-doctoral skill. Gown and mask up with complete personal protective equipment (PPE). This fruit is not called *Punica granatum* for nothing. Study the fruit carefully while your assistant unwraps and hands you your sterilized scalpel. You may delicately cut through the rind at the albedo. Once you penetrate past the outer membrane, you then have to navigate the various sections. Done wrong, she bleeds like a stuck pig. Have a plate and a heap of towels for this reason.

After carefully cutting the leathery exocarp and fleshy mesocarp from north to south, set your knife down and let your masterful fingers take over. I believe the human hand is single-handedly the most amazing tool. But I digress—on a digression. Gently but firmly tear those layers apart to expose the various sections of the precious seeds called arils. I call them rubies as they are very reminiscent of that precious stone. You can then break up an entire section packed with arils and hand it off to a mouth drooling beside you—much like handing off a liver to your surgical assistant. They'll further break it up and eat the little rubies one by one hoping the experience never ends. One must chew the explosive individual gem whole and swallow it. None of this "spit out the hard part inside" business. It is a very fruitful affair!

Here's how Paul describes the experience:

> *I admit that I haven't yet acquired the absolute*
> *fullness that I'm pursuing, but I run with passion*
> *into his abundance so that I may reach the purpose*
> *that Jesus Christ has called me to fulfill and*
> *wants me to discover. I don't depend on my own*
> *strength to accomplish this however I do have one*
> *compelling focus: I forget all of the past as I fasten*
> *my heart to the future instead. I run straight for*
> *the divine invitation of reaching the heavenly*
> *goal and gaining the victory-prize through the*
> *anointing of Jesus. So let all who are fully mature*
> *have this same passion, and if anyone is not yet*
> *gripped by these desires, God will reveal it to*
> *them. And let us all advance together to reach this*
> *victory-prize, following one path with one passion*
> (Phillipians 3:12-16, TPT).

God loved us while we were yet sinners. Because of His goodness and grace, God continues to love us so dearly and is good to us *even when we sin.* That said, we can't actively foster pet sins and harmoniously abide in God at the same time. We can't willfully rebel against Him, mocking Him by trying to serve Him *and* our idols, and not incur his discipline. Jesus said,

> *No one can serve two masters. Either you will*
> *hate the one and love the other, or you will*
> *be devoted to the one and despise the other.*
> (Mathew 6:24a).

If you sense distance between you and the Lover of your Soul, take inventory of your life. Ask Him to help you search your heart. Examine your heart, your actions, and your purity before you go militantly claiming blessings and victory in His name, while indulging in a life-dominating sin. Know well that if you are actively cherishing sin, your first prayer needs to be one of repentance, otherwise, as King David said,

> *If I regard iniquity in my heart,*
> *the Lord will not hear me*
> (Psalm 66:18).

As you repent, turning away from this "regarding" (Heb. *Râ'âh—look intently, cause to gaze at, approve, be near, enjoy, have experience with,*) God has sent his SWAT team to deliver you from it and guide you to abundant living.

> *So, as the Holy Spirit says:*
> *"Today, if you hear his voice, do not harden your hearts*
> *as you did in the rebellion, during the time of testing in the wilderness,*
> *where your ancestors tested and tried me,*
> *though for forty years they saw what I did.*
> *That is why I was angry with that generation; I said, 'Their hearts*
> *are always going astray, and they have not known my ways.'*
> *So I declared on oath in my anger, 'They shall never enter my rest.'"*
> *See to it, brothers and sisters, that none of you has a sinful, unbelieving*
> *heart that turns away from the living God. But encourage one*
> *another daily, as long as it is called "Today," so that none of you may*
> *be hardened by sin's deceitfulness. We have come to share in Christ,*
> *if indeed we hold our original conviction firmly to the very end*
> (Hebrews 6:7-14).

Grace is a typhoon force that blows
down the caverns of our hearts and lives,
before and after salvation, kicking down
doors like an invading SWAT team.

Chapter 30

The Christian's Response—
Righteousness

Therefore, get rid of all moral filth and the
evil that is so prevalent and humbly accept the
word planted in you, which can save you.
Do not merely listen to the word, and so deceive
yourselves. Do what it says. Anyone who listens
to the word but does not do what it says is
like someone who looks at his face in a mirror
and, after looking at himself, goes away and
immediately forgets what he looks like. But
whoever looks intently into the perfect law
that gives freedom, and continues in it—not
forgetting what they have heard, but doing
it—they will be blessed in what they do.
(James 1:21-25).

Not only will God help you work out sexual and all other sanctification, he will richly reward it. I am finding this to be a fact in my life. I have FOMO (fear of missing out). My Uncle Jedidiah mentality did not result in me enjoying Thanksgiving, though I was stuffing my face. It left me obese and undernourished! It will always leave us unfulfilled and steeped in toxic shame. There is no lasting pleasure in overindulgence—and *any* type and degree of pornography/idolatry—mental, emotional, and physical—is overindulgence. You are not missing out on anything!

At twenty-one years of marriage, I am enjoying intimacy with my husband more than I did in all the prior years combined. God in His miraculous economy is seeing to it that as I grow in godly self-control and discipline to mentally focus exclusively on my husband, I am more satisfied than by the sum total of any option of scintillating wayward experiences. That astounds me. I was grasping for pleasure when all the while it lay here snoring beside me!

God has turned intimacy into a worship experience. While it's always been positive, God has geared it to another level altogether. He floods me with immense gratitude for this man who is so different from me and from anything I could have planned or imagined for myself. I marvel at His creation and gifting of this visually preposterous, laughable act that has justified such names as the "horizontal hula," "the funky chicken," and "assault with a friendly weapon." I thank Him for faithfulness and restoration.

Believe in this God of whom King David proclaims,

> *Praise the Lord, my soul, and forget not all his*
> *benefits—who satisfies your desires with good*
> *things so that your youth is renewed like the eagle's*
> (Psalm 103:2, 5).

It is fruitless to try to satisfy our hunger with cotton candy—it does not satisfy! Whatever you seek in gaming, in gambling, in overspending, in people-pleasing, will deeply disappoint you after the short-lived thrill is over. Give up the search, Christian. It occurred to me, God has treasures for me and they are tied up in this man! Your treasures are bound up in obedience. I don't know what you're looking for, but I'll tell you right now it's not "out there." Hopping around from one idol or lover to the next, including virtual or mental ones, will never meet your needs. God, your jealous God, loves you too much for that. Look at this fabulous verse,

Do not worship any other god, for the Lord,
whose name is Jealous, is a jealous God
(Exodus 34:14).

Where has that one been hiding? It's actually his name! You well know that the hopping around complicates your life terribly. Appreciate and nurture what God has given you. That is your Pleasant Land. What your spouse doesn't have or doesn't do, God is able to give them or teach them how to do. He is more than happy to provide for you and knows what is best for you. God is also very capable of changing your expectations and perceived needs as you mature. He will work with what you have and who you have. As we saw in the chapter titled *20 Ways We Despise the Pleasant Land,"* God constantly gives us phenomenal blessings but we soon despise them. Let us aim to grow in the disciplines of contentment and gratitude.

*Godliness with contentment is **great** gain*
(1 Timothy 6:6, emphasis added).

We need to give up the clear idea that we can two-time God by enjoying his abundant life while indulging in idolatry. We can't abide in him and dwell in willful sin. We can't serve two masters. We saw that Jesus said that no one can serve two masters. Either you will hate the one and love the other, or you will be devoted to the one and despise the other.

If I had cherished sin in my heart, the
Lord would not have listened;
but God has surely listened and
has heard my prayer.
Praise be to God, who has not rejected my prayer
or withheld his love from me
(Psalm 66:18-20).

Who may ascend the mountain of the Lord?
Who may stand in his holy place?

The one who has clean hands and a pure heart,
who does not trust in an idol
or swear by a false god.
They will receive blessing from the Lord
and vindication from God their Savior.
Such is the generation of those who seek
him, who seek your face, God of Jacob
(Psalm 24:3-6).

Lord, who may dwell in your sacred tent?
Who may live on your holy mountain?
The one whose walk is blameless,
who does what is righteous,
who speaks the truth from their heart;
whose tongue utters no slander,
who does no wrong to a neighbor,
and casts no slur on others;
who despises a vile person but honors
those who fear the Lord;
who keeps an oath even when it hurts,
and does not change their mind;
who lends money to the poor without interest;
who does not accept a bribe against the innocent.
Whoever does these things will never be shaken
(Psalm 15).

This blameless, wholehearted living cannot be attained by human strength no matter how strong your resolve. Remember righteousness has already been imputed to you. If Experian measured such things, your spiritual credit score would be 850 because of your positional righteousness. God declared you an A+ student before you took the test. Your practical outworking of righteousness is only tenable by the power of the Spirit. Practically, you will attain perfection upon your entry into Jesus' presence. What we are talking about is living a life of faith, crucifying the flesh, keeping short accounts with God, and striving after Christlikeness. Have faith in your God, the

God of Abraham. As children of Abraham, wield your faith as he did his:

> ***Against all hope*** *Abraham in hope believed… Without weakening in his faith, he faced the fact[s]… Yet he did not waver through unbelief regarding the promise of God, but was strengthened in his faith and gave glory to God, being fully persuaded that God had power to do what he had promised! This is why "it was credited to him as righteousness." The words "it was credited to him" were written not for him alone, but also for us, to whom God will credit righteousness—for us who believe in Him who raised Jesus our Lord from the dead. He was delivered over to death for our sins and was raised to life for our justification* (Romans 4:18-25, emphasis added).

Your spiritual credit score is 850!

Chapter 31

The Church's Response—Rescue

We mustn't abandon our own on the battlefield. This is a serious mandate for the Church of Jesus Christ.

> *Finally, as members of God's beloved family,*
> *we must go after the one who wanders from*
> *the truth and bring him back. For the one*
> *who restores the sinning believer back to*
> *God from the error of his way, gives back to*
> *his soul life from the dead, and covers over*
> *countless sins by their demonstration of love!*
> (James 5:19–20, TPT).

What a high calling—no one gets left behind! Paul says,

> *Brothers, if someone is caught in a trespass, you*
> *who are spiritual should restore him with a spirit*
> *of gentleness. But watch yourself, or you also may*
> *be tempted. Carry one another's burdens, and*
> *in this way you will fulfill the law of Christ*
> (Galatians 6:1–2).

What heart should we do it in? Condemnation does not work. "As with the woman caught in adultery, Jesus recognized that stoning does not get to the heart of the problem. Mercy does," says Rochester, adding, "When discovery takes place, loving, not condemning pastoral-support, targeted counseling, and deliberate plans, and prudent steps must be taken to help the man out from relapsing."[1]

Please understand that this is a painfully difficult process. Jesus himself taught us the procedure for doing this.

> *If your brother or sister sins, go and point out*
> *their fault, just between the two of you. If they*
> *listen to you, you have won them over. But if*
> *they will not listen, take one or two others along,*
> *so that 'every matter may be established by*
> *the testimony of two or three witnesses.' If they*
> *still refuse to listen, tell it to the church; and*
> *if they refuse to listen even to the church, treat*
> *them as you would a pagan or a tax collector*
> (Mathew 18:15-17).

Paul later reiterated that we can't turn the other way and pretend nothing is going on, which is the easy thing to do. After we have done what Jesus says to do, then there is only one outcome. Bristle-alert!

> *I wrote to you in my letter not to associate with*
> *sexually immoral people—not at all meaning*
> *the people of this world who are immoral,*
> *or the greedy and swindlers, or idolaters. In*
> *that case you would have to leave this world.*
> *But now I am writing to you that you must*
> *not associate with anyone who claims to be*
> *a brother or sister but is sexually immoral or*
> *greedy, an idolater or slanderer, a drunkard or*
> *swindler. Do not even eat with such people.*
> *What business is it of mine to judge those*
> *outside the church? Are you not to judge those*
> *inside? God will judge those outside. "Expel*
> *the wicked person from among you."*
> (1 Corinthians 5:9-13).

Friends, Jesus has yet more of that chafing teaching that just makes a saved, grown woman want to say, "Yeah, no!" He was so uncompromising about this stuff that he was willing to lose followers. Much as it breaks his heart, he still is. That is why he warns us to count the cost of following him. While his burden is easy and his yoke light, it is still a burden and a yoke. Writer Wesley Hill states, "In choosing fidelity to the gospel, we agree to bear up under this burden for as long as is necessary."[2] This is where the rubber meets the road after the Holy Ghost hibby jibbies are long gone. I call it the "Jesus 6066 Mode" AKA bristle-alert. It's a heart-break that goes like this:

> *On hearing it, many of his disciples said, "This*
> *is a hard teaching. Who can accept it?"*
> *Aware that his disciples were grumbling about*
> *this, Jesus said to them, "Does this offend you?*
> *Then what if you see the Son of Man ascend to*
> *where he was before! The Spirit gives life; the flesh*
> *counts for nothing. The words I have spoken to*
> *you—they are full of the Spirit and life. Yet there*
> *are some of you who do not believe." For Jesus had*
> *known from the beginning which of them did*
> *not believe and who would betray him. He went*
> *on to say, "This is why I told you that no one can*
> *come to me unless the Father has enabled them."*
> *From this time many of his disciples turned*
> *back and no longer followed him*
> (John 6:60-66).

Pastors, let last Sunday be the last Sunday that you assumed that men, women, and children looking up at you from the pews, are living in purity. Like a kidnapping victim in a getaway car trying to make eye contact with you—to save their very life, there are eyes looking up at you from the pew, pastor, pleading for your involvement. Women and children are just as ensnared. They are the concealed cargo in the trunk of the getaway car.

Saints, this isn't just the pastor's job! That would be an impossible burden for one or just a few people to take on. We are responsible for each other. Are we to assume that the steps above only refer to sexual sin but not to "lesser" ones? I don't think so. Note that Jesus said, if anyone is caught in a sin. Period. Paul adds swindlers, slanderers, the greedy, etc. to the list.

A few months ago I met a lady at church and we enjoyed getting to know each other. We took a walk on a recent sunny afternoon and talked about deeply personal things including struggles. As we talked about shame, huge tears rolled down her cheeks. I knew I was standing at the threshold of her sanctum. She changed topics. Presently, I circled back to the tears. She was quiet for a long minute then spoke. "Every time I've shared with new friends that I've made attempts at my life, that's as far as the relationship goes." Her pool of shame had sprung a leak. She wiped the flood tears with the back of her hand.

We watched a massive gaggle of migrating geese at a pond by our path.

"We're not very good about letting others be real, are we?" I consoled.

The geese squabbled loudly.

When was the last time a member of your church confessed to struggling with lying, an anger problem, or stealing? Who do you know that would admit to shopping excessively, over-eating, or being a workaholic? Who would raise their hands for struggling with same-sex attraction or people-pleasing or hypocrisy? Where do the selfish, the jealous, and those with eating disorders go? It's a wonder Jesus died for anyone in this crowd, everyone's just got it together! Not a proud one among us under this pretty plastic steeple. What a stained-glass masquerade. Jesus despises it!

Sure we hear about it when someone has had an affair. Why do we ignore the "small" matters leading up to that and then gasp, shocked that such things could possibly happen? Why are we shocked by each other's sins? Why do we act like we have none? Why do we not know how to confess or what to do with a confession? We already saw that we're all fallen. May we do the hard, awkward work of fostering an environment where honesty and vulnerability are valued and practiced. If we can't share about the sins committed outside the body, how can we hope to share about and be healed from those committed inside the body?

It was glorious to sit on a little wooden bench by that pond and pray with my sister as she confessed her sin and took off the mantle of shame as one would a cloak. She'd borne it so long her spirit had a stooped gait. She knew God had already forgiven her but she'd continued to beat herself up about it for years. In that moment, as she prayed, groups of geese loudly took off from the pond, bearing her burdens to the sky. She stood ten feet tall. We walked the rest of the way with a deep sense of restoration to our standing in God as righteous and free.

Many Christians in today's liberal world don't even realize the depravity of their behavior. As we saw in the statistics earlier, some consider "not recycling" a more serious issue than porn. Your confession to someone could be a gateway experience, an awakening for them. We need to hear preaching and teaching about this. We need to get over the discomfort of the topic. The leaven is in the dough and it's rising! The fetus is in the womb and it's growing. Church, go bring them back!

Women and children are just as
ensnared. They are the concealed cargo
in the trunk of the getaway car.

Chapter 32

Restoration to Intimacy

We are spiritual Israel. Paul teaches,

> *It is not the children by physical descent who*
> *are God's children, but it is the children of the*
> *promise who are regarded as Abraham's offspring*
> (Romans 9:8).

> *And if you are Christ's, then you are Abraham's*
> *seed and heirs according to the promise*
> (Galatians 3:29).

> *Today, if only you would hear his voice,*
> *"Do not harden your hearts as you did at Meribah,*
> *as you did that day at Massah in the wilderness,*
> *where your ancestors tested me;*
> *they tried me, though they had seen what I did*
> (Psalm 95:7b-9).

God deals with us much like he did with that beloved nation of his that he symbolically calls his virgin daughter and wife despite her harlotry. Here is another Biblical paradox: God describes us as a daughter and also as a wife (so bear with me if I answer to Mrs. Lord Almighty. I'm owning this whole thing.)

For your Maker is your husband—
the Lord Almighty is his name
(Isaiah 54:5a).

Beloved Israel indulged in wanton idolatry, and after much warning, God, in anger, banished her to exile in Babylon. The Lord is patient with us when we don't obey him. But in due time, like a loving Father, He disciplines us—albeit less than we deserve. His heart is *always* to restore us to himself. He is still in pursuit of reconciliation with the end goal of intimacy. I couldn't do a better job of describing God's restoration in my life than God does in the book of Jeremiah. Here are some excerpts from Jeremiah 30 that describe His heart for us:

"In that day," declares the Lord Almighty,
I will break the yoke off their necks
and will tear off their bonds; no longer
will foreigners enslave them.
Instead, they will serve the Lord their God...
"So do not be afraid, Jacob my servant; do
not be dismayed, Israel, declares the Lord.
"I will surely save you out of a distant place,
...I am with you and will save you," declares
the Lord... "I will not completely destroy you.
I will discipline you but only in due measure;
I will not let you go entirely unpunished."
(Jeremiah 30).

This makes me think of a flick on a naughty toddler's hand. I thank God for his gentleness with us when we deserve wrath. Because of this great work, we can rejoice with our brother King David. Think of the passage below in light of your besetting sin:

Give thanks to the Lord, for he is good;
His love endures forever.

Let the redeemed of the Lord tell their story—
Those he redeemed from the hand of the foe,
Those he gathered from the lands,
From east and west, from north and south.

Some wandered in desert wastelands,
Finding no way to a city where they could settle.
They were hungry and thirsty,
and their lives ebbed away.
Then they cried out to the lord in their trouble,
And he delivered them from their distress.
He led them by a straight way
To a city where they could settle.
Let them give thanks to the lord
for his unfailing love
And his wonderful deeds for mankind,
for he satisfies the thirsty
And fills the hungry with good things.

Some sat in darkness, in utter darkness,
Prisoners suffering in iron chains,
Because they rebelled against God's commands
And despised the plans of the Most High.
So he subjected them to bitter labor; they
stumbled, and there was no one to help.
Then they cried to the Lord in their trouble,
And he saved them from their distress.
He brought them out of darkness,
the utter darkness,
And broke away their chains.
Let them give thanks to the Lord
for his unfailing love
And his wonderful deeds for mankind,
for he breaks down gates of bronze
And cuts through bars of iron.

Some became fools through their rebellious ways
And suffered affliction because of their iniquities.
They loathed all food and drew
near the gates of death.
Then they cried to the Lord in their trouble,
And he saved them from their distress.
He sent out his word and healed them;
he rescued them from the grave.
Let them give thanks to the Lord
for his unfailing love
And his wonderful deeds for mankind.
Let them sacrifice thank offerings and
tell of his works with songs of joy.

Some went out on the sea in ships; they
were merchants on the mighty waters.
They saw the works of the Lord, his
wonderful deeds in the deep.
For he spoke and stirred up a tempest
that lifted high the waves.
They mounted up to the heavens
and went down to the depths;
In their peril their courage melted away.
They reeled and staggered like drunkards;
they were at their wits' end.
Then they cried out to the Lord in their trouble,
And he brought them out of their distress.
He stilled the storm to a whisper; the
waves of the sea were hushed.
They were glad when it grew calm,
And he guided them to their desired haven.
Let them give thanks to the Lord
for his unfailing love
And his wonderful deeds for mankind.
Let them exalt him in the assembly of the people
And praise him in the council of the elders.

He turned rivers into a desert, flowing
springs into thirsty ground,
And fruitful land into a salt waste,
Because of the wickedness of those who lived there.
He turned the desert into pools of water
And the parched ground into flowing springs;
There he brought the hungry to live,
And they founded a city where they could settle.
They sowed fields and planted vineyards
that yielded a fruitful harvest;
He blessed them, and their
numbers greatly increased,
And he did not let their herds diminish.

Then their numbers decreased,
and they were humbled
By oppression, calamity and sorrow;
he who pours contempt on nobles
Made them wander in a trackless waste.
But he lifted the needy out of their affliction
And increased their families like flocks.
The upright see and rejoice, but all
the wicked shut their mouths.

Let the one who is wise heed these things
And ponder the loving deeds of the Lord
(Psalm 107).

About twenty years ago, Mum was coming to visit us for about a month in August. I was over the moon when I heard the news. This was speedily followed by a feeling of dread. The drinking. What would I do? I knew she had to indulge heavily every day. I didn't want that but I certainly didn't want her withdrawing while under my care either. I was just sick over it. Since she wouldn't be able to drive, I started scheming where I would get her booze and how to limit it daily. I formulated a plan. I also decided I would wait for her to initiate all this.

The first day she arrived, she was exhausted and it didn't come up. Nor on the second nor the third day. I watched her closely especially as the dreaded 4pm approached. I figured she was scoping the atmosphere and deciding how to bring it up, not to mention acclimatizing to the time zone. It must have been killing her. By the fourth day, I couldn't stand it anymore. I decided that if she didn't bring it up, I would. On day five I broached it.

"Oh honey," she chuckled. "I told you. April 11th. Remember?"

I was dumbfounded. She attended a very somber, formal, liturgical church. My sister Faith and I attended more lively evangelical churches. Mum didn't stop us but she wasn't crazy about the new-fangled ways of worship. On April eleventh that year, a charismatic evangelist spoke at Mum's church and God gave her a word of knowledge. There was healing for a lady who had fallen down a flight of stairs and broken her arm. It never healed right. Mum, completely out of character, shot up like a flash of lightning.

She'd woken up late one night. There was a landing just outside their bedroom with a wall mounted light. The landing led to an adjoining tiled staircase. Mum had her hand stretched out to pull the cord to the light. She got disoriented, reached and leaned right into the void of the staircase and plummeted to the bottom. I was just a child then. All I know is I woke up and mum had a cast on. She hated hospitals but there was no avoiding this visit.

Years later, there she was, kneeling at the church's altar. She recommitted her life to the Lord and he completely healed the pain in that arm. I was ecstatic when she shared that with me. It was just incredible. Her delight and joy bubbled over whoever she talked to. But she didn't tell the half of it.

"What does April 11th have to do with anything?" I asked quizzically.

"Before church, I'd given one of the farm-hands money to buy my booze so it would be ready when I got home after church. As soon as I got home I dumped it all. It was the last time I've handled a bottle."

My core started to convulse and huge tears rolled down my cheeks. What was she saying? How? I couldn't believe it. Yet I had seen it for five days. It was the longest time I'd seen her sober. It was unreal. We talked at length. And she kept saying, "He took my thirst."

What an amazing God. Yet another banana deliverance. He restored her soul, healed her arm, delivered her from the snare of alcoholism and who knows what else. All in an instant. Then she paused a moment while I cried a waterfall.

That day in August, another miracle happened. She acknowledged how difficult it must have been for me as child and apologized for what she put us through. This was too much. I hope you understand that in my culture, adults don't apologize to children. This was a wonder I didn't even know what to do with. She tapped into a massive vein of buried gold deep within the strata of my being. Only God can do that!

Dad sits on his wheelchair in the verandah swatting flies with his cow tail whisk. I can hear the TV in the background as he catches me up on the news. He keeps abreast of all world news. He also catches me up on his week. He marvels at a strange new world of quarantine where people can't touch each other or come and go as they please. He folds back his pant leg to reveal the stump where his leg was amputated six years ago. He rubs away the phantom pain. "If something is killing you, it's better to cut if off," he muses. It's been a rough few years for him. "But we look up to the Lord. What else can we do?" His Lord is his love now.

He has experienced immense losses in the last decade. He should have died many times over. There is no logical explanation for why he is still alive. His heart is awakening to all things of earth being sinking sand. He grieves the passing of his children, he laments the loss of his leg, and with it the will to bulldoze his way through life. He is still reeling from Mum's passing the same year he lost his leg. He was so sick he didn't realize what hit him. It's still a blur to him.

It delights me that his heart is becoming increasingly inclined to the Lord. He has let go of numerous arenas of life that I believe were a stumbling block for him. He reports how what once pleased him is now meaningless. He was a self-made man who quit primary school to support his mother and siblings when his father drowned. He survived brutal British colonialism. He was a charismatic politician and elder. A stellar orator and sage. A gifted athlete. A world traveler. He thanks God for all that but has as much affection for it as a man rocking on his porch has for traffic as it goes by.

He's experiencing a transformation. He cares what's going in the lives of others. He takes time to talk to those he once considered lesser humans than himself. He openly expresses love and affection in our conversations. He talks more freely about his powerlessness. He is coming closer and closer to an end of himself as the Lord continues to till the soil of his heart. He is undergoing a decade-long *Punica granatum* deliverance and it is glorious to watch. Only God can do that!

Hear me, Lord, and answer me,
for I am poor and needy.
Guard my life, for I am faithful to you;
save your servant who trusts in you.
You are my God; have mercy on me,
Lord, for I call to you all day long.

Bring joy to your servant, Lord,
for I put my trust in you.
You, Lord, are forgiving and good,
abounding in love to all who call to you.
Hear my prayer, Lord; listen to my cry for mercy.
When I am in distress, I call to
you, because you answer me.
Among the gods there is none like you,
Lord; no deeds can compare with yours.
All the nations you have made will come
and worship before you, Lord;
they will bring glory to your name.
For you are great and do marvelous
deeds; you alone are God.

Teach me your way, Lord, that I
may rely on your faithfulness;
give me an undivided heart, that
I may fear your name.
I will praise you, Lord my God, with all my heart;
I will glorify your name forever.
For great is your love toward me; you
have delivered me from the depths,
from the realm of the dead…
But you, Lord, are a compassionate
and gracious God,
slow to anger, abounding in love and faithfulness.
Turn to me and have mercy on me; show
your strength in behalf of your servant;
save me, because I serve you just as my mother did.
(Psalm 86:1-13, 15, 16).

Chapter 33

Practical Steps to Intimacy

There are practical steps that we can take to cull the beast of pornography in all its forms. Please note that we can perform spiritual disciplines and yet be very far from God. Beware of a performance-oriented approach. God loves you as you are. Your performance doesn't make him love you more. The goal is to love the Lord our God with all our hearts and all our minds, and all our strength. We are to love others as ourselves. This is PAPDATE material. The Lover of our Souls wants us to be consumed with him in our purposes, affections, passions, desires, appetites, thoughts, and endeavors. Unity and intimacy are the thews of our spiritual life. Out of that will come all the steps I outline below.

God is the initiator and finisher of our salvation. I loved it when, as a kid, dad took me to work with him. Our Christian walk is Abba taking us to work with him every day. He gives us stuff to do but it's his work. It's not just busy work to keep us out of trouble while he attends meetings. It's important stuff he has as do as he trains us to be like him. Out of this relationship, there will be an outflowing of several spiritual disciplines. God is not whist about how he wants us to love him. He has gone to great lengths to make it abundantly clear. We find his invitation in his Word. Then he calls us to count the cost of that.

Being in a relationship with a person entails loving them the way *they* want/need to be loved as long as that isn't harmful to them or you. If my husband insisted on taking me to the mall, I'd be the most miserable bride on earth. I'm a Goodwill kinda gal. Take me junkin' and I'm happy as a clam at high tide. Sure I want the fancy stuff; I'm just willing to wait for it to show up at the thrift store for a price I'm willing to pay. Or if he had me spend hours traipsing mountains, which he loves to do—just shoot me now! My husband only knows that because I told him. So let's study those we love and aim to love them as they desire and need to be loved.

Recalling his military career, Rochester orders us to be vigilant, "Keeping your head on a swivel is to watch and pray…because the devil is serious"[1]—a lion on the prowl. Christian, keep your head on a swivel—just as the Angel of the Lord instructed Samson's mother to be *shomer*. Prayer is an indispensable discipline in our Christian walk. The apostle Paul, after describing the Armor of God, says,

> *And pray in the Spirit on all occasions*
> *with all kinds of prayers and requests.*
> *With this in mind, be alert and always*
> *keep on praying for all the Lord's people*
> (Ephesians 6:18).

Each of us is also to constantly meditate and fill our minds with the Word of God. We need to systematically read his word. We have a habit of picking and choosing what we want. I'm afraid there isn't a single other best-seller that's as picked at as a pile of produce at the end of the day. Here's another Jesus 6066 moment—God's Word isn't a 'catch and release' program where we take what we want and release what doesn't suit our sensitivities. If it's about being in a love relationship with him, we either take the word in its entirety or we leave it. If it's about choosing a "good" way to be a "good" person living a "good life" that's different. Lots of people do that and you're entitled to it. But that's not Christianity.

Scripture is God's outline of how he wants to be loved by us. He's not asking us to love him perfectly or get off the bus. He's asking us to nurture a heart that seeks diligently after him—tripping and falling all the way, getting up with his patient help and continuing on his path, till he carries us across that great threshold. It breaks his heart to have people walk away, but I think he'd rather you walked away than deceived yourself that you were in relationship when you weren't.

> *Be very careful, then, how you live—not as unwise*
> *but as wise, making the most of every opportunity,*
> *because the days are evil. Therefore, do not be*
> *foolish, but understand what the Lord's will is. Do*
> *not get drunk on wine, which leads to debauchery.*
> *Instead, be filled with the Spirit, speaking to one*
> *another with psalms, hymns, and songs from the*
> *Spirit. Sing and make music from your heart to the*
> *Lord, always giving thanks to God the Father for*
> *everything, in the name of our Lord Jesus Christ.*
> (Ephesians 5:16-20).

If you think you're a Jesus lover, picking and choosing what you're going to subscribe to in Scripture may be a sure way to tell if you're deceived. It is in Scripture we find His resuscitating breath— our very lifeline,

> *teaching, rebuking, correcting, and training in*
> *righteousness so that the servant of God may*
> *be thoroughly equipped for every good work*
> (2 Timothy 3:16–17).

> *I have hidden your word in my heart*
> *that I might not sin against you.*
> (Psalm 119:11).

We must also confront the pain from our past. That may be our failure or someone else failing us. Very few of us will outwardly reveal that we are seriously wounded inside or attempt to find help. Human, if you've been alive for any length of time, you are hurt. Many are even wounded. John Steinbeck says, "…Once a boy has suffered rejection, he will find rejection where it does not exist or worse, draw it forth from people simply by expecting it."[2] We nurse our wounds with the soiled bandages of denial and shame. We downplay our childhood trauma, not realizing that we carry it on our backs to this day.

We may be stuck in the shame that we didn't know how to grow past. This fallen world can fling us around mercilessly and spit us out. It is our responsibility to resist the temptation to withdraw from life and relationships. Wounds from our past leave us vulnerable to all kinds of other attacks, as though we're not hurting enough. From her years of experience being sex trafficked, Bender notes that, "Vulnerable people are highly at risk for human trafficking."[3] 'The vulnerable' are the spiritually and emotionally wounded, and it's as if they exude an odor that's an attractant for further victimization and abuse. Like sharks to blood, or bullies to a child with his head hung low, those stifling inner tears of failure from the past are at high risk for further wounding. Keep in mind that Satan is a brutal trafficker.

No matter what the source of your wounding is, do the hard work of seeking healing. Join a life group and live in authentic community. Have someone in your life that lovingly calls out the issues in your life. Practice saying "Thank you" when people correct you, instead of responding with defensiveness. Invite people to correct you. In my life, God used "Purely His Ministries" by Michelle Caswell, one of many high-quality Christian programs that address root issues of sin that keep us bound from going "all in" with Jesus. Another phenomenal resource is Dr. Neil Anderson's *Winning the Battle Within.* It outlines 7 practical, powerful steps to freedom in Christ. Dr. Anderson is the founder of Freedom in Christ Ministries (FICM.)

We must engage in tearing down provisions we've made that contribute to or foster our sinful habits. We can then erect provisions for righteousness. Here are some practical ways:

1. Above all else, trust Jesus. He knows and wants what's best for you. Surrender to him and seek his help. Tony Evans teaches, "Once we let go of self-ownership, we open the door to God coming in and helping us clean up the mess we've made."[4] Don't try to do this the other way around. Don't put the cart before the horse. You don't need to clean up before you come to him.

2. Live your life "before the Lord". Make him your true treasure, your *raison d'être*, your pillar, your hope, your motivation, your master, your glory, your joy, your all in all!

3. Explore your past. I was struck to find a common thread of predominant sins in my family history when I did this. I'd never connected the dots. Though we have numerous sins, it quickly became clear that family member after family member from generations past to current had fallen prey in these few specific temptations. That was very enlightening to me. Determine that with God's help and power, the buck stops with you, and do battle for your family.

4. What Jesus said regarding salvation applies to practical sanctification as well.

    > *Enter through the narrow gate. For wide*
    > *is the gate and broad is the road that leads*
    > *to destruction, and many enter through it.*
    > *But small is the gate and narrow the road*
    > *that leads to life, and only a few find it*
    > (Matthew 7:13).

    As followers of Jesus, we are admonished,

    > *If anyone desires to come after me, let him deny*
    > *himself, and take up his cross daily, and follow me*
    > (Luke 9:23).

    This, friends, paradoxically, is the abundant and victorious life, not worldly success. Your glory, beyond comparing to anything here on Earth, awaits you in heaven. Discipline and self-denial are signatures of a Jesus follower. Practice this in several arenas of your thought life—your imagination, your decision-making, your eating, your Bible reading time, controlling your temper, tendencies to control/manipulate people, etc.

As individuals, we need to fasten our belt of truth. Each of us must decide if we are going to continue like indulgent Uncle Jedidiah on the one extreme, or grow towards an attitude of discipline and self-control, like the soldiers of the cross that Christ has called us to be. From that stance, we will then either make provision for sin and wear suspenders to Thanksgiving and eat as though we'll never eat again, or resolve to enjoy a sufficient portion of what we are allowed to, and know when enough is enough. Work out your spiritual muscles by learning to say "no" to yourself and your sinful desires and "yes" to the things of God. Wake up and fight! Glory awaits you soon enough.

5. Don't just roll over and succumb to temptation. Tackle it at the threshold. Be *shomer* and expect to be tempted. Have and use a peep-hole in the door of your heart. Don't be caught unaware. Don't open the door, even to tell it you're not interested. Shoot your ballistic missiles of Scripture at it from a distance. Call for backup if you need it. Flee if it's threatening to break in. Be a soldier, vigilant and ready for action. If you fall for the temptation, don't camp in it or in shame. Remember productive shame is a crosswalk on a busy highway—get across quickly. Call on the name of the Lord to deliver and forgive you. Do it a thousand times a day if you need to. Don't give up!

6. As a body, when we take communion, which we can celebrate at every meal, we have a great opportunity to examine ourselves and constantly confess our sins to God and to each other.

7. Be gracious to one another. Forgive each other. Consider these phenomenal truths put out by Dr. Anderson in Gospel Light's Steps to Freedom in Christ. This is some of the most outstanding, in-depth, and practical work I have seen regarding forgiveness:

> It is inevitable that we will suffer at the hands of others no matter how righteous we live. Physical and emotional abuse can leave one

feeling bitter, anger (sic) and resentful. Our old fleshly nature seeks revenge and repayment, but the Holy Spirit says, "Forgive them just as Christ has forgiven us." "But you don't know how bad they hurt me," cries the victim. The wise pastor responds, "As long as you hang on to your bitterness, they are still hurting you. Forgiveness is what sets you free from your past and stops the pain. You don't heal in order to forgive; you forgive in order to heal."

Forgiveness is not forgetting. God says, "For I will forgive their wickedness and will remember their sins no more" (Heb. 8:12). That means God will not use our past sins against us in the future. He will remove them as far from us as the east is from the west (Ps. 103:12). We haven't forgiven another person if we continuously bring up their past and use it against them. Forgetting may be a long-term by-product of forgiving, but it is not the means by which we forgive. Forgiving is not tolerating sin. God forgives, but He never tolerates sins. We must forgive those who have wronged us, and then we should set up scriptural boundaries to stop further abuse.

Forgiveness is resolving to live with the consequences of another person's sin. But that's not fair! Of course it isn't fair, but you will have to anyway. Everybody is living with the consequences of somebody else's sin. We are all living with the consequence of Adam's sin. The only real choice is to do that in the bondage of bitterness or the freedom of forgiveness. If we are required by God to forgive as Christ has forgiven us, then how did Christ forgive us? He took our sins upon Himself. No person has truly forgiven another unless he has taken that person's sin upon himself. As long as we refuse to forgive, we are emotionally chained to past events and the people who hurt us. Forgiveness is to set the captive free and then realize that we are the captives. It is for our own benefit that we forgive others.

But where is the justice? The cross is what makes forgiveness morally correct. Christ died once for all our sins; his sins, her sins, your sins and my sins. But I want justice now! We will not have perfect justice in this lifetime. That is why there is a coming final judgment. But I want revenge! "Do not take revenge my friends, but leave room for God's wrath, for it is written: 'It is mine to avenge; I will repay,' says the Lord" (Rom. 12:19). But why should I let them off my hook? That is precisely why you should forgive, because you are still hooked to them. If you let them off your hook, are they off God's hook? What is to be gained in forgiving others is freedom from our past. God will make it right in the end.

Forgiving others does not mean that we don't testify in court against another. Nor does it mean that we don't confront a brother who is living in sin for the purpose of carrying out church discipline. Forgiving others makes our own heart right before God and allows us to experience our freedom in Christ. Only then can we righteously testify in court and confront others.[5]

8. Parents, start sex education when your children are babies. Call body parts by their real names. Teach children that their bodies are beautiful and amazing. There are no "bad," "dirty," or "naughty" parts, just some that can be shown and others that are private. The church must be involved in teaching quality, honest sex-education to our teens and young adults. Safe sex is

non-existent outside of marriage. The world is busy training and empowering prospective pornographers in how to beat the system with condoms and assurances of "marvelous medical breakthroughs to treat STDs, thus defying the institution of marriage as set forth in the Bible. This demonic reasoning has infiltrated into the church,"[5] says Rochester.

9. As a body, we need to start talking about pornography and idolatry seriously, from the top down and bottom up. Our leaders need people in their lives that ask the tough questions about purity and single-minded devotion to Jesus. Who is asking you the hard questions? Who are you asking the hard questions? We need more honest accountability among men, women, and children. Share truth, share struggles, share victories. We must create an atmosphere of sharing. In this way the church will be the fence at the top of the cliff and not just the ambulance at the bottom of it!

10. In sexual matters, cover your nakedness. Don't be a stumbling block to brothers and sisters by displaying body parts that need to be covered. Stop being suggestive in your appearance, your words, and your actions. A precious sister taught me what she's taught her son: that if a person is not aware or decent enough to cover their own nakedness, we are to cover it for them. How do we do that? Look the other way. Go the other way. Change the channel. Change the conversation. Do a Joseph and run out of your coat if Potiphar's wife grabs you. Teach this powerful principle to your young children. You may well save their lives.

11. Unmarried people, shacking up is pornography and has no value. It doesn't matter how in love you are or how long you've been together. Get married. A wedding doesn't have to be flamboyant or expensive. If money is holding you up from getting married, have your pastor marry you in a brief private ceremony after church one day. Then have a big party when you can afford it, if you need that. Beloved, get to the bottom of the social or finan-

cial issues contributing to this choice in your life. Is it another relationship complicating your current one? Is it the large tax break you get? Can you trust Jesus to breakthrough all that for you or are you determined that you've got it under control in your own strength?

12. Too many couples are entering marriage pregnant with the porn monster. The Church needs to wake up and start addressing this problem in pre-marital and in marriage counseling. We have to arm couples and parents with the tools they need to slay this monster. Many couples don't realize it's an issue in their loved one's life and counseling can be the perfect place to bring it up and address it.

13. On the home front, marital discord is undoubtedly the chief reason why married people engage in the various forms of pornography. Be people of grace and peace. Extend what Rochester calls "the olive branch instead of the meat-cleaver."[6] Don't be petty, angry or contentious. We can drive each other away without even knowing it. Instead, compromise, reconcile, and live in harmony as Psalm 133:1 admonishes. It is,

> *Better to dwell in the corner of a housetop than*
> *in a house shared with a contentious woman*
> (Proverbs 21:9).

Be strong and courageous without being headstrong. Spur each other on to good works, without spurring each other for spurring's sake, which can drive a spouse to the "housetop" of idolatry.

> *Be kind and compassionate to one*
> *another, forgiving each other, just*
> *as in Christ God forgave you*
> (Ephesians 4:32).

14. See God as a primary and vested partner in your marriage. Relish Cathy Goekler's phenomenal words,

> "If the *"I do"* at the marriage was a commitment
> to another person alone, the union is
> automatically weak. We're emotional creatures.
> In emotional states we make poor decisions.
> If our vows were made to God *and* to the
> other person, then at least one-third of the
> union will always be in His right mind and
> available to get the mess sorted out… One of
> God's functions in your marriage is filling you
> up with His love so you don't demand love
> from your mate that she can't give you and
> you can't give her. *"Love never fails."*[5] is about
> God's love, not human love. When we know
> we're loved by God absolutely, then we aren't'
> trying to get someone else to love us absolutely.
> We're free to enjoy what we each *can* give
> instead of always pecking for what we can't."[7]

15. Gary Chapman discusses 5 principles that he calls Reality Living. The third one says you cannot change others but you can influence them.[7] Give up controlling your spouse. Let them be who they are. They don't need to be like you. Your marriage doesn't need two of *you*! Moreover, you are not God; therefore, you can't change them. The Holy Trinity doesn't have any employment openings currently. They will be sure to notify you when they do. You can spur people on to good works but trying to constantly change your spouse is a clear rejection of them, the gift God has given you. Furthermore, maybe God gave you your spouse the way they are to put up with you the way you are.

Accept one another, then, just as Christ
accepted you, in order to bring praise to God
(Romans 15:7).

16. Dr. Chapman, discusses our basic needs as love, freedom, significance, recreation, and peace with God. When these areas are fulfilled, our emotional tanks are filled. God, our spouses, and other people in our lives fill these tanks. Be mindful of your own tank levels as well as your spouse's. Work assertively to monitor and maintain each area, depending on its importance to you. Reductions in levels of fulfillment in these areas may cause strain in a relationship, and give various forms of pornography a foothold.

    Chapman's book *The Five Love Languages* is another excellent tool that people can use to come to a better understanding of their own and other people's communication and love styles and so enhance relationships.

17. People, put down the smut! Women, replace Cosmopolitan magazine with Corinthians and Harlequin novels with Hebrews. Men, trade in Penthouse for Proverbs and Grisham for Galatians.

18. Women, offer your husband good sex. Men, offer your wives beautiful sex. The old joke goes:

    > "Doctor: Are you sexually active?
    > Patient: No, I just lie there."

    That's funny. But it's not. No matter your age, let the days of lying like a limp rag during sex be a thing of the past. Address the issues that contribute to your lack of desire or involvement. Speak to your doctor about medical matters that affect you sexually. Decide in your heart to make this an act of worship and blow your spouse away. You don't have to engage in outlandish, ridiculous antics, either. Simple sex can be amazing if your heart is in it.

    In their fabulous book, Dillow and Pintus guide Christian women to grow toward being responsive, adventurous, uninhibited, expressive, and sensuous lovers[9] regardless of your age. Give yourself permission to be sensuous. You get to be! God has sanctioned it for you. Take off the attitude of tedium. Strip off the dreary mindset of sex being a never-ending chore. I remember that for years, whenever my husband was feeling amorous, I would roll my eyes, drop my tone an octave and groan, "Again?" with as much melancholic drama as I could muster. Ask God to renew your mind and its attitudes. In the moment, ask Him to help you when you don't have the desire.

A lady in their book challenged me. She claimed that at sixty years of age, she was enjoying her body more than ever. What? Crepe-like skin on baggy arms and saggy body parts and all? Yup, with cellulite to boot! Rachel Hollis reminds us that, "having a low opinion of your body is so damaging to your ability to enjoy sex. I used to worry about whether or not my tummy was tight or if my butt looked okay in those panties. You know what Dave was thinking when I took off my clothes? *Boobies!*"[10]

Your man does has had it up to here hearing you go on and on about how fat you are, and how unattractive. Don't you realize that your body is a wonderland? That's Hannah TK chapter 1 verse 1. Highlight it. Your body is marvelous and thrilling and amazing. Get that in your head and memorize it! Love what you've got and stop being ridiculous. That or do something about your body. Another wondrous miracle of God is that as things on your body head south, your husband's vision gets worse. So he really has no idea what you're talking about. Roll with that.

19. For a struggling Christian, spouses are the first line of defense and are most vested. Spouse, walk in the truth and don't lie to yourself. If you suspect your spouse is involved in pornography/idolatry in its various forms, expose it. (That said, if you are prone to unfounded jealousy, knock it off. Train your brain to trust. It is utterly exhausting to live with a spouse who sees things that don't exist and is constantly suspicious. Ask the Lord to help you overcome that snare.) Denial is a serious problem in our marriages. One spouse suspects that things aren't quite right but says nothing. How many stories have we heard of children

who were molested for years and a parent or grandparent knew and never said a word? This is inexcusable. We are slaying our children at the altar of pornography, sacrificing them to Satan, the god of this world, in cold blood. Our silence and avoidance are exacerbating these issues.

Of course, we must be "wise as serpents" in the manner in which we handle matters like these, or in the way we confront each other when we suspect sin. This can be the difference between further division or healing. In sexual matters, here are some warning signs (these may apply to other besetting habits.)

- A married couple may have separate bank accounts, but more importantly, one person's expenditure is secret from the spouse. This is especially a problem if one of the spouses isn't completely on board with this arrangement.
- Erratic communication breakdown is a clue. Many spouses report that they knew that something wasn't quite right when their spouse was cheating on them. If the emotional atmosphere in the house or relationship changes dramatically from time to time, the couple needs help.
- Unexplained late hours at work, especially if coupled with abnormal closed communication where you can't reach your spouse for a significant amount of time
- Jumpy behavior such as sudden changes of TV channels or computer screens when you enter the room
- Keeping close company with known pornographers
- Abstaining from sex is a huge red flag. The apostle Paul teaches that regular sexual intimacy should be the norm except for stints of fasting and prayer.

Now for the matters you wrote about: It is good for
a man not to have sexual relations with a woman.
But since sexual immorality is occurring, each
man should have sexual relations with his own
wife, and each woman with her own husband.
The husband should fulfill his marital duty to his

wife, and likewise the wife to her husband. The wife does not have authority over her own body but yields it to her husband. In the same way, the husband does not have authority over his own body but yields it to his wife. Do not deprive each other except perhaps by mutual consent and for a time, so that you may devote yourselves to prayer. Then come together again so that Satan will not tempt you because of your lack of self-control
(1 Corinthians 7:1-5).

20. While fighting for your marriage, seek wise counsel and do not discuss your marriage with busybodies and gossips with worldly mindsets. Instead, seek counsel from a wise, older, godly saint. Use discretion in all matters.

21. Don't blame your spouse for your behavior. We established that you are a volunteer, not a victim. Don't behave like a victim. If your spouse claims they engage in idolatry because you made them (e.g. how you treat them, or because of your appearance, etc.) that's garbage. Adults, take responsibility for your own actions and seek help where needed. It is infantile to blame others for our sins.

22. Don't make desperate, fleshly attempts to appease a pornographer. You can't compete with idolatry. Remember Tenbergen's cardboard butterfly, fickle and fake as it is, you can't compete with it. The desire for it is a disordered brain. As a wife, do not do "things seen in porn to keep your husband interested." Rochester admonishes, don't let your "husband make you do things that you are not comfortable with. Never allow your minds to harbor the thought that if you don't "perform," your husband will reject you. Chances are if you decide what he wants out of compulsion, and it doesn't work out, then he'll go back to porn anyway."[11] Do not cater to or endorse sinful behavior in

those you love. Point them to the light, don't shove them deeper into the mire by going along with their behavior.

23. God's word is clear regarding homosexuality. It displeases him, to put it mildly. If you have same sex attraction, as in all other matters of idolatry, get on the same page as God and believe that your Maker knows what is best for you. Choose him over your desires. Work overtime to

> *demolish arguments and every pretension that sets*
> *itself up against the knowledge of God, and we take*
> *captive every thought to make it obedient to Christ*
> (2 Corinthians 10:5).

24. Emotional affairs are not a naughty but innocuous pastime. If you are struggling with one, flee with everything you have. Sin is crouching at your door. Quit putting yourself out there. Certainly don't find a way to let your "crush" know about it. Put your flesh to death by praying for that person's faith and for their marriage, if they have one. That'll kill two birds with one stone. Pray for their purity. Determine to give your own spouse, if you have one, that same degree of attention. If you don't keep nurturing it, it probably won't last forever.

25. Believe that God has a plan for you through delivery from the trap that has ensnared you. Ask for his help. He has a plan. Be convinced that he will see you through, just as he helped Abraham, "against all hope." Once loosed, you can run into the Death Den and help others out! Remember,

> *Everything exposed by the light becomes visible—*
> *and everything that is illuminated becomes a light*
> (Ephesians 5:14).

Your confession and resulting story will be your authority to shine light for others in darkness so they can come to freedom.

26. If a Christian will not repent of his sin and make a concerted effort to make amends with ALL the people he has hurt, the Bible clearly outlines what needs to happen to him. It is the same thing that Jesus, the friend of sinners, did.

> *I wrote to you in my letter not to associate with*
> *sexually immoral people—not at all meaning*
> *the people of this world who are immoral,*
> *or the greedy and swindlers, or idolaters. In*
> *that case you would have to leave this world.*
> *But now I am writing to you that you must*
> *not associate with anyone who claims to be*
> *a brother or sister but is sexually immoral or*
> *greedy, an idolater or slanderer, a drunkard or*
> *swindler. Do not even eat with such people.*
> *What business is it of mine to judge those*
> *outside the church? Are you not to judge*
> *those inside? God will judge those outside.*
> *"Expel the wicked person from among you*
> (1 Corinthians 5:9-12).

Like sharks to blood, or bullies to a child
with his head hung low, those who stifle
inner tears of failure from the past are
at high risk for further wounding.

Chapter 34

A Wake-Up Call

The World Health Organization reports that we have 5.1 million confirmed cases of Covid-19 worldwide.[1] There were 7.58 billion people on earth in 2019.[2] That means that approximately 7out of 10,000 people are infected. Saints, compared to this pandemic, which has brought the world to its knees, the statistics we saw regarding pornography are staggering! And that's just one form of one type of idolatry. We can no longer afford to wave this off, as those who first waved Covid-19 off as a mere flu. The stakes are too high.

Church of God, a real pandemic is ravaging the camp. A cancerous monster is incubating in the womb of our hearts. Too many stand in the pulpit or smugly sit in the pews and in Bible studies conscientiously cultivating the growth of this malignant fetal monster in the warm, dark womb of secrecy. It deeply grieves our Savior. It's hamstringing our work and our impact in reaching the world for Christ. Ever got behind the bumper sticker that says, "Jesus is alright, it's his followers I can't stand"? I'm afraid much of that may have to do with one aspect or another that we've discussed in this book. Friend, we have a choice and must valiantly stand up against the idolatry and self-centeredness we harbor in our hearts. We must shine the healing light of exposure on it. We must repent and be sanctified.

Come, let us bow down in worship, let us kneel
before the Lord our Maker; for he is our God
and we are the people of his pasture, the flock
under his care. Today, if only you would hear his

> *voice,* **Do not harden your hearts** *as you did*
> *at Meribah, as you did that day at Massah in*
> *the wilderness, where your ancestors tested me;*
> *they tried me, though they had seen what I did*
> (Psalm 95:7b-9, emphasis added).

Are you napping in death's den, snoring away on Delilah's lap? No good awaits you there. No matter how much pleasure she brings you, her plans are to steal, kill, and destroy you. Her pleasure is bait. Empty, destructive calories. It's only a matter of time. You don't belong there. Run, Christian, run!

> *The hour has already come for you to wake up*
> *from your slumber, because our salvation is nearer*
> *now than when we first believed. The night is*
> *nearly over; the day is almost here. So let us put*
> *aside the deeds of darkness and put on the armor*
> *of light. Let us behave decently, as in the daytime,*
> *not in carousing and drunkenness, not in sexual*
> *immorality and debauchery… Rather, clothe*
> *yourselves with the Lord Jesus Christ, and do not*
> *think about how to gratify the desires of the flesh*
> (Romans 13:11b-14).

If you've read this far, I pray that your passions, appetites, purposes, desires, affections, thoughts, and endeavors are freshly attuned to the directorship of the Holy Spirit. I pray that you have a grander picture of how sweetly and deeply you are loved; how powerfully you are empowered for godliness by the Lover of your Soul. I pray that your faith has been furthered. I pray that your knowledge has increased. I pray that your hope has been set on fire. Reread it and share it.

Unsettle me.

These are the two words rattling about in my brain today. I almost wish it was a more glamorous prayer…

The funny thing is I've spent my whole existence trying to find a place to settle down. People to settle down with. And a spirit about me worthy of all this settled down-ness.
All of this is good. A contented heart, thankful for its blessings is a good way to settle.
But there are areas of my life that have also settled that mock my desires to be a godly woman. Compromises if you will.
Attitudes that I've wrapped in the lie, "Well, that's just how I am. And if that's all the bad that's in me, I'm doing pretty good."
I dare you, dear soul of mine, to notice the stark evidence of a spirit that is tainted and a heart that must be placed under the microscope of God's word. Yes, indeed, unsettle me Lord.
Unearth that remnant of unforgiveness.
Shake loose that justification for compromise.
Reveal that broken shard of pride.
Expose that tendency to distrust.

Unsettle me in the best kind of way. For when I allow your touch to reach the deepest parts of me—dark and dingy and hidden away too long—suddenly, a fresh wind of life twists and twirls and dances through my soul.

I can delight in forgiveness and love more deeply. I can discover my gentle responses and find softer ways for my words to land.

I can recognize the beauty of humility and crave the intimacy with God it unleashes.
I can rest assured though harsh winds blow, I will be held.
Goodbye to my remnants, my justification, shards, and tendencies. This is not who I am— nor who I was created to be.

Goodbye to shallow love, sharp words, self-focus, and suspicious fears. I am an unsettled woman who no longer wishes to take part in your distractions or distructions (sic).
Welcome deeper love, softer words, unleashed intimacy, and the certainty I am held.[3]

May the zealous spirit of Phinehas, in the book of Numbers chapter 8, burn within us when pornography, in all its forms is flagrantly flaunted. He thrust a fornicating couple through with a javelin, effectively stopping God's judgement in the form of a plague that ravaged the camp. We need many a modern-day Phinehas to stand up in our churches to call out and address the pandemic. We need valiant children, men, and women to put a check to it in their own lives.

Arise, mighty warriors; awaken, children of the King. Be *shomer*. This is no time to be napping in the den of death. Get off Delilah's murderous lap. Be holy, as He is holy. Be strong and courageous. It won't be long, stand firm then! In a chapter where Jesus spoke twice about marriage, he summarizes the greatest commandment:

> *Jesus replied: "'Love the Lord your God with all your heart and with all your soul and with all your mind.' This is the first and greatest commandment. And the second is like it: 'Love your neighbor as yourself.' All the Law and the Prophets hang on these two commandments* (Matthew 22:37-39).

Now may the God of peace, who through the blood of the eternal covenant brought back from the dead our Lord Jesus, that great Shepherd of the sheep, equip you with everything good for doing His will, and may He work in us what is pleasing to Him, through Jesus Christ, to whom be glory for ever and ever. Amen
(Hebrews 13:20).

May God Himself, the God of peace, sanctify you through and through. May your whole spirit, soul and body be kept blameless at the coming of our Lord Jesus Christ. The one who calls you is faithful, and **He will do it**!
(1 Thessalonians 5:23, 24, emphasis added).

Beloved, take off your muddy gumboots and make yourself comfortable while I make us a cup of chai. We are waiting to hear your story. What are you waiting for?

"The law of the Lord is perfect, refreshing the soul.
The statutes of the Lord are trustworthy,
making wise the simple.
The precepts of the Lord are right,
giving joy to the heart.
The commands of the Lord are radiant,
giving light to the eyes.
The fear of the Lord is pure, enduring forever.
The decrees of the Lord are firm,
and all of them are righteous.

They are more precious than gold,
than much pure gold;
they are sweeter than honey, than
honey from the honeycomb.
By them your servant is warned;
in keeping them there is great reward.
But who can discern their own errors?
Forgive my hidden faults.
Keep your servant also from willful
sins; may they not rule over me.
Then I will be blameless, innocent
of great transgression.

May these words of my mouth and
this meditation of my heart
be pleasing in your sight,
Lord, my Rock and my Redeemer"
(Psalm 19:7-14).

References

CHAPTER 2—*In The Temptress's Arms*

1   TerKeurst, Lysa. 2011. *Made to Crave.* Grand Rapids: Zondervan.

CHAPTER 3—*Of Pornography and Idolatry*

1   *Helps Word Studies, s.v.* "pornography," accessed June 30, 2019, https://Bible-hub.com/greek/4202.htm.
2   *The NAS New Testament Greek Lexicon, s.v.* "porneia," accessed June 30, 2019, https://www.Biblestudytools.com/lexicons/greek/nas/porneia.html.
3   Anderson, Neil. 2008. *Winning the Battle Within.* Eugene: Harvest House Publishers.
4   *Blue Letter Bible, s.v.* "spirit," accessed June 30, 2019, https://www.blueletterBible.org/lang/lexicon/lexicon.cfm?t=kjv&strongs=h7307.
5   Rochester, Fred. 2009. *Secret Sexual Sins: Understanding a Christian's Desire for Pornography.* Denver: Outskirts Press. 2009.

CHAPTER 4—*The State of the Heart*

1   Gallagher, Steve. 2004. *A Biblical Guide to Counseling.* Dry Ridge: Pure Life Ministries.
2   Ibid.
3   Tozer, A. W. 2008. *Mornings with Tozer: Daily Devotional Readings,* compiled by Gerald B. Smith. Chicago: Moody Publishers.
4   Harris, Laird, Archer Jr., Gleason L., and Bruce K. Waltke. 2004. *Theological Wordbook of the Old Testament.* Chicago: Moody Press.
5   Genesis 6:5.
6   Matthew 5:28.
7   Harrell. *The True Nature.*
8   Ibid.
9   Shaw, Mark. 2018. *The Heart of Addiction: A Biblical Perspective.* Bemidji: Focus Publishing.

CHAPTER 5—*The Pandemic of Pornography in the Pew and the Pulpit*

1 Crombie, Noelle. "No Mercy." *The Oregonian*, October 8, 2019.

CHAPTER 6—*My Besetting Sin*

1 2 Samuel 6: 5, 14, 16, 17, 21.
2 *Dictionary.com, s.v.* "beset," accessed March 30, 2020, https://www.dictionary.com/browse/beset?s=t.
3 Maddox, Maeve. "Daily Writing Tips." A Besetting Sin. Accessed February 2, 2020.
   https://www.dailywritingtips.com/a-besetting-sin/.

CHAPTER 7—*Mine Was a Happy Childhood Until…*

1 Van Cleave, Steven et al. 1987. *Counseling for Substance Abuse and Addiction*, edited by Gary R. Collins, 93. Dallas: Word Incorporated.
2 Kolber, Aundi. 2020. "When You're in Need of a Fresh Approach to Move Out of Anxiety, Stress, and Survival Mode." Accessed May 11, 2020. https://annvoskamp.com/2020/05/when-youre-in-need-of-a-fresh-approach-to-move-out-of-anxiety-stress-and-survival-mode/

CHAPTER 8—*The Anatomy of Salvation*

1 2 Peter 3:9.
2 John 20:31.
3 Augustus M. Toplady. 1776. "Rock of Ages." https://library.timelesstruths.org/music/Rock_of_Ages/.
4 Spurgeon, Charles. 1888. "David Dancing before the Ark Because of His Election." Accessed March 1, 2020. https://www.spurgeon.org/resource-library/sermons/david-dancing-before-the-ark-because-of-his-election#flipbook/.

CHAPTER 9—*Sin Leading to Death*

1 1 Corinthians 11:30.

CHAPTER 10—*The Anatomy of Porneia*

1 Gibbons, Luke. 2018. "15 Statistics About the Church and Pornography That Will Blow Your Mind." Last modified September 18, 2018. https://www.charismanews.com/us/73208-15-statistics-about-the-church-and-pornography-that-will-blow-your-mind.
2 Kinnaman, David. 2016. "The Porn Phenomenon." Last modified February 5, 2016. https://www.barna.com/the-porn-phenomenon/.

3   Weaver, Andrew, Hosenfeld, Charlene, and Harold Koenig. 2007. *Counseling Persons with Addictions and Compulsion: A Handbook for Clergy and Other Helping Professionals.* Cleveland: Pilgrim Press.

4   Gallagher, Steve. 2004. *"A Biblical Guide to Counseling the Sexual Addict."* Dry Ridge: Pure Life Ministries.

CHAPTER 11—*The Physiology of Addiction—Part 1*

1   Herculano-Houzel, Suzana. 2009. "The Human Brain in Numbers: A Linearly Scaled-up Primate Brain." Frontiers in Human Neuroscience, vol. 9, no. 31. https://www.ncbi.nlm.nih.gov/pmc/articles/PMC2776484/.

2   "Brain Basics: The Life and Death of a Neuron." 2019. The National Institute for Neurological Disorders and Stroke. Last modified December 16, 2019. https://www.ninds.nih.gov/Disorders/Patient-Caregiver-Education/Life-and-Death-Neuron.

3   Gage, Fred H. 2002. "Neurogenesis in the Adult Brain." Journal of Neuroscience. 1 February 2002. 22 (3) 612-613; DOI: https://doi.org/10.1523/JNEUROSCI.22-03-00612.2002.

4   Paolo, Calabresi, Picconi, Barbara, Tozzi, Alessandro, and Di Filippo, Massimiliano. 2007. "Dopamine-mediated regulation of corticostriatal synaptic plasticity." *Trends in Neurosciences*, 30, no. 5: 211–219. Accessed January 19, 2020. https://www.sciencedirect.com/science/article/abs/pii/S0166223607000483.

5   Nestler, Eric J, Barrot, M., Self, D. W. 2001. "DeltaFosB: a sustained molecular switch for addiction." *Proceeding of the National Academy of Science U S A.* 98 (20): 11042-6. https://www.ncbi.nlm.nih.gov/pubmed/11572966.

6   Lewis, Marc. 2015. *The Biology of Desire.* New York: Public Affairs.

7   Fehlhaber, Kate. 2012. "The Reward Pathway Reinforces Behavior." Last modified October 31, 2012. https://knowingneurons.com/2012/10/31/the-reward-pathway-reinforces-behavior/

8   Villines, Zawn. 2017. "What Does the Frontal Lobe Do?" *Medical News Today.* Last modified June 29, 2017. https://www.medicalnewstoday.com/articles/318139#Effects-of-damage-to-the-frontal-lobe.

9   Lewis, Marc. 2017. "Addiction and the Brain: Development, Not Disease." *US National Library of Medicine, National Institutes of Health, Neuroethics.* 10 (1): 7–18. https://www.ncbi.nlm.nih.gov/pmc/articles/PMC5486526/

CHAPTER 12—*The Physiology of Addiction—Part 2*

1   Grant, Jon, and Samuel Chamberlain. 2013. "Expanding the Definition of Addiction: DSM-5 vs. ICD-11." *World Psychiatry* 12(2): 92–98. https://www.ncbi.nlm.nih.gov/pmc/articles/PMC3683251/.

2   Regier, Darrel, Kuhl, Emily, and David J. Kupfer. 2013. "The DSM-5: Classification and criteria changes." *World Psychiatry.* https://www.ncbi.nlm.nih.gov/pmc/articles/PMC5328289/.

[3] Grant and Chamberlain. "Expanding the Definition."

[4] Regier, Kuhl, and Kupfer. "The DSM-5."

[5] Grant, Jon E., Murad Atmaca, Naomi A. Fineberg, Leonardo F. Fontenelle, Hisato Matsunaga, YC Janardhan Reddy, Helen Blair Simpson, Per Hove Thomsen, Odile A van den Heuvel, David Veale, Douglas W Woods, and Dan J Stein. 2014. "Impulse control disorders and "behavioral addictions" in the ICD-11." *World Psychiatry* 13(2): 125–127. https://www.ncbi.nlm.nih.gov/pmc/articles/PMC4102276/.

[6] McVey, Steve, and Quarles, Mike. 2012. *Helping Others Overcome Addictions.* Eugene: Harvest House.

CHAPTER 13—*Adverse Childhood Events (ACES)*

[1] Perry, Jackie. 2018. *Gay Girl, Good God.* Nashville: B&H Publishing Group.

[2] Piper, John. 2013. "The Renewed Mind and How to Have it." Accessed May 26, 2020. YouTube video. 3.23. https://www.youtube.com/watch?v=ApIg22vig-BI&t=1024s.

[3] Anderson, Neil. 2008. *Winning the Battle Within.* Eugene: Harvest House Publishers.

[4] Van Cleave et al. *Counseling for Substance Abuse.*

[5] Stevens, Jane. 2017. "Addiction doc says: It's not the drugs. It's the ACES… adverse childhood experiences," Last modified May 2, 2019. https://ACES-toohigh.com/2017/05/02/addiction-doc-says-stop-chasing-the-drug-focus-on-ACES-people-can-recover/.

[6] Barret, Dierdre. 2010. "Supernormal Stimuli." The Scientist. Last modified February 19, 2010. https://www.the-scientist.com/daily-news/supernormal-stimuli-43491.

[7] Moore, Beth. 2015. *Believing God.* Nashville: B&H Publishing Group.

[8] Perry, *Gay Girl.*

CHAPTER 14—*God's SWAT Team Comes for You*

[1] Hunt, Michael. 2012. The Significance of Numbers in Scripture. Last modified May, 2012. https://www.agapebiblestudy.com/documents/The%20Significance%20of%20Numbers%20in%20Scripture.htm

[2] All Hebrew words translated using Riversoft Information System developers. "MySword." Study the Bible on your Android mobile device (cellphone or tablet) offline, Mysword for Android 11.1. https://www.mysword-bible.info/ Accessed on July 1, 2020.

[3] 1779. "Amazing Grace." John Newton.

CHAPTER 15—Of "Holey" Rugs and Filthy Carpets

[1] Harrell, William. 2009. "The True Nature of the Christian's Heart." Banner of Truth. Last modified January 27, 2009. https://banneroftruth.org/us/resources/articles/2009/the-true-nature-of-the-christians-heart/.

[2] Gaffigan, Jim. 2016. "Working Out" November 11, 2016. YouTube Video, 8:47. https://www.youtube.com/watch?v=8tNyWyrkaiI&t=524s

[3] Evans, Tony. n.d. "Power Versus Authority." Tony Evans the Urban Alternative (blog). Accessed February 12, 2020. https://tonyevans.org/power-verses-authority/.

[4] Francesca Battistelli. 2017. "Defender." https://francescamusic.com/.

[5] "2 Timothy 1:7 Commentary." Precept Austin. Last modified April 29, 2020. https://www.preceptaustin.org/2_timothy_17.

[6] Anderson, *Winning the Battle*.

[7] Hunt, June. 2011. *How to Defeat Harmful Habits: Freedom from Six Addictive Behaviors*. Eugene: Harvest House Publisher.

[8] Ibid.

CHAPTER 16—What's So Wonderful about Sex?

[1] Chapman, Gary. 2008. *Desperate Marriages: Moving Toward Hope and Healing in Your Relationship*. Chicago: Northfield Publishing.

[2] Reinke, Tony. 2017. *12 Ways Your Phone is Changing You*. Wheaton: Crossway.

[3] Ibid, 95.

[4] Kimberling, Kim. 2015. "7 Deadly Sins and Your Marriage—# 5 Lust." Awesome Marriage. Last modified August 7, 2015. https://awesomemarriage.com/blog/7-deadly-sins-and-your-marriage-5-lust?rq=Lust.

[5] Gresh, Dana. 2009. "Yada, Yada, Yada!" Last modified November 16, 2009. https://liesyoungwomenbelieve.com/yada-yada-yada/.

[6] "Study Guide for Matthew 5 by David Guzik." Blue Letter Bible. Accessed September 2, 2019. https://www.blueletterBible.org/Comm/archives/guzik_david/StudyGuide_Mat/Mat_5.cfm

[7] Matthew 22:37-40.

CHAPTER 17—God's Goals vs. Satan's

[1] Perry, *Gay Girl*.

CHAPTER 18—Overindulging Does Not Mean Cherishing

[1] Alexandra Katehakis. *Mirror of Intimacy*. Daily Meditation email. January 5, 2020.

2   Alexandra Katehakis. *Mirror of Intimacy.* Daily Meditation email. January 10, 2020.
3   Crombie. "No Mercy."
4   Lemmel, Helen Howarth. 1922. *The Heavenly Vision.* Retrieved August 26, 2020. https://www.hymnal.net/en/hymn/h/645.

CHAPTER 19—*My Mission*

1   Casting Crowns. 2005. "Stained Glass Masquerade." Track # 4 on Lifesong. Billboard Christian Albums, CD. https://www.google.com/search?q=stained+-glass+masquerade+lyrics+casting+crowns&oq=st&aqs=chrome.1.69i59l2j69i-57j0l5.2732j0j8&sourceid=chrome&ie=UTF-8

CHAPTER 20—*7 Reasons Why We Engage in Porn*

1   Rochester, *Secret.*
2   Ibid.
3   Janssen, Erick. "Why People Use Porn." Frontline. Accessed July 19, 2019. https://www.pbs.org/wgbh/pages/frontline/shows/porn/special/why.html
4   Bender, Rebecca. 2020. *In Pursuit of Love: One Woman's Journey from Trafficked to Triumphant.* Grand Rapids: Zondervan.
5   Gallagher, *Counseling the Sexual Addict.*
6   Shaw, *The Heart of Addiction.*
7   Kolehmainen, Hannah. 2020. "Dreams—Part 1. The Secret Counsel." Last modified 3/24/2020. https://tribalminded.com/2020/03/24/my-dream-the-secret-counsel/.
8   Shaw, *The heart of addiction.*
9   Hunt, *Defeat Harmful Habits.*
10 Shaw, *The heart of Addiction*

CHAPTER 21—*13 Problems with Porn*

1   "Proverbs 6." Bible Study Tools. Accessed October 14, 2019. https://www.Biblestudytools.com/commentaries/matthew-henry-complete/proverbs/6.html.
2   Reinke, *12 Ways your Phone.*
3   Anderson, *Winning the Battle.*
4   Brooks, G. R. 1995. "The Centerfold Syndrome: How Men Can Overcome Objectification and Achieve Intimacy with Women." San Francisco: Bass. Cited in Yoder; V. C., Virden, T. B., & Amin, K. (2005). Internet Pornography and Loneliness: An Association? Sexual Addiction and Compulsivity, 12, 19-44. doi:10.1080/10720160590933653
5   Anderson, *Winning the Battle.*

6   "How The Porn Industry Capitalizes On the Loneliness and Depression of Its Consumers." Accessed October 10, 2019. https://fightthenewdrug.org/why-porn-leaves-you-lonelier-than-before/.

7   Reinke, *12 Things your Phone*.

8   Hunt, *Defeat Harmful Habits*.

9   Rochester, Secret.

10   Anderson, *Winning the Battle*.

11   Johnson, Eric. "Seattle is Dying." Accessed April 15, 2020. YouTube Video 20:30, 22:13, 25:22. https://www.youtube.com/watch?v=bpAi70WWBlw.

12   Gallagher, *Counseling the Sexual Addict*.

13   Reinke, *12 Ways*.

14   Rochester, *Secret*.

15   Lewis, *The Complete C. S. Lewis Signature*.

16   Anderson, *Winning*.

17   Rochester, *Secret*.

18   Kirk, Marshall, and Madsen, Hunter. *After the Ball—How America Will Conquer Its Fear and Hatred of Gays in The Nineties*. New York: Plume, 1990.

19   Gallagher, *Counseling the Sexual Addict*.

20   C. S. Lewis, *The Complete C. S. Lewis*.

CHAPTER 22—*20 Ways We Despise the "Pleasant Land"*

1   Barrett, "Supernormal Stimuli."

CHAPTER 23—*Temptation*

1   Rochester, *Secret Sexual Sin*.

2   Blue Collar Comedy. "You Might Be A Redneck." YouTube Video 5:52. Accessed April 15, 2020. https://www.youtube.com/watch?v=PX4XrcKyBN, 4.

3   Rochester, *Secret Sexual Sin*.

4   Ibid.

5   Gallagher, *Counseling the Sexual Addict*.

6   Goekler, Cathy. 2013. *Rev Your Wife's Engine*. Bloomington: Westbow Press.

7   Gallagher, *Counseling the Sexual Addict*.

CHAPTER 24—*The Purpose of Shame*

1   Burgo, Joseph. "Why is Shame Good." Last formatted April 18, 2019. https://www.vox.com/first-person/2019/4/18/18308346/shame-toxic-productive.

2   Vaknin, Sam. "Narcissism, Shame, Happiness." EC Psychology and Psychiatry. Last modified March 01, 2019. https://www.ecronicon.com/ecpp/pdf/ECPP-08-00426.pdf.

CHAPTER 25—*We're All Pornographers*

1. Keyes, Richard. 2008. "Defining Idolatry." The Idol Factory. Last modified February 3, 2008. http://uptown.apostles.nyc/sermons/2008/02/defining-idolatry/.
2. Nowalk, Nick. 2015. "Idolatry and Sexual Immorality: Cause and Effect." Last modified December 30, 2015. https://www.christianunion.org/publications-media/christian-union-the-magazine/past-issues/fall-2015/1036-idolatry-and-sexual-immorality.
3. Gallagher, *A Biblical Guide to Counseling*.
4. Lewis, C. S. 2002. "Mere Christianity," in The Complete C. S. Lewis Signature Classics. New York: Harper Collins.
5. Calvin, John. 1960. *Institutes of the Christian Religion,* edited by John T. McNeill. Philadelphia: Westminster.
6. Barrett, Deirdre. 2010. "Supernormal Stimuli." *The Scientist.* Last modified Feb 18, 2010. https://www.the-scientist.com/daily-news/supernormal-stimuli-43491.
7. *Thayer's Greek Lexicon, s.v.* "convict," accessed March 1, 2020, https://Biblehub.com/greek/1651.htm.
8. Spurgeon, *David Dancing*.

CHAPTER 26—*Dr. Exposure*

1. Rochester, *Secret*.
2. Ibid.
3. Perry, *Gay Girl*.
4. Chandler, Greg. 2013. "The Stench of Sin" Goodlane Church of Christ. Last modified December 26, 2013. https://www.teachingtruth.org/resources/Bible-articles/2013/12/26/the-stench-of-sin.
5. Spurgeon, "David Dancing."
6. Ibid.

CHAPTER 27—*Repentance*

1. Anderson, Winning the Battle.
2. Piper, "The Renewed Mind." 12.45.
3. Goekler, Cathy. "Capable." Email. 2020.
4. The Oregonian. 2020. "Mercy Corps board: 'We apologize unreservedly' to Tania Culver Humphrey." Last modified February 5th, 2020. https://www.oregonlive.com/news/2020/02/mercy-corps-board-we-apologize-unreservedly-to-tania-culver-humphrey.html

CHAPTER 28—*Standing Firm*

1 Gallagher, *Counseling the Sexual Addict.*
2 Rochester, *Secret Sexual Sins.*
3 Subby, Robert. 1987. *Lost in the Shuffle—The Co-dependent Reality.* Deerfield Beach: Health Communications.
4 Shaw, *The heart.*
5 Covenant Worship. 2020. "Just One Drop." Single. Colorado: Integrity. (Retrieved from https://rocketlyrics.com/song/5e5416b3da7dd1006829bad5.)
6 Hebrews 9:22.
7 Hebrews 10:4.
8 John 19:30.

CHAPTER 29—*The Solution of Sanctification*

1 Gallagher, *Counseling.*
2 Goekler, *Rev,* 11.

CHAPTER 31—*The Church's Response—Rescue*

1 Rochester, *Secret.*
2 Hill, Wesley. 2010. *Washed and Waiting.* Grand Rapids: Zondervan.

CHAPTER 33—*Practical Steps to Intimacy*

1 Rochester, *Secret Sexual Sins.*
2 Steinbeck, John. 1952. *East of Eden.* New York: Penguin Books.
3 Bender, *In Pursuit of Love.*
4 Tony Evans. "Give it All Away." The Urban Alternative. Accessed April 1, 2020, https://tonyevans.org/give-it-all-away/.
5 Anderson, Neil. "Forgiving Others." Freedom in Christ Ministries. Accessed May 2019. https://ficm.org/neilsblogs/forgiving-others/.
6 Rochester, *Secret.*
7 Goekler, *Rev you Wife's Engine.*
8 Chapman, *Desperate Marriages.*
9 Dillow, Lorraine, and Linda Pintus. 2002. *Intimate Issues.* Colorado: Waterbrook Press.
10 Hollis, Rachel. 2018. *Girl, Wash Your Face.* Nashville: Nelson Books.
11 Rochester, *Secret.*

CHAPTER 34—*A Wake-Up Call*

[1] "Corona Virus Disease (Covid-19) Situation Report—124." Last modified May 23, 2020.
https://www.who.int/docs/default-source/coronaviruse/situation-re-ports/20200523-covid-19-sitrep-124.pdf?sfvrsn=9626d639_2.

[2] Dupre, Sam and Vickstrom, Erik. 2019. "Annual World Population Growth Slowing, Projected to Soon Slip Below 1% for First Time Since 1950." Last modified July 10, 2019. https://www.census.gov/library/stories/2019/07/esti-mated-seven-point-five-eight-billion-people-world-population-day-2019.html.

[3] TerKeurst, *Made to Crave*.

About the Author

Hannah Thuku Kolehmainen, PhD. is a footloose, heart-firm lover of life. Raised in Kenya, she relishes tribal thinking and living. Her passions include teaching, writing, painting, wood-burning, culinary arts, and gardening. She has worked in psychiatry and physical rehab as an occupational therapist as well as in geriatrics. She received her PhD in Christian counseling.

With the power of Scripture, great humor, and painful candor, she shares from a broken life, now restored by Jesus. As a speaker and teacher, she is propelled to share His goodness and plan for us. She has a fervent desire for Christians see themselves as extensions of the story of the Bible, overcome crippling hurdles, and bear fruit as compelling ambassadors for the King of kings.

She and her husband and two sons live in Oregon.